SO-BYU-369

DISCARD

When Genres Collide

Alternate Takes: Critical Responses to Popular Music

A series edited by Matt Brennan and Simon Frith

When Genres Collide

Down Beat, Rolling Stone, and the
Struggle Between Jazz and Rock

Matt Brennan

Bloomsbury Academic
An imprint of Bloomsbury Publishing Inc

B L O O M S B U R Y
NEW YORK · LONDON · OXFORD · NEW DELHI · SYDNEY

Bloomsbury Academic

An imprint of Bloomsbury Publishing Inc

1385 Broadway	50 Bedford Square
New York	London
NY 10018	WC1B 3DP
USA	UK

www.bloomsbury.com

BLOOMSBURY and the Diana logo are trademarks of Bloomsbury Publishing Plc

First published 2017

© Matt Brennan, 2017

All rights reserved. No part of this publication may be reproduced or transmitted in any form or by any means, electronic or mechanical, including photocopying, recording, or any information storage or retrieval system, without prior permission in writing from the publishers.

No responsibility for loss caused to any individual or organization acting on or refraining from action as a result of the material in this publication can be accepted by Bloomsbury or the author.

Library of Congress Cataloging-in-Publication Data
Names: Brennan, Matt.
Title: When genres collide : Down Beat, Rolling Stone, and the struggle between jazz and rock / Matt Brennan.
Description: New York : Bloomsbury Academic, 2017. | Series: Alternate takes : critical responses to popular music | Includes bibliographical references and index.
Identifiers: LCCN 2016035477 (print) | LCCN 2016037064 (ebook) | ISBN 9781501326141 (pbk. : alk. paper) | ISBN 9781501319020 (hardback : alk. paper) | ISBN 9781501319037 (ePDF) | ISBN 9781501319044 (ePUB)
Subjects: LCSH: Musical criticism–United States–History–20th century. | Jazz–History and criticism. | Rock music–History and criticism.
Classification: LCC ML3785 .B76 2017 (print) | LCC ML3785 (ebook) | DDC 781.66/165–dc23
LC record available at https://lccn.loc.gov/2016035477

ISBN:	HB:	978-1-5013-1902-0
	PB:	978-1-5013-2614-1
	ePub:	978-1-5013-1904-4
	ePDF:	978-1-5013-1903-7

Series: Alternate Takes: Critical Responses to Popular Music

Cover design: James Brown
Cover image © James Brown

Typeset by Integra Software Services Pvt. Ltd.
Printed and bound in the United States of America

For Anna

Contents

List of Figures

All attempts have been made to contact copyright holders and gain permission for images.

Acknowledgments

This book is based on my doctoral research, which was financed by a Faculty of Arts Studentship from the University of Stirling in the first three years and a doctoral award from the Social Sciences and Humanities Research Council of Canada in the final year. I am grateful for the support of these two institutions, without which I would have been back on the boat to Canada years ago instead of working as a popular music scholar in Scotland. Thanks also to Frank Alkyer at *Down Beat*, Bill Sagan at Wolfgang's Vault, and Debbie Paitchel at Wenner Media for permission to reprint the magazine covers.

I would like to thank the following interviewees for their time and advice: John Burks, Robert Christgau, Alan Heineman, Jon Landau, Greil Marcus, Dan Morgenstern, and Langdon Winner.

A book like this requires a fair bit of digging around in archives. I would like to thank Andy Linehan at the British Library as well as Joe Peterson and Tad Hershorn at the Institute of Jazz Studies for their assistance. Thanks also to Paul Archibald for help with the layout.

I could not have completed this book without help, advice, and good conversation from former teachers and current colleagues who have lived in Scotland at some point, particularly Kirstin Anderson, Adam Behr, Mark Brownrigg, Szu-Wei Chen, Martin Cloonan, Annette Davison, Kyle Devine, Tami Gadir, Sean McLaughlin, Nikki Moran, Pedro Nunes, Mark Percival, Nick Prior, Inez Templeton, Arnar Thoroddsen, Tomke Veenhuis, Tom Wagner, Sean Williams, and John Williamson. I would also like to acknowledge my popular music conference buddies from around the world for their advice, encouragement, and good jazz and rock times, particularly

Beverly Diamond, Kevin Fellezs, Bruce Johnson, Keir Keightley, Lee Marshall, Catherine Tackley, Steve Waksman, and Justin Williams. Thanks also to the anonymous reviewers of this book for their helpful suggestions.

Special thanks to my PhD supervisor and mentor Simon Frith, and to my colleague and friend Janine Rogers, who encouraged me to pursue an academic career in the first place. I would not have been able (or had the guts) to write a book without your help, advice, and support.

Finally, I would like to thank my friends and family for their support, especially my parents Terry and Ann, who have always worked selflessly to support their son: most of the opportunities I have had in life so far, I owe to them. Extra special thanks to Anna Miles for keeping me sane as I tried to "quickly" turn my PhD thesis into a book—the result is dedicated to you.

Some of the material here first appeared in article form in *Popular Music History* (2006), the *Jazz Research Journal* (2007), and *Popular Music and Society* (2013).

Introduction

Raucous Jazz (Rock Is Jazz?)

*Jazz is the result of the energy stored up in America. It is a very
energetic kind of music, noisy, boisterous, and even vulgar. One thing is
certain. Jazz has contributed an enduring value to America in the sense
that it has expressed ourselves. It is an original American achievement
which will endure, not as jazz perhaps, but which will leave its mark on
future music in one form or another.*

GEORGE GERSHWIN, 1930[1]

Rock 'n' roll is the most raucous form of jazz, beyond a doubt.

DUKE ELLINGTON, 1955[2]

My first inkling of the tension that lay between jazz and the rest of popular
music came one autumn night at a small club in Montreal. I was a freshman
studying jazz drumming at university, and part of our assigned coursework
was to put together a small jazz "combo," perform a set at the club, and face
an adjudication from a faculty member in the audience. We muddled as best
as we knew how through our set of jazz standards taken from the *Real Book*
(a popular anthology of sheet music for jazz repertoire), tumbling awkwardly
through the chord changes of "Spring Is Here," "Lonnie's Lament," and "Blue
Monk." In fact, we only really began to cook when we closed our set with a half-
decent rendition of "Chameleon," the jazz-funk hit by Herbie Hancock. When
we got off stage and crammed ourselves into the club's storage room to hear
the appraisal from our jazz teacher, I remember thinking that "Chameleon"
was easily our strongest performance of the evening. I was disappointed, then,

when our teacher chastised us for choosing it and concluded with a warning to "save that funk stuff for your paying gigs."

As a naïve seventeen-year-old, I got over my initial reaction (what paying gigs?) and realized that despite plenty of jazz-funk and fusion charts existing in our *Real Book* alongside what was ostensibly other jazz repertoire, clearly there were boundary lines that I had yet to learn. Over the years, I did learn more about the history of American vernacular musics, but the problem of the boundary between jazz and other popular genres persisted. It seemed to be common sense for music historians to recognize the interactions between folk, blues, country, and rock 'n' roll, but jazz was represented more often than not as the odd one out. The relationship between jazz and rock seemed to be particularly problematic, and my attempts to unpick and understand the on-again, off-again affair between these two genres have ultimately led to writing this book.

The book aims to address two historical puzzles. The first concerns the history of the relationship between jazz and rock scholarship. Why are these two fields so resistant to one another, with limited interdisciplinary dialogue despite the many similarities between them? The second puzzle concerns the history of jazz and rock journalism. Jazz and rock have intersected, overlapped, and collided in dramatic ways at various points in history, and yet they have been treated quite differently in the press. I propose that these two puzzles are related, and my underlying argument is that we cannot take for granted the fact that jazz and rock would ultimately become separate musical cultures.

As Tony Whyton has argued, the birth of jazz and its development as a culture provoked many of the key debates that continue to inform how we make sense of American popular music almost a century later. In the first half of the twentieth century, jazz culture sparked heated discussions about the interaction between African-American and European musical traditions, art and commerce, authenticity and "manufactured music," low and high art, function and form, and many other oppositional values. These tensions did not end with jazz, but continued to be discussed in popular music genres that followed, including rock 'n' roll, rock, soul, disco, hip-hop, and electronic dance music. Or as Whyton succinctly puts it, "jazz served to shape the way in which popular music is discussed and understood today."[3]

If this is indeed true—if jazz was so important—why was there such a rupture between jazz and the new music called rock 'n' roll in the 1950s, and later rock in the 1960s? Why do so many music documentaries inform us that for all intents and purposes, Anglo-American popular music began in 1955 (or thereabouts) when Elvis Presley first swiveled his hips to screaming fans? Why wasn't rock 'n' roll absorbed as just another sub-genre of jazz, like swing or bebop before it? As the quote from Duke Ellington at the outset of this chapter demonstrates, some jazz musicians did perceive rock 'n' roll—at least at first—as merely the latest in a long line of musical fashions to fall under the umbrella label of jazz (albeit a particularly "raucous" version of it). The Ellington quote comes from an essay he wrote titled "The Future of Jazz," and although the *Duke Ellington Reader* notes that it was published in an issue of the *Music Journal* in 1962 (under the different title "Where Is Jazz Going?"), in fact the piece first appeared seven years earlier as part of the program notes for the 1955 Newport Jazz Festival. This is an important distinction to make: Ellington is not assessing rock 'n' roll in the year that the Beatles released "Love Me Do," but in the months after Bill Haley released "Rock Around the Clock" and just shy of a year before Elvis made his television debut on the Ed Sullivan show. In 1955, there was not yet a consensus on how to define the genre, but the essay clearly situates rock 'n' roll within a larger jazz tradition, as Ellington himself elaborates:

> Recently I was asked whether I felt that jazz had moved a great distance away from its folk origins. With the present state of Rock 'n' Roll music I don't know how anyone can even consider asking such a question! Rock 'n' Roll is the most raucous form of jazz, beyond a doubt; it maintains a link with the folk origins, and I believe that no other form of jazz has ever been accepted so enthusiastically by so many. This is probably an easy medium of musical semantics for the people to assimilate. I'm not trying to imply by this that Rock 'n' Roll shows any single trend, or indicates the only direction in which things are moving. It is simply one aspect of many.[4]

Ellington's appraisal raises more questions than it answers. What kinds of tensions arise when a particular type of music is claimed to belong to a folk tradition on the one hand but is also clearly a mass culture phenomenon ("accepted so enthusiastically by so many") on the other? And what sorts of problems are caused by a potentially new, "easy" to enjoy sub-genre of jazz arriving at a time when critics are busy making a case for the value of jazz as a complex and even "difficult" high art? As David Ake et al. have noted, such questions were typical of jazz commentators in the 1950s, who asked "whether jazz was best understood as a folk expression, a commercial dance style, or an art form deserving of serious treatment alongside highbrow European compositions."[5] My argument is that in order to understand how such debates contributed to the formation of jazz and rock as music genres, we must view the formation of jazz *in relation* to the formation of rock 'n' roll (and later rock) and vice versa.

To solve the mystery of why "rock 'n' roll" didn't remain just another sub-genre of "jazz," I propose to return to the moments when jazz and rock were being discussed in the press as new and emerging genres, examine the arguments afresh, and recover the other ways popular music history could have been written (and in fact has been written) that call the oppositional representation of jazz and rock into question. I want to examine in particular the two oldest surviving and most influential American jazz and rock periodicals: *Down Beat* and *Rolling Stone*. What are now represented as inevitable musical and cultural divergences between these two genres were actually constructed under very particular institutional and historical forces, and the American jazz and rock press were among the most significant early forces to contribute to the development of dominant jazz and rock discourses. I am not only proposing that we rethink the relationship between the histories of jazz and rock; I am also advocating that a greater effort be made to bridge the gap between the communities of scholars who teach and research jazz and rock—in other words, the gap between jazz studies and popular music studies. Simon Frith has observed that "in the academy 'jazz studies' and 'popular music studies' have evolved as different and rarely overlapping research and teaching areas...the separation of jazz and popular music studies is an indisputable fact of academic life, and the reasons for this are an interesting topic for the sociology of knowledge."[6] Before addressing the historical rift between jazz and rock as genres, then, I want to spend the rest of this chapter sketching an outline of how jazz and the rest of popular music came to be treated separately in the academy.

The marginalization of popular music in jazz studies

Jazz is curiously absent from the field of popular music studies. This is despite the fact that jazz was the first music to raise many of the concerns now considered to be fundamental to studying popular music. Jazz was one of the first musics to seriously challenge the boundary between the worlds of commercial entertainment and legitimate art. It was also one of the earliest musical forms to develop an international community of young fans who cherished records as much as live performance and consumed their music as a mass cultural commodity. And perhaps most importantly for the study of popular music, jazz was arguably the first popular style to generate a fully fledged art world with a community of critics, articulate musicians, and avid readers producing an unprecedentedly rich popular music discourse in books, magazines, newspapers, and mimeographs (or what would later be called "fanzines"). No other style of popular music had so much ink spilled to debate its value, and never before had so many terms, concepts, and arguments contributed to a sophisticated discussion of the tension between art and commerce that arose when music became disseminated as mass culture. To understand the roots of the key debates in popular music studies, one must understand the cultural history of jazz. However, to understand why jazz studies have nevertheless remained largely distinct from the rest of popular music studies, we need to examine the historical migration of jazz into the academy.

Although a handful of dedicated critics, scholars, and musicians had been working toward the legitimization of jazz from early on in its history, it would not be until well into the second half of the century that jazz began to make significant inroads into schools and universities. The earliest scholars in the academy to study and teach jazz came from a variety of disciplines: among these were Len Bowden, who led a jazz band at the Tuskegee Institute (now Tuskegee University) as early as 1919; Marshall Stearns, a professor of medieval English literature who began teaching a jazz history class at New York University in 1950; Howard Becker, a professor of sociology who conducted pioneering ethnographic studies of jazz musicians in the early 1950s; and Gunther Schuller, a composer and musicologist who produced some of the best musicological analyses of early jazz in the 1960s. In his overview of jazz education, David Ake notes that while select American colleges—such as Berklee, Westlake, and North Texas—taught jazz performance as early as the 1940s, "these examples stood as exceptions, not as the rule in American colleges, universities and conservatories," the vast majority of which excluded jazz from their curricula until at least the 1970s.[7] Indeed, Ake goes on to remark that some of the more prestigious conservatories "not only omitted the genre, but also actually forbade the playing of jazz on school property, with transgressions possibly leading in extreme cases to students' expulsion from the institution."[8]

Jazz was first discussed at the Music Educators National Conference (MENC) as early as 1956, but it was not until 1968 that MENC formally sanctioned jazz education by welcoming the newly founded National Association of Jazz Educators (NAJE) to become a permanent part of its program. The inaugural NAJE newsletter proclaimed that "to all of you who have looked upon jazz as a legitimate form of musical challenge .... 1968 will be the year to remember."[9] According to its Constitution, among the aims and goals of the NAJE were: "(1) to foster and promote the understanding and appreciation of jazz and popular music and its artistic performance; (2) to lend assistance and guidance in the organization and development of jazz curricula in schools and colleges to include stage bands and ensembles of all types; and (3) to apply jazz principles to music materials and methods at all levels."[10]

In its early years, the NAJE seemed to advocate teaching the performance of rock as well as jazz in school music ensembles, especially in the writings of Sidney Fox, an educational consultant who became the General Music

Chairman for the NAJE in 1970. Fox encouraged teaching all forms of Western popular music in schools in order to stimulate a musical interest in youth who were otherwise switched off:

> Only about 8 per cent of students in the junior high and senior high schools are actively involved in music ... The other 92% received little or no experience in music in the school. For these students, the music educator is the local disc jockey. It is these students to whom our work must be geared ... [A special committee] has already begun consideration of this problem ... and urged the consideration [of] the "entire magnificent field of Man's musical behaviour for serious and systematic exploration: gospel, folk-rock, art songs, Broadway, pop, soul music, traditional and modern jazz, blues, symphonic literature, chamber music, country western, opera, guitar music, piano, harp (harmonica), the Nashville Industry ... and any and all music in Western culture."[11]

Fox's all-embracing ethos of music education was certainly not shared by all, and his conference speeches were sometimes reportedly met with vocal resistance, but at least in the early newsletters of the NAJE, Fox found a comfortable forum to advocate the teaching of jazz and many other forms of popular music, including rock, under the umbrella of "jazz education."

Jazz education grew steadily throughout the 1970s, and by the early 1980s jazz enjoyed a much improved status in both educational institutions and government foundations as a preeminent American classical art—well worthy of a place in music departments and conservatories. The National Endowment for the Arts, which began supporting jazz artists in 1970, instituted the American Jazz Masters Awards in 1982, given out to jazz artists endorsed by their musician peers, as well as scholars and critics. The early 1980s also marked the rise of an important new "historicist jazz" movement ushered in by the young Wynton Marsalis, who had just released his debut album as a leader. Marsalis was trying to forge a new path for jazz after it had splintered into two polarized musical directions, avant-garde modernism and jazz-rock fusion, in the 1960s and 1970s; Marsalis departed from both by embracing the past and actively attempting to construct a jazz tradition that prioritized music created before the conflicting styles and cultural ideologies of the 1960s (free jazz, avant-garde, soul-jazz, jazz-rock, etc.) had fragmented jazz audiences, critics, and musicians. In his conception of the jazz tradition and the new historicist jazz movement, Marsalis made a significant contribution to both the stabilization and institutionalization of the music. As Scott DeVeaux explained,

> the Marsalis phenomenon made it possible to reposition jazz in American culture. As a product of both the Julliard Conservatory and the classic hard bop "conservatory," Art Blakey's Jazz Messengers, and the winner of Grammy awards in both jazz and classical music (the latter for recordings of trumpet concertos), Marsalis drove home the idea that jazz had come of age as an alternative "classical music"—separate from the European tradition, but of equally enduring quality and artistry.[12]

Or as Marsalis himself put it in 1984 in a televised Grammy award acceptance speech:

> I'd like to thank everyone [at the record label] ... for presenting my work with the quality that is necessary to get to the elite jazz audience. And I would like to thank all the guys in the band, because without the band I wouldn't be able to play anything, because this music is very difficult ... Last, but certainly not least, I'd like to thank all the great masters of American music—Charlie Parker, Louis Armstrong, Thelonius Monk—all the guys who set a precedent in Western art, and gave an art form to the American people, that cannot be limited by enforced trends or bad taste.[13]

As Marsalis implies in his less than subtle condemnation of contemporary popular music industry and its audience (the "enforced trends" of post-jazz popular music promoted by the recording industry and the "bad taste" of the undiscriminating record-buying public), along with its "coming of age" came the strategic distancing of jazz from other forms of popular music. Whereas the NAJE (which became the International Association of Jazz Educators [IAJE] in 1989) was originally founded on the premise that the study of any kind of music could be proven worthwhile, jazz educators now increasingly rallied round an ideology that distinguished jazz as different from (and greater than) other forms of American popular music. This move was in part rationalized as a necessity: unlike rock and pop, jazz—at least the jazz that fell outside of the categories of "smooth" and "fusion"—was perceived to be in constant danger of disappearing as a commercially sustainable music. The dilemma for jazz supporters was whether to continue to hope for the revival of jazz as a commercially popular art form, perhaps infused by some of the vitality of rock or hip-hop, or to define jazz in opposition to commercial music and systematically cleave any associations between jazz and pop, consequently making it easier to argue the case for jazz as a music that could not survive as a distinct art without the proper state support and academic refuge.

As Ake has documented, the cultural value of jazz music continued to grow over the next two decades: "the 1987 Congressional Act declaring jazz 'a rare and valuable national American treasure,' along with the fact that jazz performers increasingly share[d] performance spaces and grant dollars with their more established classical colleagues, both symbolize[d] and solidifie[d] jazz's prominence in and beyond [America]."[14] In 1988, Wynton Marsalis established the Lincoln Center Jazz Orchestra, the most visible of a number of newly established ensembles devoted mainly to the music of deceased jazz legends such as Louis Armstrong, Duke Ellington, and Thelonius Monk. The development of jazz as a repertory music represented yet another shift toward the models of the classical music world. Ake examined the writing of Mark Gridley, author of the best-selling university textbook *Jazz Styles*. In an essay directed to college-level music educators, Gridley aimed to make a clear distinction between jazz and the rest of popular music:

The moral of the story is, don't assume that anyone understands the differences between jazz and pop. If you run into resistance establishing a jazz curriculum or in trying to obtain funding for a jazz concert series, remember those who hold the purse strings might be withholding the money only because they are confused about what jazz is and because they see the music as so commercially successful and plentiful that it does not need their patronage. They may also see it as not warranting study because pop music by definition is not serious.[15]

According to Gridley, then, jazz was worthy of academic attention, whereas pop and its offspring (including rock) *by definition* lacked the same level of musical sophistication.

Since the late 1980s, two important trends have emerged in the academic study and teaching of jazz. The first is the emergence of something close to a dominant jazz discourse, consolidated primarily by the work of documentary maker Ken Burns and Jazz at the Lincoln Center director Wynton Marsalis. In 2000, Burns released what was meant to be a definitive nineteen-hour television documentary called *Jazz*, which caused controversy upon its release mainly because the documentary was almost entirely devoted to jazz made before 1961, compressing the following forty years of jazz history into a single concluding episode. The narrative of *Jazz* reflected the neoclassical vision of musicians like Wynton Marsalis and conservative critics like Stanley Crouch, who were both key consultants in the making of the documentary. Despite attracting criticism from many scholars and journalists, *Jazz* was nevertheless adopted as an essential, if not the definitive text in jazz history classes around the world, even by many of those scholars who openly criticized it.

The second significant trend in jazz scholarship and education in the last two decades has been the emergence of interdisciplinary or "new" jazz studies. Sherrie Tucker suggests that this movement, which sought to study and define jazz not simply as music but as culture, emerged at the end of the 1980s and began to consolidate by the mid-1990s:

Just as the "Jazz Tradition" narrative coalesced in a particular moment of institutionalization of jazz, so has the critical response to it that we sometimes call "academic jazz studies, or interdisciplinary jazz studies," or "New Jazz Studies" ... [Recent years have] seen the spread of academic jazz studies beyond the band rooms, bebop combos, and jazz appreciation classes that are the legacy of "Jazz Tradition," to its current array of emanations from lecture halls and seminars from a variety of non-Music departmental prefixes, where participants theorize anti-canonical figures such as Sun Ra; and study topics like race, gender, nationalism, and politics.[16]

It is against this backdrop that we must consider the current position of jazz and its relationship to the study of popular music in the academy: on the one hand jazz was historically cut off and defined against popular music, while on the other a more recent generation of interdisciplinary jazz scholars have questioned the construction of the jazz tradition. New Jazz Studies is hardly new anymore and shares many similar approaches and concerns with the rest of popular music studies. This makes it all the more strange that the two fields continue on the whole to operate independently of one another. It is the naturalization of this divide in popular music studies which I will turn my attention to next.

The marginalization of jazz in popular music studies

As we have seen, some scholars within jazz studies have actively argued that jazz should be set apart from the rest of popular music for aesthetic, institutional, and economic reasons. It is more difficult to explain why more popular music researchers have not acknowledged the many parallels between these two areas of scholarship, especially given the interdisciplinary emphasis in popular music studies. In their recent *Sage Handbook of Popular Music*—a 600-page overview of the key debates for popular music studies in the twenty-first century—editors Andy Bennett and Steve Waksman sketch an outline of the roots of the field as follows:

The foundations of popular music studies were established over a period of ten years between the late 1960s and the late 1970s, punctuated at intervals by the publication of highly influential books such as Dave Laing's (1969) *The Sound of Our Time*, R. Serge Denisoff and Richard A. Peterson's (eds.) (1972) *The Sounds of Social Change*, Wilfred Mellers's (1973) *Twilight of the*

Gods and Simon Frith's (1978) *The Sociology of Rock* (republished in 1981 as *Sound Effects*)… Complementing the evolution of popular music studies in this formative period was the stimulus provided by emergent forms of music journalism from 1966 onward. As rock grew to a position of dominance in the wider field of Anglo-American popular music production during the 1960s its economic rise was accompanied by a new set of journalistic outlets, designed to explain its cultural and political impact.[17]

There are several assumptions worth interrogating here: were there no serious book-length studies of popular music prior to the late 1960s? As for music journalism, were there no critics who took popular music seriously before 1966? Finally, was rock really the first genre to spur the creation of new journalistic outlets to examine the cultural and political impact of popular music? This is not to criticize the editors or the handbook—indeed, Bennett and Waksman are deservedly respected as leaders in their field, their book ranks among the best overviews of its kind published in recent years, and their outline above is likely an accurate account of how most scholars working in popular music studies currently understand the field and its origins. It also illustrates, of course, how jazz scholarship and jazz journalism have been essentially omitted from the narrative of popular music studies.

Neither is this a one-off representation: in a book of similar scope published just after the millennium titled *Popular Music Studies*, editors David Hesmondhalgh and Keith Negus (once again two highly respected popular music scholars) present an overview of the history of the field which claims it was not until "the late 1960s and early 1970s" that the publishing industry was commissioning "influential and serious studies of the history, social significance and aesthetics of popular music, often from writers bridging the journalism/academic divide."[18] As examples of this trend, they cite Dave Laing's *The Sound of Our Time*, Charlie Gillett's *The Sound of the City*, and Greil Marcus's *Mystery Train*.[19] All three of these works were influential, of course, but they are also examples which promote a highly rock-centric version of American popular music history, and their use as examples, therefore, creates a rock-centric orientation for the roots of popular music studies—this is an odd move not least because Hesmondhalgh and Negus make a call in the same essay to avoid placing rock-centric limitations on the field.[20]

While both overviews are spot on in highlighting the crucial relationship between music journalism and the origins of popular music scholarship, they also position the beginning of the rock era in the late 1960s as ground zero for taking popular music seriously, unwittingly demonstrating how jazz is routinely snubbed as a major form of popular music to which popular music studies owe an enormous intellectual debt. Hesmondhalgh and Negus argue, for instance, that "in studying popular music we are dealing with an unstable, contested and changing category," not only due to debate about what qualifies as "popular" or even "music," but also because the traditional categories of art, folk, and popular music "are a continual source of musicological disagreement and ideological dispute."[21] Despite this claim, however, there appears to be an assumption that jazz does not merit consideration as a form of popular music even though it was jazz that first challenged the boundaries between such categories long before rock 'n' roll emerged as a distinct genre. As Lawrence Levine put it, "jazz in fact is one of those forces that have helped to transform our sense of art and culture … a music that in fact bridged the gap between all of the categories that divided culture."[22]

That jazz and rock discourses are usually treated as resistant—rather than related—to one another in popular music studies may be partly to do with their ideological pitfalls, which are usefully (if cartoonishly) illustrated by the terms of derision used to deflate overly zealous jazz and rock fans and writers. Since the 1980s, for instance, those involved in the project of cleaving jazz from "pop music" have sometimes been labeled as "jazz snobs." The *Urban Dictionary* defines a jazz snob as "an annoying or stubborn person whom denies any, or most, kinds of music other than jazz. Has a self-indulgent illusion of sophistication about himself and, in particular, his tastes."[23] This description highlights the stereotypical gendered, elitist traits of the jazz snob but also crucially how he holds jazz in opposition to other forms of (one imagines, popular) music. The term was also immortalized in John Zorn's memorably titled 1990 composition "Jazz Snob Eat Shit." (As an avant-garde musician who borrows equally from jazz, rock, noise, and hardcore, and other music genres, Zorn and his music actively transgress the fringes of music genres.)

On the other hand, since the mid-2000s the term "rockism" (originally coined by UK music critics in the early 1980s) has been used by American music critics to describe rock-centric tendencies in popular music writing. According to Douglas Wolk, rockism can be defined as "treating rock as normative. In the rockist view, rock is the standard state of popular music: the kind to which everything else is compared, explicitly or implicitly."[24] More recently, Miles Parks Grier has argued that the term connotes more broadly "the jurisdiction straight white men exercise over matters of taste in popular music."[25] Interestingly, both jazz snobbery and rockism are linked by a common underlying ideology that assumes jazz and rock, respectively, to be authentic musical cultures contrasted against mass-produced, manufactured commercial "pop," actively turning a blind eye to their own obvious participation in music as a form of commercial production. However, there are also key differences between the two: Jody Rosen has observed that "rockism was a product of its own historical moment, a time when rock critics had to face down snobs on both their right and left flanks who dismissed the idea that pop music could ever be art at all."[26] By the second half of the 1960s, the snobs rock critics had to face included a significant contingent of jazz critics, several of whom ironically had to fight in previous decades for jazz, a contemporary popular music of its time, to be considered as art. Unfortunately, the consequence of this struggle was for rock critics to invent a new starting point for popular music history—the birth of rock 'n' roll. Perhaps the greatest sin of rockism is to assume that popular music begins in 1955.

A non-rockist, jazz-friendly (and hopefully not overly jazz-snobbish) account of the intellectual roots of taking popular music seriously might include the numerous seminal jazz and blues-focused books on American popular music that predated rock histories. In terms of bridging the academic/journalistic divide of popular music writing, for instance, it would be remiss not to mention Nat Shapiro and Nat Hentoff's *Hear Me Talkin' to Ya*, Marshall Stearns' *The Story of Jazz*, Amiri Baraka's (née. Leroi Jones) *Blues People*, and Francis Newton's *The Jazz Scene*.[27] These were among the books (rather than Laing, Gillett, Marcus, and so on) that first grappled with the implications of American popular music being socially and aesthetically significant.

The same goes for scholarly treatises on popular music, where it would be negligent not to mention musicological work like Gunther Schuller's *Early Jazz: Its Roots and Musical Development*, as well as forebears such as Hughes Panassié, Winthrop Sargeant, and André Hodeir.[28] All of these early jazz scholars were challenging established musicological conventions and treating a popular music—often transcribing recordings and performances rather than composed scores—with unprecedented analytical attention.

In the sociology of popular music, many of the earliest and most influential texts in the field focused on jazz. The most famous example is the work of Theodor Adorno, who, as a musicologist, philosopher, and member of the Frankfurt School, would end up having a profound influence on the sociology of rock and pop, despite having written his seminal critiques of popular music and the culture industry well before the birth of rock 'n' roll as a genre. Instead, Adorno pointed the finger at jazz, and not, I would argue, by accident.[29] Adorno perceived jazz to be the best example of a revolution in the production of culture; jazz was the first form of twentieth-century popular music to challenge the previously comfortable boundary between commercial entertainment and legitimate art. The development of recording technology caused a transformation in musical aesthetics that allowed the performer to be prioritized as an artist instead of the composer, and it was jazz (as opposed to rock) that first demonstrated the change. Jazz was also the first focus of Howard Becker, whom Hesmondhalgh and Negus accurately describe as pioneering the sociology of popular musicians with his study of dance musicians aspiring toward jazz.[30] Becker was merely the best known of several early sociologists of popular music who used jazz cultures to explore issues of group, race, class, status, and power.[31]

The sociology of jazz—and Adorno and Becker in particular—was an important influence on a second wave of sociologists interested in popular music such as Richard Peterson and Simon Frith, who took the pioneering work on jazz by popular music sociologists and significantly developed it while applying it to newer popular genres such as country and rock.[32] However, popular music studies subsequently took a trajectory that distanced it from jazz scholarship, and this was due in part to rise of the discipline of cultural studies: as institutions like the Centre for Contemporary Cultural Studies at the University of Birmingham (led by Richard Hoggart and later Stuart Hall) and theorists like Dick Hebdige and Lawrence Grossberg became increasingly important in popular music scholarship, so too did the sociology of music (and its jazz heritage) lose some of its dominance in popular music studies.

To return to the overview written by Hesmondhalgh and Negus, the authors conclude that over time the field of popular music studies has become united by a common goal:

> To rescue popular music from being treated as trivial and unimportant, whether as music (which some would see as trivial because of its "merely" ritual or entertainment function) or as popular culture (which some would see as debased because of its commercial origins, supposed lack of complexity and dubious aesthetic merit). The study of popular music has tended to effect this rescue operation in a certain way, via a commitment to a politicization of music: by attempting to show that music is often—some would say always—bound up with questions of social power ... [which are often] closely bound up with questions of cultural value, about who has the authority to ascribe social and aesthetic worth to what kinds of music, and why.[33]

This goal, of course, also perfectly describes the struggles experienced in the history of jazz scholarship, but the link is rarely made for some reason. I am not trying to suggest that popular music studies scholars are hostile toward jazz, and certainly not in the same way that jazz writers like Gridley are antagonistic toward the rest of popular music, but there does appear to be a tendency, even when calling for the field to move beyond its focus on rock and pop, to reinforce the study of rock and pop as the natural starting point for popular music studies, and to render jazz studies invisible.

Popular music studies made a significant step toward becoming an organized academic movement in 1981, when scholars from around the world gathered to create the first formal organization for the field, the International Association for the Study of Popular Music (IASPM). Like the IAJE in the jazz world, the original mandate of IASPM embraced the study of all forms of popular music, including jazz. IASPM intentionally adopted a philosophy of inclusion rather than exclusion, encouraging scholarship of popular music genres and cultures from around the globe and embracing an interdisciplinary approach to their study. But it was also formed in reaction against the established postsecondary music education system, which dismissed certain kinds of music scholarship. When searching for a definition of "popular music" at the Second International Conference on Popular Music Studies, Philip Tagg tried to address the problem:

> Let us consider "popular music" to be all that music traditionally excluded from conservatories, schools of music, university departments of musicology, in fact generally excluded from realms of public education and public financing in the capitalist world: this state of affairs is the reason for the existence of IASPM anyhow and "popular" is a shorter way of saying "traditionally excluded..." and the like![34]

As Tagg suggests, popular music scholars were faced with resistance by the gatekeepers of the musical academy. However, if jazz scholarship was finding some footholds in the academy by the 1980s, it was also still perceived by most IASPM scholars as belonging to the field of popular music studies.

A similar philosophy could be found in the journal *Popular Music*, which was founded in 1981 by Richard Middleton, a musicologist whose early research focused on the blues, and David Horn, a librarian who specialized in American musical history with an interest in the relationship between jazz and the songs of Tin Pan Alley—neither saw jazz as being a separate field from popular music scholarship. As board member Simon Frith later recalled in an interview, the journal's editorial board attempted to solicit research representing as many strands of popular music as possible for its first five annual issues, but it seemed unusually difficult to find scholars from the jazz field who were interested in contributing to the journal.[35] IASPM member and music scholar Charles Hamm became especially concerned by the late 1980s that the popular music studies community was not placing sufficient emphasis on popular music history outside of the rock genre. (Hamm later published an article that provided evidence for his claims by doing a content analysis of the articles published in *Popular Music* and noting that the vast majority of its content was focused on music after 1955, leading him to conclude that "the new and vital field of popular music studies has developed as an ahistorical discipline.")[36]

The post-1955 orientation of popular music studies has been replicated not just in peer-reviewed journals but in edited collections and textbooks as well. By the end of the 1990s, popular music studies had taken on a distinctive rock-pop orientation, which has been reflected and consequently reinforced in the market for university textbooks. Cambridge University Press, for instance, has released separate *Cambridge Companion* books for "jazz," "blues," and "rock and pop," reflecting distinctions in popular music scholarship as a whole. As we saw earlier, textbooks which imply in their titles that they cover "popular music" in a broad sense tend to have a distinctly post-1955 rock-pop focus. These books both reflected the interests of their authors and were commissioned to respond to market demand— presumably what teachers asked for according to how the popular music scholarship had become organized—but they resulted in strengthening the divisions in the field.

The establishment of jazz studies and popular music studies as scholarly fields has inevitably led to a growing body of work by writers (e.g., Philip Ennis, Kevin Fellezs, Bruce Johnson, Keir Keightley, George McKay, Steven Pond, Sherrie Tucker, and Elijah Wald) challenging the conventions of these fields and revisiting key periods in history to raise questions about genre formation.[37] I hope to contribute to this discussion by making the argument that the divide between jazz and rock can be explained in part because the split was naturalized in the discourse of the music journalism.

Music journalism as the first draft of music history

Just as journalism is sometimes referred to as the first draft of history, music journalism can be considered the first draft of music history.[38] Historians have routinely relied on the music press to get a sense of how musical and cultural events were covered in print media as they were unfolding. The music press has also been influential in its construction of the language and concepts used to discuss popular music in everyday life; because they are writing music history as it happens, journalists and critics are often given the first shot at selecting which cultural moments are important enough to appear in print and, therefore, remain in cultural memory, as well as selecting which interpretive themes are best suited to framing these events. Furthermore, many popular music critics worked in more than one profession, creating portfolio careers as journalists, critics, publicists, historians, radio and television personalities, talent scouts, record producers, university lecturers, and other kinds of work that cumulatively endowed them with a privileged influence in not just covering but shaping various aspects of genre cultures. As we shall see, this was especially the case for those who worked during the formative years of the two case-study magazines this book will examine, *Down Beat*[39] and *Rolling Stone*, respectively, the two oldest surviving and most influential of American jazz and rock periodicals.[40]

The history of music journalism is central to understanding the formation of popular music genres, especially the further back in history one goes: in the pre-internet era the music press played a disproportionate role in shaping popular music discourse, spreading it to a mass audience, and crucially preserving a document of that discourse for posterity. There are several important existing accounts of the individual histories of *Down Beat* and *Rolling Stone*. I owe a debt to John McDonough, who wrote a long essay on the history of *Down Beat*, for example, which appeared in a commemorative book to celebrate the sixtieth anniversary of the magazine.[41] Meanwhile, several histories of *Rolling Stone* have been produced, including Robert Sam Anson's *Gone Crazy and Back Again* and Robert Draper's *The Rolling Stone Story*.[42] The histories written by Anson, McDonough, and Draper have been useful in providing background information for my own analysis, but unlike my research, they are focused on each magazine in isolation. More recently, Devon Powers has produced an excellent account of the early rock criticism in the *Village Voice*.[43] Broader overviews of jazz criticism (John Gennari's *Blowin' Hot and Cool: Jazz and Its Critics*) and rock criticism (Ulf Lindberg et al.'s *Rock Criticism from the Beginning*) also exist, as well as a handful of studies that consider jazz and rock discourses (the work of Bernard Gendron, Fabian Holt, and Steve Jones are all notable here).[44] My own book builds on this work by mapping a history of journalism that covers both jazz and rock journalism in relation to one another, focusing on significant moments of overlap, interaction, and conflict between jazz and rock writing that resonate into the present.

Of the scholarship on music journalism that preceded this book, the studies by Lindberg et al. and Gennari are illustrative of the discursive gap I am trying to bridge. In his analysis of jazz and its critics, Gennari proposes that "one of the ways to create a less static model of jazz—and perhaps even to grant more agency and power to jazz musicians—paradoxically is to shift the focus from the musicians to the jazz superstructure."[45] The jazz superstructure for Gennari is the sum total of the debates between critics, historians, and educators of jazz, and their attempts to construct meaning for the genre: not only defining its musical properties, but its history, discourse, and artistic and sociological significance. Gennari describes the history of negotiations over the many meanings of jazz, and in so doing explores with considerable skill the densely entangled issues that make up the cultural politics of America—what he calls "the knotty intersections of black, brown, beige, and white; complex dynamics of race, gender, class, nationality, and power; interlocking cultures of sound, image, and word."[46]

Interestingly, however, Gennari writes that even though he grew up as part of the rock 'n' roll generation, rock criticism was far less interesting to him than jazz criticism:

Somehow this jazz writing seemed more important, more necessary than the writing about rock and pop music. Many rock musicians were well-known celebrities; we saw them on television. We loved their music because it was accessible. Those of us who were musical dabblers played rock and funk because they felt like native languages, and because we knew we could connect with an audience of our peers. If we ventured into jazz, it was a second language, and it came with no guarantee of an audience. These jazz writers crucially helped us to understand jazz and, equally important, to imagine ourselves part of a community of people for whom the music mattered more than anything else.[47]

Gennari goes on to suggest that "of all the great American vernacular musics, only jazz has cultivated intellectual discourse as a core element of its superstructure."[48] While this may have a grain of truth in it—rock, for instance, is far more commercially viable than jazz and, therefore, less dependent on critics for exposure, whereas jazz has survived partly because critics legitimized it as an art worthy of state support—it begs the question of what a rock "superstructure" might look like. Furthermore, it leaves unexamined whether the key issues in jazz discourse might not also exist in rock discourse.

Perhaps one could look to the Scandinavian authors of *Rock Criticism from the Beginning* for an answer, as they certainly make the case that the field of rock criticism is a substantial intellectual discourse in its own right. Lindberg et al. conducted an historical survey of American and British rock criticism, focusing on the specialist music press and books, which strived "to move beyond an insider's view and situate rock in a wider cultural context":

> [Our book's] point of departure is the assumption that critics, as Regev (1994) argues, have played an important role for the elevation of rock music into at least "semi-legitimate" art. This achievement was made possible by diverse alliances: the critics became spokesmen for musicians or trends whose ambitions seemed "serious," as well as for "progressive" social forces (working-class youth, white trash, African Americans); now and then they received support from agents in more established cultural fields disposed to spot nuggets in unexpected places. The outcome was both a construction of rock music as different from and more valuable than other popular music and a parallel construction of criticism itself as a "serious" business.[49]

If these two sets of arguments sound similar, it is because they *are* similar: reading Gennari's jazz criticism book and Lindberg et al.'s rock criticism book alongside one another, it is immediately clear that there are many parallels in the trajectories of jazz and rock criticism. There are differences too, of course: jazz has come closer than rock to achieving the status of a fully legitimate art; jazz was constructed by critics as primarily an African-American form of music rather than working-class or white; the rise of jazz and rock criticism took place in different historical eras; and rock's economic significance easily dwarfs that of jazz. Despite these differences, however, there remains a remarkable similarity between jazz and rock criticism here that begs for a more extended comparison.

I should note that up to this point I have used the terms "music criticism" and "music journalism" somewhat interchangeably. Lindberg et al. have argued that these actually are two different enterprises: *music criticism* is music writing that has argumentative and interpretive ambitions but is more journalistic than academic (i.e., reviews, in-depth interviews, overviews, debate articles, essays, or "think pieces"); *music journalism*, on the other hand, might simply be news reporting, practical information, or passing commentary.[50] However, I think this distinction is difficult to sustain in practice: the business of the music press ultimately depends on its success in matching advertisers with a readership—and a successful music magazine is one that matches the right kind of reader with the right kind of advertiser through the creation of particular curated content. Selecting which news stories and practical information to include and what to exclude is itself a critical act, as we shall see in the following chapters. Drawing a line between criticism and journalism is not necessarily useful when analyzing the music press, and I hope to demonstrate that what initially seem like journalistic or editorial choices are inevitably also a form of criticism with particular consequences for the formation of music genres, canons, and cultures.

Music genres and the categorization of jazz and rock

What are we talking about when we talk about jazz and rock? Are they musical cultures, genres, styles, discourses, or something else? Following the pioneering work of Franco Fabbri, my starting premise is that genres such as jazz and rock cannot be defined in purely musicological terms: music genres are always formed socially as well as musically, and the musical and social aspects of genre are indivisible.[51] As Fabian Holt had argued, music genres are "always collective ... (a person can have his or her own style, but not a genre). Conventions and expectations are established through acts of repetition performed by a group of people, and the process of genre formation is in turn often accompanied by the formation of new social collectivities."[52] Rather than discuss music genres *per se*, it is more accurate to talk about *genre worlds* or *genre cultures*:

> It makes sense to view popular music genres as small cultures because they are defined in relation to many of the same aspects as general culture. Genres are identified not only with music, but also with certain cultural values, rituals, practices, territories, traditions, and groups of people.[53]

Understanding how music genres work is not simply an academic exercise. For David Ake et al., "genre designations play a fundamental role in shaping how we teach, learn, create, access, and assess music."[54] Holt similarly argues that genre is "a tool with which culture industries and national governments regulate the circulation of vast fields of music. It is a major force in canons of educational institutions, cultural hierarchies, and decisions about censorship and funding."[55] And as Kevin Fellezs suggests, popular music genres can act as "a logic through which ideas about race, gender, social class are created, debated, and performed through musical sound and discourse."[56] Genre is arguably the key structuring device for how popular music is made and heard, taught and learned, bought and sold, and supported or suppressed.

David Brackett's theorization of music genres adds an important and valuable temporal emphasis to genres as *events* that unfold and change over time. He advocates a genealogical approach to genre: "rather than focusing on *what* constitutes the contents of a musical category, the emphasis here falls on *how* a particular idea of a category emerges and stabilizes momentarily (if at all) in the course of being accepted across a range of discourses and institutions."[57] As Brackett points out, music genres cannot be formed by only one segment of a musical culture. Instead, they emerge from a collective dialogue, "a way of communicating about music between artists, music industry middle-people, and audiences, none of whom are strictly separable":

> If the roles that they perform differ, all of these agents inhabit the same, or similar, or overlapping, social worlds. If the labels that are used to group musical utterances together are not broadly legible, they will not gain

currency. The process through which this occurs has no single agent or point of origin: an individual (no matter how powerful) cannot will a genre label into existence. Genres are therefore neither "top down," in that they cannot be imposed by the music industry if the connections projected by the categorical labels are not legible to the public; nor can genres be "bottom up," created by consumers willy-nilly in a voluntaristic feat of individual will. The counterposing of "top down" and "bottom up" is not meant to eviscerate the effects of power, but rather to indicate that the effects of power transcend the role played by the idealized agency of music industry executives as well as consumers.[58]

In this book, I want to focus on the moments where this process of collective dialogue struggles to achieve consensus, and to discuss not just the winners of such conflicts but also the losers. The histories of jazz and rock illustrate just how dramatically genre boundaries can stretch over time, but also the points at which they break under stress—how genres can flirt with one another but ultimately go their separate ways. Why didn't rhythm and blues and then rock 'n' roll become get subsumed into the expansive list of jazz sub-genres in the 1950s? Similarly, if rock had become a hegemonic economic and cultural force in popular music by the late 1960s, why didn't it devour jazz whole? And why didn't jazz and rock hybridize at some stage into a single genre culture that encompassed all of American popular music, despite several critics predicting that this was bound to happen? Kevin Fellezs has chronicled the development of jazz-rock fusion in the 1970s, but notes that ultimately fusion was rejected from the canons of both jazz and rock and still sits uneasily in between the two genres.[59] As he puts it, "the failure of fusion as a genre is indicative of [the struggles of fusion artists] to bear the tensions multiple loyalties exerted."[60] This book is not about jazz-rock fusion, but rather about the failure of jazz and rock to fuse despite sharing many characteristics with one another.

I argue that the questions above can be fruitfully explored by focusing on the music press as a snapshot of genre cultures. As I noted earlier, successful music magazines have historically matched advertisers to a readership through written content usually focusing on a particular genre world. Key sectors of the *music industry* (e.g., instrument manufacturers, record labels, and concert promoters) relied on *staff employed by the magazine* (editors, reporters, critics, designers, and photographers) to cover, critique, interview, and represent *artists* (musicians and the professional music-making world that they inhabited) and ultimately reach a target audience of *music fans* (the usually non-professional music listeners and makers who made up the consumer market who might buy the advertised instruments, records, and tickets). This is not simply a one-way discussion with critics leading the discourse: music journalists might report on corruption within the same music industry on whom the magazine depended for advertising revenue. Musicians frequently voiced disagreement with critics in interviews and resisted being pigeonholed into genres. Meanwhile, readers of *Down Beat* and *Rolling Stone* wrote letters to the editor, which were published each month debating the contents of the previous issue (albeit a debate that was curated by the editorial staff of each magazine). As such, the music press was not simply the voices of critics, but a microcosm of a much wider genre culture with a range of different constituencies; moreover, longstanding music magazines such as *Down Beat* and *Rolling Stone* provide a regular snapshot (taking into account the power of critics, journalists, and editors of framing the snapshots) of the interactions between these constituencies over time.

I have chosen to examine five critical periods in history when the meanings of "jazz" or "rock" were being challenged. Chapter 1 examines how jazz in the first half of the twentieth century prefigured rock culture and embodied many of the discursive characteristics that would later be used to claim rock was a "revolutionary" popular music. It will consider the emergence of music as mass culture and early jazz criticism, the swing era and the birth of *Down Beat*, the rise of a jazz art world, and how jazz art discourse after the birth of bebop defined its boundaries in ways that marginalized pop in the jazz tradition.

Chapter 2 looks at how *Down Beat* reacted to the decline of the big band era and struggled to survive as a commercial music publication in the 1950s, adopting a reactive, flexible editorial policy that followed new trends in popular music. It will examine *Down Beat's* brief history of country music coverage and how it positioned country music within the context of jazz-oriented magazine.

It will then consider how *Down Beat* covered rhythm and blues, and especially how critics treated "aranbee" differently than country music in the magazine, dismissing it as an embarrassing and unwanted cousin of jazz. The chapter also provides an account of how the Maher Printing Company diversified its magazine portfolio and charts the brief existence of sister magazines to *Down Beat* such as *Up Beat*, *C & W Jamboree*, and *Record Whirl*. Finally, the chapter considers how the emergence of the jazz education market allowed *Down Beat* to reorient itself toward young learning musicians instead of practicing professional musicians, and how this change, coupled with an economic resurgence for jazz in the mid-1950s, led the magazine to return to being a primarily jazz-focused publication.

Chapter 3 focuses on the year 1967 as a pivotal year in the American jazz press, when two important publications, *Down Beat* and *Jazz* (later *Jazz & Pop*), deliberately changed their editorial policies to include rock coverage. It will demonstrate the role of instrument manufacturers in pressuring the staff at *Down Beat* to adopt an editorial policy that was more inclusive of rock in an attempt to reach the huge market of students buying rock instruments such as drums, electric basses, and guitars, and how these commercial machinations affected the discourse and aesthetic the magazine promoted. The chapter also examines the controversy that rock's cultural accreditation caused among jazz critics, examining the cases of Leonard Feather and Ralph Gleason, who took opposing critical stances on the value of rock.

Chapter 4 traces the birth and meteoric rise of *Rolling Stone* as a rock authority. It examines the landscape of the American music press out of which the magazine emerged and how it defined itself in opposition to existing music discourses, including jazz discourse. It will also propose that the conflict between jazz and rock discourses in the late 1960s was reminiscent (with key differences) of the conflict within jazz discourse between "moldy fig" traditionalists and modernists earlier in the century.

Chapter 5 focuses on the interactions between jazz and rock through the lens of live music. It proposes that the 1969 Newport Jazz Festival was a pivotal moment in the emerging culture war between jazz and rock and examines the frequently ignored critics who encouraged the prospects of a jazz-rock merger years before the term "fusion" entered the critical lexicon.

I want to conclude by returning to Duke Ellington's provocation that "rock 'n' roll is the most raucous form of jazz, beyond a doubt." In a way, the underlying thrust of this book is to explain how Ellington could credibly make such a claim in 1955 due to the cultural debt owed to jazz by rock 'n' roll up to that point in history, but also how it would become untenable for him to make the same claim by 1970, when, despite their earlier resonances, jazz and rock genre cultures had undergone a series of collisions through the 1950s and 1960s which revealed the fault lines between them.

1

Jazz Culture as a Precursor to Rock 'n' Roll Culture

*Every parent remembers the hysteria attendant on the swing era
and the Benny Goodman band whose fans danced in the aisles of
the New York Paramount much as today's fans dance to R&B. And
the prophets of doom regarded that with as much dismay as do
today's critics of R&B.*

RALPH GLEASON, 1958[1]

*[Rock] music is a source of both an emotionally intensified sense of
self (as artists are heard to articulate their listeners' own, private
fears and feelings) and collective excitement, an illicit, immediate
sense of solidarity and danger, an unbourgeois innocence of caution,
an uncalculated directness and honesty.... What is on offer is the
fantasy community of risk—such a use of music has a long history:
in the 1920s and 1930s, middle-class adolescents were, for similar
reasons, drawn to jazz.*

SIMON FRITH, 1981[2]

I argued in my introduction that jazz scholarship followed a largely separate
path from the rest of popular music studies. The rift between jazz and popular
music has also manifested itself in the conventionally accepted history of
American popular music: both popular and academic histories have tended
to separate jazz—especially jazz created before World War II—from the

prehistory of rock 'n' roll. Too many music documentaries to mention begin
with a representation of the 1950s as a stultifying musical wasteland until rock
'n' roll revolutionized popular music culture. In the mythology perpetuated
by such accounts, the roots of rock 'n' roll were a blend of musical sources:
African-American rural country blues and urban rhythm and blues, hillbilly
country and western music, and polished pop from Tin Pan Alley. According
to music historian Chris McDonald, if jazz gets acknowledged at all in this
framework, it is often positioned within a "simplified, perhaps caricatured,
image of Tin Pan Alley, which gets portrayed as an exclusively white,
middle-class milieu, somehow isolated from the diversity and turbulence
of the larger American society."[3]

Some scholars have challenged the common-sense blues + country +
pop representation of the roots of rock 'n' roll. Gene Santoro, for example,
proposes that American popular music history should be understood as a
tangled web of interactions between jazz, blues, country, and rock, while
Philip Ennis argues that at least six distinct musical streams contributed to
the formation of rock 'n' roll: pop, black pop, country pop, jazz, folk, and
gospel.[4] However, more often than not, jazz culture—with its connotations of
big bands and dance ballrooms—is represented as the musical culture from
which rock 'n' roll *broke away*. Chris McDonald suggests that jazz and its
culture are left out as an influence on rock 'n' roll for another reason as well:

> jazz criticism and scholarship has been so invested in raising jazz's status
> to an art music that its most commercial [pre-World War II] forms have
> been given little serious coverage. On the other hand, many popular music
> scholars have been invested in portraying rock and roll as a "revolutionary"
> genre, and have therefore sought to show disjuncture, not parallels, with
> popular music from before 1950.[5]

This chapter makes the case for the importance of jazz as a key cultural
precursor to rock 'n' roll. In the interwar years, the words "teenage," "teenager,"
"subculture," and "youth culture" were not yet widely in use, but that is not to
say that the phenomena they described did not exist.[6] Like rock 'n' roll, jazz
was simultaneously vilified and valorized as mass culture, generating fans

around the world who were at least as interested in the cultural commodities of recorded discs as they were in live performances. It was a teenage youth culture thought by dominant culture to be subversive and morally corrupt, prefiguring the teenage "revolution" of the baby boomer generation. It was also a powerful signifier of racial politics in America, and a commercial music that was valued for its perceived anti-commercial authenticity (or dismissed when such qualities were seen to be lacking). Indeed, these similarities between jazz and rock 'n' roll as genres are precisely the characteristics by which rock 'n' roll is normally argued to be a "revolutionary" musical moment.

I will examine these issues by focusing on how they were represented in the press coverage of jazz in its heyday, which is to say I will also consider how jazz generated such an unprecedented and rich discourse in the form of the music press—a new attendant culture of magazines, critics, and readers who routinely tackled tensions and themes that were to become central to all future discussions of popular music. This last point is crucial, as even though jazz did not make a mass impact on the same scale as rock 'n' roll culture—perhaps giving an opportunity for some to challenge its status as a truly "mass culture"—the discourse and debates that accompanied jazz culture are indisputably relevant to and resonant of subsequent popular music cultures, including rock 'n' roll. Given of the wealth of research on American jazz culture in the first half of the twentieth century, this chapter also pulls together the relevant work that best illustrates the numerous ways in which jazz culture prefigured rock 'n' roll culture.

The early reception of jazz

The early critical reception of jazz needs to be contextualized within broader musical discourses occurring in the United States during the late nineteenth and early twentieth centuries. Paul Lopes has researched the rise of American popular music from the perspective of *Metronome*,[7] a national music periodical that was first published in January 1885 and targeted at the growing class of professional musicians. According to Lopes, *Metronome*'s readership of musicians struggled with what they perceived as a lack of public respect for the time and effort required for their profession, and defended their work by appealing to European standards of musical excellence:

> [These musicians] viewed their role as providing the finest music available in America, what musicians and educators referred to as "good" music. "Good" music referred to the European music repertoire and legitimate techniques of professional bands and orchestras. Since most professional musicians performed for the general public, however, popular tastes and popular music constantly challenged the conception of their role in creating and promoting "good" music.[8]

Popular bandleaders during this time such as John Philip Sousa therefore "performed an eclectic repertoire and prided themselves on mediating the various tastes of their audiences while bringing 'good' music to the public."[9]

In the first two decades of the twentieth century, critics in *Metronome* contrasted the "good" music of the "cultivated" European tradition against ragtime and early jazz. The latter genres were represented as a threat to "good" music because, it was argued, they unashamedly appealed to the lowest common denominator of public taste. Or as one article in *Metronome* puts it, composers of good music were being threatened by songwriters who "prostitute their talents by the writing of degrading ragtime and suggestive songs to please the taste of the perverted public.... The classical composer starves in his attic, while the illiterate one-fingered piano pounder gathers in the shekels from a generous public."[10]

The quote above is an example of an attack on *jazz as mass culture*, and is the first of three types of attack on jazz that I want to highlight in this section. Lopes draws on the research of Lawrence Levine to demonstrate that the late nineteenth century marked the beginning of a "significant transformation in the relation between high art and popular art."[11] In the case of music in the United States, Lopes argues that this movement was led by elite members of American society who aimed "specifically to distance themselves from popular entertainment and the popular classes," and developed a "high art" world through the establishment of symphony orchestras, grand operas, music societies, schools, and special journals.[12] The emergence of this new art world would widen the discursive gap between "good" music and the "corruptive" influence of popular music.

The early twentieth century was not only a time of transformation in the world of professional music making. It was also a time of great innovation in mediating technologies that significantly changed the ways music was disseminated to audiences, as Neil Leonard explains:

> Before 1917 Americans heard jazz "live," that is, played directly to them, in dance halls, saloons, barrel houses, brothels, lumber and turpentine camps, riverboats and at minstrel and vaudeville shows, carnivals, parades and funerals. After the war people still hear it "live," but more and more it reached them "canned," that is, through mechanical sound-reproducing devices: the player piano, the phonograph, the radio and the film sound track. Conceived at the end of the nineteenth century, these devices were developed and widely marketed in the first part of the twentieth century. They grew up with jazz and strongly influenced its diffusion and evolution.[13]

Various popular music scholars have argued that postwar rock 'n' roll and rock—as opposed to earlier popular music genres—were defined in part by a new kind of relationship with recording technology. Reebee Garofalo, for instance, has claimed that "rock 'n' roll differed from previous forms of music in that records were its initial medium ... [recording] technology exists as an element of the music itself."[14] Meanwhile, Theodore Gracyk viewed recordings to be a key component of the rock aesthetic, with the genre's major musical developments always having "occurred in recording studios, as in the cases of Presley, Dylan, and the Beatles."[15] David Brackett argues that the roots of this transition predate rock 'n' roll; instead, he uses the term "sonic aesthetic" to describe a period in the early 1940s in which trade papers recognized the importance of coin-operated jukeboxes as a way of measuring the popularity of music, leading to "an emerging discourse [that] tentatively recognized recordings as texts":

> This sonic aesthetic, based on the unique qualities of sound associated with particular performers and performances, could only circulate

beyond a specific performance space on radio broadcasts or mechanically reproducible recordings—sheet music could not communicate subtle timbral differences, let alone the microrhythmic nuances responsible for different grooves (easily felt by dancers but elusive for transcribers), or the pitch inflections that enliven melodies with otherwise limited pitch content (easily hummed along with by well-trained listeners but not amenable to even-tempered notation).[16]

Interestingly, however, jazz scholars have also made similar arguments, but trace the roots of this important shift even further back in history to the first decades of the twentieth century. Scott DeVeaux argues, for instance, that the development of recording technology caused a transformation in musical aesthetics which allowed the performer to be prioritized as an artist instead of the composer, and that it was jazz (as opposed to rock, rock 'n' roll, or jukebox era music) that first demonstrated the change:

> With the widespread introduction of recording technology into the popular market in the first decades of the twentieth century, music sound itself became a tangible object. In the process, the nuances of performance—which included African-American techniques of timbral variation, pitch bending, and swing as well as European rubato and expressive phrasing—could finally be made permanent. This had the potential to greatly expand the reach and prestige of the performer. In particular, recordings made possible the rise of the improvising jazz soloist, whose powers of on-the-spot creation are so compelling that the copyrighted music nominally performed seems to recede into irrelevance. As Evan Eisenberg has argued, "records not only disseminated jazz, but inseminated it ... in some ways they created what we now call jazz."[17]

Although scholars point to different historical moments when discussing the changing dynamic between notation, live, and record-oriented music cultures, as early as 1921 phonograph records had become a significant way for Americans to listen to music. Leonard claims in that year alone "over 100 million records were manufactured, and Americans spent more money for them than for any other form of recreation."[18] However, the nascent record industry quickly faced intense competition from the rise of the radio, and with the sound quality of live radio broadcasts exceeding the quality of acoustic recording technology during that time, the two industries fought fiercely for consumers rather than complementing one another as they would later in the century. Despite their rivalry records and radio both began to change the way (not least the speed) in which music spread across the nation. Those aspiring musicians who were lucky enough to have access to recordings were able to teach themselves aspects of jazz performance by imitating the records of their favorite players, permitting them "to learn music without bothering with the formalism, discipline, technique and expense of traditional training."[19] In this way, the "Jazz Age" of the 1920s gave rise to certain foundational characteristics of a musical youth culture that are normally argued to appear only in much later musical cultures such as rock 'n' roll. As Burton Peretti notes, "jazz inspired adolescent white males to create cliques of appreciation and instrument playing, which led many of them to musical careers. Phonograph records and instrument instruction inspired high school boys ... to form bands."[20] These "cliques of appreciation" included record-collecting clubs, where young men gathered and argued with passion over the merits of hot jazz recordings. John Gennari documents how record-collecting clubs became a popular phenomenon across the United States by the mid-1930s, although several jazz fans who grew up in the 1920s, such as Marshall Stearns (who would become one of the most important early academic historians of jazz), remembered similar listening gatherings from their adolescent years as early as the 1920s.[21] Finally, I would suggest that any such shift away from a "song-as-text" paradigm oriented around sheet music toward a "sonic aesthetic" (to use Brackett's term) oriented around specific performances was already a part of live music culture. Jazz fans did not seek out hot jazz, live or recorded, because the *songs* were different, but because hot jazz bands transformed songs through distinctive performances (it should be remembered, for instance, that radio stations frequently broadcast live performances rather than recordings in the first half of the twentieth century and were just as able to transmit a sonic aesthetic as recordings).

It was not just young men for whom jazz was a crucial part of their social world. Chris McDonald notes that women also shaped their identities through their choices in entertainment and leisure; the young woman who epitomized the challenging of traditional gender roles through jazz in the 1920s was known as a "flapper," whom McDonald describes as "the vanguard of youthful femininity during the Jazz Age ... Behavior associated with jazz and the speakeasy context—dancing the Charleston, smoking in public, drinking—was quite daring for women of the time, and became emblematic behavior of flappers."[22] This brings me to the second common type of attack against jazz, which was to cast *jazz as an agent of moral corruption*. It was not just the radical subculture of flappers for whom jazz and dancing were important. Paula Fass argues that the 1920s were a time of unprecedented freedom for a young woman, who "was freer to engage in a variety of physical and mental experiences than ever before because the group that needed to approve of her behavior was not the tradition-oriented adult world of family and community but the experimental peer group."[23] For both young men *and* women, dancing was the most important of all social pastimes, as it represented an opportunity for young men and women to meet, and as Fass puts it, "the dancers were close, the steps were fast, and the music was jazz."[24] One of the more extreme descriptions of jazz as a moral problem is an article titled "Does Jazz Put the Sin in Syncopation?," which appeared in the *Ladies Home Journal* in 1921. This article cites some rather dubious "science" as evidence for the supposed negative effects of listening to jazz:

> A number of scientific men who have been working on experiments in music-therapy with the insane, declare that while regular rhythms and simple tones produce a quieting effect on the brain of even a violent patient, the effect of jazz on the normal brain produces an atrophied condition on the brain cells of conception, until very frequently those under the demoralizing influence of the persistent use of syncopation, combined with enharmonic partial tones, are actually incapable of distinguishing between good and evil, between right and wrong.[25]

It has been well documented that much of the mainstream press coverage of ragtime and jazz was unfavorable during its early years in the first decades of the twentieth century.[26] In one of the earliest sociological studies on the reception of jazz writ large, Morroe Berger noted that in addition to critiques of jazz that tried to link the music to connotations of "crime, vice and greater sexual freedom than is countenanced by the common rules of morality," another commonly voiced critique (and the third type of attack on jazz I want to examine) dismissed *jazz as an aesthetically primitive form of music.*[27] This argument dismissed jazz as simplistic and lacking musical sophistication and tended to be voiced by "musicians (and those on the periphery of the profession) associated with 'classical music' and forms of popular music other than jazz ... [who opposed jazz because] it was produced by musicians who were not educated in the familiar tradition, and did not conform to rules of public conduct developed by centuries of the concert stage" (despite the fact that many important jazz musicians were classically trained, they were generally written about as if they were not).[28] Studies of early American jazz criticism by Berger and other scholars are powerful reminders of how popular music discourse carries ideological baggage and how aesthetic judgments are often hinged on unspoken moral assumptions.[29] In the case of early reactions to jazz, music criticism was frequently used to naturalize racist ideology. Newspaper editors might think twice about publishing an outright racist polemic, but they did publish articles that represented jazz music as primitive, unsophisticated, and morally suspect. Early critiques of jazz were therefore sometimes merely a thin veil concealing racist stereotypes of the broader African-American culture with which jazz was associated. Furthermore, mass culture critiques of the commercialism of ragtime and jazz often carried implicit arguments or became conflated with criticisms of African-American culture as a whole, whereby criticisms of appealing to "the masses" or "the lowest common denominator" carried a subtext that African-American musical tastes and practices were somehow inferior to their Euro-American counterparts.

Jazz began to spark increasing debates about African-American vernacular music as a legitimate art form. There was no doubt that jazz was popular—the controversy was whether it had musical value or not, and the question of value was split along racial lines. Musicologist Scott DeVeaux argues that "the musical techniques that set jazz apart from European art music are precisely those that derive from black American musical folkways (and ultimately from Africa): swing, call-and-response patterns, vocalized timbre, 'blue notes', improvisation, and so forth."[30] While European art music had a history of criticism and canonization of "art" works, there was a poverty of literature that treated African-influenced music with the same level of reverence. It was for this reason that when white orchestras and composers like George Gershwin and Paul Whiteman began to incorporate syncopated rhythms and blue notes into European arrangements using symphonic instrumentations, the bourgeois art community took notice. Sometimes the primitivist argument was made implicitly, especially when discussing symphonic jazz, such as the work of Paul Whiteman or George Gershwin; this was the case when Walter Damrosch, then the director of the New York Symphony Society, wrote the following regarding the premiere of Gershwin's *Rhapsody in Blue*:

> To my mind it is epoch-making, in that he has succeeded in elevating the much-discussed, much-loved and much-hated music which commonly goes under the name of jazz, into the higher realms of art.... If the gifted Gershwin can carry his mastery of the American dance and imbue it with the finer emotions and aspirations of humanity, all I can say is more power to his elbow.[31]

For some champions of symphonic jazz, then, it was up to white, classically trained musicians to save a vital but vulgar folk music from itself by "elevating" it into "the higher realms of art." Other critics took a less racially one-sided view, notably Joel Augustus (J.A.) Rogers, whose essay "Jazz at Home" appeared in *The New Negro*, a landmark anthology published in 1925 containing fiction, poetry, and essays on African-American art and literature. *The New Negro* became the definitive text of the wider Harlem Renaissance movement, which sought to create a new and progressive black identity shaped by leading African-American intellectuals and artists themselves. Rogers suggested that jazz was quickly becoming an American art form but included black bandleaders, from the classically oriented Will Marion Cook to Harlem hot jazz bandleader Fletcher Henderson, among its chief innovators:

Musically jazz has a great future. It is rapidly being sublimated. In the more famous jazz orchestras like those of Will Marion Cook, Paul Whiteman, Sissle and Blake, Sam Stewart, Fletcher Henderson, Vincent Lopez and the Clef Club Units, there are not of the vulgarities and crudities of the lowly origin or the only too cheap imitations.[32]

For other critics, however, the "lowly" nature of jazz was its best feature. According to Ron Welburn, one early music critic to put forth such an argument was Roger Pryor Dodge, a professional dancer who penned occasional articles for *The Dancing Times*. Writing in 1929, Dodge championed the music of Louis Armstrong and Duke Ellington rather than Gerswhin and Whiteman. As Dodge puts it, black jazz differed

> from the civilized and elegant versions of the symphonic jazz band. For the negro has taken the least possible contribution from the notes of the melody. He distorts it beyond recognition, makes of it a new synthesis, and his product is a composition—whereas that of the symphonic band is no more than a clever arrangement.[33]

As Welburn notes, Dodge crucially considers improvisation to be a positive rather than negative musical characteristic of jazz, but perpetuates an equally problematic racist ideology by associating improvisation with what he calls "the primitive innate musical instinct of the negro" in contrast to the "civilized" symphonic jazz band.[34] Unfortunately, such racially essentializing arguments would reoccur through much jazz criticism in the first half of the century.

Both Rogers and Dodge were American, and along with European counterparts (particularly in the UK and France) were among the first to take jazz seriously, and in so doing articulated some of the themes that critics would later develop in the pages of the American jazz press in the 1930s. The tensions between low and high art, vernacular and cultivated musical traditions, race relations, the morally corruptive effects of popular song, and mass culture were all already topics of debate in popular music discourse. It was jazz, not rock 'n' roll, that first drew such issues into the spotlight because it fused together otherwise disparate cultural spheres, resulting in a clash of values: jazz brought together black and white audiences, African-American and Euro-American instrumental techniques, virtuosity, and complex arrangements with improvisation and dance rhythms. Indeed, the intensity and frequency of these debates, as well as consumer demand for jazz journalism, would only grow when jazz experienced another surge in popularity in the mid-1930s, ushering in the swing era and the birth of a dedicated American jazz press.

The swing era and the birth of *Down Beat*

The nationwide impact of rock 'n' roll is often attributed to the mass media through which it was disseminated, with the television debut of Elvis Presley on the Ed Sullivan show in 1956 frequently cited as a breakthrough moment for the genre. But over two decades before Presley's appearance on Ed Sullivan, a different kind of mass media watershed occurred in jazz history when the Benny Goodman band's nationwide radio broadcasts set young audiences from coast to coast abuzz with the sounds of big band swing. In August 1935, the Benny Goodman orchestra played to an ecstatic crowd of young fans at the Palomar Ballroom in Los Angeles. Goodman's band had been on the verge of failure only a few months earlier, but on the advice of a young jazz impresario named John Hammond, Goodman hired a struggling black bandleader, Fletcher Henderson, to create arrangements of hot jazz for his big band. According to Gene Lees, the three-hour time difference between the east and west coasts played a key role in Goodman's success, whose radio broadcasts in the east were heard late at night, when many listeners would have been asleep: "but they were broadcast on network at a much earlier hour in the west, and by the time the Goodman band reached Palomar on its American tour, young Californians had become excited about their 'swing' music."[35] Goodman brought the big band swing of black bands to a mass white audience and in so doing untapped an unprecedented youth market for music.

There are many parallels to be found between the youth subcultures of American swing of the second half of the 1930s and rock 'n' roll in the mid-

1950s. As a letter to the editor in the *New York Times* put it in February 1939, "swing is the voice of youth striving to be heard in this fast-moving world of ours. Swing is the tempo of our time. Swing is real. Swing is alive."[36] Historian Lewis Erenberg has researched the rise of swing-oriented youth culture in 1930s America through compiling a rich oral history of correspondence from hundreds of swing fans recollecting their experiences. Their memories paint a convincing picture of how swing stimulated the development of a vibrant youth subculture. A lack of jobs resulting from the Great Depression in the 1930s meant that both working-class and middle-class youth were far more likely to stay enrolled in school rather than leaving early for work, and high-school students comprised the main following of swing bands. One such youth, Jack McNulty, recalled how in the late 1930s "every aspect of my life and that of my friends, revolved around big bands, jazz dancing, jitterbugging, in my formative teens … our heroes, our dress, look, styles, morals, sex lives [were based on immersion in bands and] the lives they showed us."[37] Erenberg also noted how long before the advent of the transistor radio in the 1950s, teenage swing fans were asserting their own cultural identity through arguments with their parents about what to listen to on the radio:

> To avoid such battles, many teens simply went and purchased their own radios. [One fan] Jean Lukhard noted that "most of us had our own little radios at bedside (mine was a little white Philco named Oscar)." So popular were band shows that parents of high schoolers often prohibited radios in their childrens' rooms. As one parent put it, "It's not that I object to swing. But I don't think they should study to it or go to sleep to it." Yet many did. Every night, [another swing fan named] Elliot White fell asleep with "the radio tuned to late-night broadcasts."[38]

Erenberg's collected correspondence with swing fans describing their experiences from the era poses a direct challenge to received assumptions about the "revolutionary" behavior of 1950s teenagers. Just like future generations of rock 'n' roll fans, many teenagers during the swing era recalled that bands and music were central to their formation of identity, which they actively shaped at dances, listening to their own radios, and developing a distinct youth music culture that distinguished them from their parents.

The swing era was chronicled in numerous magazines created to meet demand from both musicians and fans for the latest news, criticism, and debate about swing culture. The most important of these papers was *Down Beat*, which continues to be published in the present day, making it the oldest surviving American jazz periodical. *Down Beat* was launched in 1934 by the unlikely character of Albert J. Lipschultz, whose primary business was selling insurance to working Chicago musicians and who came up with the idea of a musician's newspaper as a means to expand his business.[39] *Down Beat*'s first months of publication contained no reviews or criticism and focused more on sweet dance bands than on hot jazz. Lipschultz sold the magazine to Glenn Burrs by the autumn of that year, which was fortunate timing for Burrs: he quickly adapted the magazine's focus to cover the swing craze ignited by the Goodman band in 1935. Burrs hired Carl Cons, who had a penchant for sensationalist headlines, as an associate editor and business manager to cover not only the big band craze but also the politics and gossip that surrounded it. Historian David Stowe conducted a survey of the various periodicals that covered jazz during the 1930s, but concludes that *Down Beat* did more to shape critical and popular opinion on jazz than any other publication of the era:

> Other journals directed primarily at musicians also made swing the focus of their coverage, while the trade journals *Variety* and *Billboard* included extensive coverage of the swing industry. Some publications were directed less at musicians than at swing enthusiasts of various levels of sophistication: *Swing* for jitterbugs, *Tempo* and *Jazz Hot* for Hot Club members, and, by 1940, the *H.R.S.* [Hot Record Society] *Rag* and *Jazz Information* for serious listeners and collectors. In addition, some general-interest publications ran regular articles on jazz by well-known writers: the *New Republic*, *Colliers*, *Saturday Evening Post*, the *New Yorker*, *Mademoiselle*. But *Down Beat* combined the most in-depth coverage of swing developments with a quality of Chicago earnestness, yellow sensationalism, risqué girlie photos, and distinctively freewheeling editorial atmosphere that made the exchange of sharp polemics irresistible to both writers and their audience. "Hardboiled and sentimental, inaccurate and thorough, unpredictable

and consistent, patriotic and rebellious, idealistic and cynical," charged one writer, "the paradoxical 'Beat' is the image of the screwball business it serves and the direct reflection of the God-damndest staff that ever handled a magazine."[40]

By the late 1930s, *Down Beat* had established itself as a national paper for dance band musicians and hot jazz enthusiasts (for a time the front page title for the publication was *Down Beat: The Musician's Bible*). The paper featured lessons on instrumental technique and transcriptions of solos alongside music industry news, cultural commentary, and a healthy dose of gossip (the September 1937 issue, for instance, published what would have presumably been considered a saucy photo exposé on "Musicians and their wives on the beach"). In 1936 *Down Beat* also launched an annual readers poll with a range of categories for swing and sweet bands. It also attracted contributing writers from the UK, such as Stanley Dance and Leonard Feather, the latter of whom moved to New York and ran the magazine's East Coast office out of his apartment. Other jazz fans who ended up publishing their first national writing in *Down Beat* included Charles Frederic Ramsey, George Avakian, and Ahmet and Nesuhi Ertegun—all of whom later went on to influential careers in the recording industry (Ramey produced records for Folkways, Avakian led the popular music division for Columbia Records, while Ahmet Ertegun founded Atlantic Records where he was later joined by his elder brother Nesuhi).[41]

There was also by this time a regular record review section called "Disc-Cussin" edited by critic Paul Eduard Miller. (A prolific jazz writer, Miller also published a *Yearbook of Popular Music* in which he used the terms "jazz," "hot music," and "popular music" interchangeably.)[42] Nearly all songs in his "Disc-Cussin" column were summarized in terms of whether a particular solo or composition was breaking new ground—at the end of the review section was a summary of the "Best New Compositions of the Month" and "These fine solos recommended"—and the most common critical put-down was to declare the tune "conventional," as in this appraisal of new Louis Armstrong sides: "With the best band Armstrong has ever had behind him, these latest efforts are pitiful.... Fine musicians ... all sit by wasting their talents on

Figure 1.1 *Benny Goodman cover issue of* Down Beat, *January 1938. Copyright 1938 © by Maher Publications. All Rights Reserved. Used by Permission.*

conventional accompaniments for the maestro."[43] Arrangements had to be "startlingly good" to merit attention, as opposed to tunes merely "patterned after the ideas" of other popular bands. Miller argued, however, that "when considering [Fletcher] Henderson, let's not forget that the originator of a style cannot be accused of being conventional now that his style has become commercialized."[44] The tendency to value new, original alternatives to formulaic, commercial sounds was clearly an important part of critical discourse at this time; Rex Stewart's "Back Room Romp" "starts off with a brand new idea, and it is to be regretted that with such a fine beginning the tune is permitted to slip into the category of typical Ellington stomps in the call-and-answer manner."[45] Bunny Berigan's treatment of "Mahogany Hall Stomp "is smooth and well played, yet almost every name band now recorded has at least these two characteristics."[46] Two novelty tavern tunes "have been waxed by [Artie] Shaw's outfit. Just why, it is difficult to understand, but for coin machine operators, this platter will be a surefire nickel-getter."[47]

Of all the American jazz critics writing in the 1930s, no one had greater influence than John Hammond, who carried added credibility as a talent scout with industry connections, an impresario, and a political agitator who consistently put a spotlight on the racial politics—and particularly the injustices—of jazz culture. Born into a wealthy white family, Hammond attended Yale for a year and a half before dropping out, but thanks to an annual trust income, Hammond was able to pursue his jazz obsession without any hardship. As a writer, Hammond contributed to a large number of publications both in the United States and in Britain, including the *Chicago News*, *Down Beat*, *Gramophone*, *Melody Maker*, and *Music and Rhythm* (which he co-founded). Hammond's critical values were often extreme and controversial. In addition to being a staunch campaigner for racial equality in the music industry, Hammond was also keenly interested in left-wing politics and wrote for such papers as the *New Masses* and the *Daily Worker*. However, as Stowe suggests, "perhaps most controversial among Hammond's critical positions was his outspoken belief that blacks played superior swing."[48] The importance of this particular contribution to jazz discourse cannot be underestimated. Hammond saw that racism in the music industry allowed white jazz bands to enjoy commercial success on a level that was simply unavailable to black bands. As a result, black bands were forced to constantly innovate to remain competitive. As Stowe points out, "much of the appeal of black bands was precisely their 'otherness' ... the canon of authenticity promoted by Hammond and others valued precisely those musical qualities that set African-Americans apart from their white imitators."[49]

Hammond's crucial contribution to jazz discourse, then, was in reinforcing the association of *authenticity* and *artistry* with the black innovators, in opposition to music that, as a result of becoming popular (a feat that in a white-controlled culture industry was much more likely for white musicians), was so imitated that it became conventional, *mechanical*, and *commercial*. Of course, Hammond was not the creator of these discursive values—he was not even the first to apply them to jazz discourse—but he was a key critic if only due to the sheer breadth of his influence. Such influence was not unproblematic, as Christopher Wells has noted in an incisive critique of Hammond and other white jazz critics working at the time:

> The emerging power of jazz critics in the 1930s came through a particular blending of those roles through which cultural brokerage takes shape; these critics built hybrid careers as journalists, critics, historians, and impresarios. Through this multifaceted identity, they shaped public perceptions of artists, acquired control of performance and recording opportunities, and initiated the discourse that would define the jazz canon. Their races (generally white), genders (generally male), and social positions (often elite, generally well educated) afforded them access to potent platforms from which to both espouse opinions and advance projects. Through these media, they constructed specific expectations for the performance of authentic hot jazz. (181)[50]

The power of Hammond and other critics allowed them to create a discourse that "promoted and encouraged, but also fetishized, difference… [critics gave themselves] license to define and police black aesthetics."[51] Hammond's critical opinions carried such significant weight largely because of his position as a music industry insider responsible for scouting some of the finest jazz artists of the decade. Although historian John Gennari put Hammond on a par with critic Leonard Feather as "arguably the two most consequential behind-the-scenes players in the music's history,"[52] Feather saw things differently. In a *Down Beat* column published in 1956, Feather described Hammond's contribution as follows:

the most important jazz critic of all, *anywhere* ... because John doesn't just write about his beliefs, he acts on them, and because of his actions we had a Benny Goodman and a Teddy Wilson and boogie-woogie and a Billie Holiday and a couple of dozen other discoveries—and, most important of all, the slow but sure decay of Jim Crow in jazz. John could write a million words and they wouldn't have a fraction of the value of those contributions.[53]

The racial segregation of Jim Crow laws was symptomatic of a wider catalogue of racial injustice in interwar jazz culture. Even the invention of the genre label "swing" (as opposed to "jazz") was indicative of the tendency toward segregation. The music of bandleaders like Chick Webb, Duke Ellington, and Fletcher Henderson bore all the hallmarks of swing years before the "Swing Era," of course, but it was only when Benny Goodman, a talented white bandleader, began working with Henderson and performing the black bandleader's arrangements under the advice of John Hammond that the potential market of that music to a mass white audience became evident, and as a consequence of its mass appeal, the popular press generated a new label to describe the phenomenon: just as "rhythm and blues" tended to get categorized as "rock 'n' roll" once Bill Haley and Elvis Presley began performing it, so too did much jazz become categorized as "swing" through Goodman's popularity.

Swing was clearly big business by the end of the 1930s, but even at its commercial peak, the prospect of black bands reaping their share of rewards from the boom was always in question. Helen Oakley (one of the only female jazz critics writing at the time) noted in 1938 that "colored attractions are now definitely in demand throughout the entire country ... and they have become unmistakable box office draws." Yet according to Erenberg, "except for a few top units, by 1939 mass interest in swing pushed white bands ahead of black orchestras in earning capacity and audience recognition."[54]

Some white jazz fans sought out black jazz bands over white bands, of course, because like John Hammond, they viewed jazz made by black musicians as more authentic. But the ideology of "pure" jazz being created by "authentic" black bands masked a problem: black bands were often recording and performing hot jazz because they had no other choice. As Scott DeVeaux argues, black bands would have been very willing to record sweet music, waltzes, and other "commercial" music had they not been discouraged by the recording industry.[55] The Fletcher Henderson orchestra, for instance, was well known in the live performance circuit as having an excellent repertoire of waltzes:

> [But] little of this is reflected in the recorded output of black bands—or in their public image. "It seems to be congenitally impossible for Negro dance musicians to play straight," reported *Fortune* in 1933. In the recording studio they were encouraged—or required—to conform to the stereotype. Black musicians naturally resented this, if only because dignity seemed to lie in versatility—the ability to play hot and straight. As one industry observer wrote of Fletcher Henderson, "The contrast of jazz and erudition is what makes for the effect." "Somewhere in the vaults of some record company," noted Rex Stewart, "there may still exist recording gems which the Henderson band made and that were rejected because they were considered too perfect musically for a negro orchestra....Few people remember how extensive and beautiful Henderson's waltz book was. No band of that era could cut the band playing waltzes."[56]

David Stowe provides additional detail on the racial discrimination practiced by record labels:

> For a time the recording industry discouraged musical "passing." What was permissible in live performances and, by extension, on remote broadcasts was discouraged in the recording studio, ostensibly because executives believed that the audience for race records—African-Americans, they assumed—would not accept it....Hoping to enlarge his "breakthrough" audience by recording a ballad, [saxophonist] Andy Kirk was discouraged by Decca founder Jack Kapp, who told the bandleader, "You've got something good going for you. Why do you want to do what the white boys are doing?"[57]

Anxieties over whether black or white bandleaders could play (or should be allowed to play) certain genres—be it sweet jazz, ballads, waltzes, upbeat swing, or improvised hot jazz—could also be found on the pages of *Down Beat*. David Brackett has argued that one of the editorial projects of *Down Beat* in this period was "the search for an 'authentic' form of white jazz," and that some critics were equally concerned with the perceived inferiority of white jazz musicians.[58] Debates about whether particular music genres had "essential" characteristics often belied deeper questions about whether the racial categories of "black" and "white" were a matter of essential versus cultural difference. Swing was popular for the same reason it was controversial—musical conventions associated with African Americans were now deeply entangled with the mainstream of American popular music. Jazz culture, therefore, became a site where the racial and cultural politics of the era were expressed through debates about the aesthetics of swing music, racial integration in big bands, and racism in the music industry. Such debates showed how assumptions about racial difference were not only reinforced and policed but could also be challenged and disrupted.

The rise of a jazz art world

The period during which swing music was experiencing the height of its commercial success coincided with jazz fans becoming increasingly obsessed by the perceived corrupting impact of the forces of commercialization. A journal called *H.R.S. Society Rag* was launched in 1938 with the aim of rekindling an interest in 1920s jazz, and its writers openly criticized swing era music as a weak, commodified dilution of the "real thing." The *Rag* was merely the first of a number of specialist journals that were created to cater specifically to a small but growing movement of revivalists and collectors of old jazz records. They defined themselves, according to Bernard Gendron, as the "only authentic alternatives to the two dominant mainstream jazz journals, *Down Beat* and *Metronome*, which were altogether beholden to the swing phenomenon."[59] Gendron suggests that "these purists were driven not only by nostalgia but by a revulsion toward the swing music industry, which by shamelessly pandering to the mass markets had in their eyes forsaken the principles of 'true' jazz."[60] Meanwhile, Erenberg describes "a growing army of record collectors, stimulated by the Hot Record Clubs' advocacy of reissues and historical accuracy, intersected with radical jazz critics in their insistence on the superiority of the unadulterated sounds of New Orleans and Chicago jazz."[61]

By 1942, the mainstream swing publications were striking back, with *Metronome* critic Barry Ulanov labeling the revivalists as "moldy figs." Leonard Feather interviewed jazz musicians for their perspective on the debate, including Louis Armstrong, who, to the disappointment of many revivalists, declared in an interview that "swing" and "jazz" were basically the same thing as far as he was concerned:

> To me as far as I could see it all my life—Jazz and Swing is the same thing....In the good old days of Buddy Bolden....It was called Rag Time Music....Later on in the years it was called Jazz Music—Hot Music—Gut Bucket—and now they've poured a little gravy over it, called it Swing Music....No matter how you slice it—it's still the same music.[62]

Jazz revivalists framed the battle as a fight between "true jazz," an authentic folk music, against desecrated, commercialized swing. Meanwhile, swing enthusiasts argued that "the best in jazz has been and always will be successful, commercial," viewing the debate as one of fusty musical traditionalists versus progressive innovators pursuing new sounds.[63]

Some jazz musicians, such as Charlie Parker and Dizzy Gillespie and their colleagues, experimented with new musical forms and sounds so brilliantly that they invented a bold, rhythmically complex, harmonically adventurous small group style at the jam sessions in after-hours clubs of New York that would later be labeled as "bebop." Although bebop is sometimes mythologized as a musical revolution led by musicians reacting against the commercialization of jazz and instead pursuing art for its own sake, Scott DeVeaux has demonstrated in detail that much like the hot jazz musicians of the 1930s, musicians created bebop for a host of reasons—some artistic, some entrepreneurial, but rarely with the intentional approach of separating art from commerce.[64] This did not stop the music press from creating a sensationalist rivalry between bebop on the one hand and traditional jazz—which was also sometimes called

"Dixieland"—on the other. As Bernard Gendron has argued, *Down Beat* and *Metronome* deliberately fueled the dispute to sell magazines:

> [The jazz press] spiced up its pages with headlines like "Police Avert Clash of Dixieland and Bebop," "A Jazz Purist Guilty of Collecting Re-bop!" and "Bop Gets Monday Night Home in Dixie Hangout," while provoking a public argument between Dixielander turned bebopper Dave Tough— "Dixieland Nowhere Says Dave Tough"—and the revivalist leader Eddie Condon—"Condon Raps Tough for 'Rebop Slop'".... [It was also good copy] for the jazz press to provoke criticisms of bebop by other musicians, and many obliged, including Fletcher Henderson, Hot Lips Page, Nat "King" Cole, Lester Young, Artie Shaw, and Benny Carter [as well as Benny Goodman, Tommy Dorsey, and Louis Armstrong].[65]

The new genre of bebop embraced a modernist aesthetic not unlike that of the twentieth-century avant-garde classical world. Progressive jazz musicians like Thelonius Monk openly praised the works of Stravinsky and Schoenberg rather than the popular music on the charts, while Miles Davis spent time at Julliard studying European art music. The trend was indicative of a growing reaction among black musicians against traditional racial stereotypes; as Gendron put it, "since it was often assumed that black musicians only played from instinct, many boppers developed their technical virtuosity and theoretical skill."[66] Critics in the jazz press, of course, quickly latched onto this development. One of the most outspoken proponents of jazz as modern art music was *Metronome* editor Barry Ulanov, who "announced that *Metronome* from then on would be subtitled the *Review of Modern Music*."[67]

As swing gradually began to decline from the charts and well-established big bands broke up over the course of the 1940s, bebop appeared in the middle of the decade as though it might succeed swing and break through to a mainstream audience. Although no bebop record ever made the popular charts, the press had developed an appetite for both the aesthetic debate over the music's value and the controversy surrounding some of its leaders, including Dizzy Gillespie's stage mannerisms and eccentric fashion sense, and the drug problems and police arrests of other bop musicians such as Charlie

Parker. According to Gendron, however, most notable of all was the power of the press, promotion, and advertising to construct the meaning of the music being performed:

> Though having considerable control over their musical product, the musicians seem to have had little control over its public meaning. Their own comments about their music were filtered through the jazz press, or worse the mass magazines, quoted out of context, and redistributed in the printed texts to fit the ideologies and marketing strategies of authors and publishers. The bebop musicians neither possessed their own means of discursive dissemination, nor as "mere" jazz musicians were they endowed by society with sufficient cultural credentials to offset those of the critics. Indeed, they were sorely dependent on these critics for increases in their own cultural accreditation.[68]

Bebop never crossed over to the pop charts or a mainstream audience, of course; instead it was championed by critics in the press as an art form, and as such marked a turning point—jazz, which throughout the 1930s had been discussed as a popular art, had now acquired high art discourse.

As music critics continued to make the case for bebop as an art form, other musicians who would have previously been situated firmly within the boundaries of "jazz" gradually found themselves pushed to the margins of the genre. David Ake has argued that one such performer was saxophonist and singer Louis Jordan.[69] Although Jordan's bands were rooted in the blues, rhythmically swung the majority of their numbers, and featured excellent improvised solos—three of the traditional hallmarks of jazz—Ake cites a plethora of history books, recording anthologies, and documentaries that completely ignore Jordan in their presentations of jazz history.[70] On the other hand, he notes that Jordan holds a prominent place in histories of rhythm and blues (or "R&B") and rock 'n' roll as a founding father. However, unlike other R&B progenitors who managed to remain viewed as being part of the jazz tradition, such as Lionel Hampton, Fats Waller, and Count Basie, Jordan rose to fame just as jazz was in the process of being reconstructed by critics and musicians as an art music:

Louis Jordan's influential bands attracted extraordinarily large audiences, swung furiously, and featured fine soloists, [so] how can we explain historians' reticence to also grant Jordan credit as a significant *jazz* musician? ... [The problem] hinges predominantly on Jordan's historical location. That is to say, while R&B precursors Hampton and Basie continued to perform through the rise of the bebop style in the 1940s and for many years thereafter, they had already established themselves as significant contributors. Louis Jordan's fame, however, coincided almost perfectly with the emergence of bop, and I argue that the seeming lightheartedness of Jordan's music flags him as a problematic figure for critics attempting to paint jazz since the 1940s as a serious art form.[71]

Despite his music containing many elements of jazz, Louis Jordan did not fit into the context of bebop, which would gradually become represented as the definitive jazz sub-genre of the 1940s. As Ake contends, there were many specific factors that made Jordan and his music a problematic fit for retrospective accounts of 1940s jazz. In terms of the blues structures of his songs, most New York–based bebop musicians who were his contemporaries "consciously avoided blues chord changes and stylistic devices," opting instead for more complex chord progressions; Jordan's music on the other hand, despite swinging and featuring solos, was deliberately *simple* and *fun*.[72] As for swing rhythm, Jordan's music was intentionally *danceable* (a key reason for its popularity), which stood in contrast to the new rhythmic innovations developed by bop drummers who aimed to break up the flow of a steady beat.[73] Finally, Jordan was recognized as much for his *singing* as he was for his saxophone playing, and singers had long been marginalized by their fellow musicians and critics in the jazz world.[74] As Ake notes, despite the fact that singers have always remained far more popular with the record-buying public than instrumentalists in jazz, this "has not altered the equally inescapable fact that vocalists go largely overlooked in jazz history texts. With the exception of Armstrong, Holiday, and to a lesser extent Sarah Vaughan, singers are viewed with suspicion by jazz writers: Singers aren't 'real musicians,' they're 'entertainers.'"[75] For all of these reasons, Ake argues that Louis Jordan has been all but absent from jazz histories: "if we follow the evolutionary narrative constructed by many historians—that the complexity and seriousness of the bebop style demonstrates jazz's claim to art-music status—then Louis Jordan's seemingly frivolous approach must lie outside of that elite world."[76]

Scott DeVeaux has made a similar argument using the example of Slim Gaillard.[77] As a guitarist, pianist, vocalist, and entertainer, who frequently used comedy in his songs, Gaillard posed many of the same problems as Jordan for jazz critics. Like Jordan, Gaillard was a competent improviser and "capable of soloing effortlessly on the endless variants of the 'I Got Rhythm' chord progressions he favored," but the arc of his career coincided with the rise of bebop:

> With bebop, jazz became serious business. In the 1930s, we can tolerate a degree of foolishness—the eccentric, clowning behavior of Fats Waller is one example. But after a certain point, the foolishness is left behind. Jazz becomes an art music. It is artistically focused, musically virtuosic. Music that doesn't get the message no longer counts....The stuff that is left out goes somewhere else. And where it goes is not hard to find. Think back on Gaillard: the verbal trickery, the physical humor...the habit of sitting on the boundary between the races, the sense of insider's knowledge (What he presents is something only hepsters should know); even the electric guitar playing! All suggest a line that points away from jazz to rhythm-and-blues (a category defined by *Billboard* in 1949), toward Chuck Berry and Little Richard, and ultimately to...rock 'n' roll. Gaillard, Jordan, and Cole *do* have a place in history. It's just not the same history.[78]

The additional complication in a jazz tradition that leaves out Louis Jordan and Slim Gaillard is its relationship with what was termed "race music"—the term used by *Billboard* and other trade papers prior before they replaced it with "rhythm and blues" in 1949. As David Brackett has documented, "race music"—the unsubtle code label used by the recording industry to designate popular music perceived to be associated with African Americans (either as producers or consumers)—was an important category for the industry from the mid-1920s until it became "rhythm and blues" at the end of the 1940s.[79] This was enshrined in *Billboard* charts in 1942, when "the paper began, albeit in a tentative fashion, to produce a representation of the popularity of 'race records' ":

> This development showed that race music had achieved a level of commercial importance such that the music industry felt it advantageous to track it in some fashion. The chart, dubbed "The Harlem Hit Parade" (HHP), "based on sales reports" from a variety of record shops (one assumes, in African American neighborhoods), continued from October 1942 until February 17, 1945, when it was replaced by a "Most Played Juke Box Race Records" chart.[80]

Some artists included on race record charts included "country blues" artists such as Tampa Red and Washboard Sam, but others, such as Jordan and Gaillard—as well as Eddie "Cleanhead" Vinson, Nat "King" Cole, Joe Turner, and Lionel Hampton—clearly had a footing in jazz as well as pushing forward styles like boogie woogie and jump blues. Interestingly, Brackett also notes that white artists—including Bing Crosby, Tommy Dorsey, Harry James, Glenn Miller, and Glenn Haymes—counter-intuitively appeared on the race records chart as well.[81] Brackett argues that swing and jazz "played an important role in facilitating the crossover between race music and the mainstream" at the beginning of the decade, but "whereas in the early 1940s, swing dominated both the discourse around jazz and the recordings in the popular mainstream, the understanding of the identity of jazz had become more complex" after bebop.[82]

Leonard Feather and Barry Ulanov, the two chief critics writing for *Down Beat* and *Metronome,* respectively, during that time, were among the most vocal champions of bebop and the construction of jazz as a serious art, and by mid-century, both had produced influential histories of jazz that applied an evolutionary narrative to jazz, representing its trajectory over time as moving away from primitivism toward an increasingly sophisticated, modernist music.[83] John Gennari has done a comparative analysis of jazz histories created from the 1930s to the 1950s and concluded that the accepted narrative of jazz in such books contributed to a turning point in jazz discourse, where "the broader public's engagement with jazz in the years after World War II increasingly took on its own more conventional academic overtones."[84] Gennari goes on to contrast the more "impulsive, melodramatic, and slangy" discourse of jazz fan magazines with the history books "written under the influence of mid-twentieth-century academic humanities and social science."[85] However, oftentimes these two kinds of jazz writing could be found side by side within the same publication: the news reporting in *Down Beat* and *Metronome* may still have carried sensationalist headlines, but it becomes obvious when examining the columns of critics like Feather and Ulanov that the magazines were actually a forum to debate and develop ideas about jazz as art that would later appear in their book-length histories of jazz.

By the late 1940s the main news headlines in *Metronome* and *Down Beat* were charting "one major economic crisis after another as each of the mighty orchestras of the Swing Era was first rumored to be dying and then, with the major exception of Duke Ellington's orchestra, did in fact disband."[86] The factors for swing's economic decline are numerous, but certain key events had an undeniable impact. The draft during World War II meant that there was a scarcity of musicians at the same time that touring expenses rose as a result of restrictions imposed on the use of commodities such as rubber and gas. The war also ended the depression in 1943, meaning that men and women who had previously lacked the economic security to start families now found themselves in a position to do so, and started marrying in record numbers. An increasing amount of the population began to stay at home and adopt family lifestyles, which unfortunately coincided with vast numbers of veteran musicians returning home to flood the dance band market, leaving many bands playing to near empty auditoriums.

None of this was helped by the field of jazz suffering from an identity crisis at the time. Whether it was Dizzy Gillespie playing bebop or Stan Kenton making progressive big band arrangements, musical departures from more danceable (and popular) jazz styles were simultaneously used in the press as "the scapegoat for the commercial demise of jazz" and given the task "of saving jazz from its economic miseries"; however, as Gendron points out, "there was clearly an incompatibility between the imperative to become as European and avant-garde as possible, on the one hand, and to become as commercially successful as possible, on the other."[87] Throughout the crisis, *Down Beat* itself was trying to navigate its own survival as a music publication. Although *Down Beat* has aligned itself with jazz for most of its existence, it has gone through many transformations and editorial policies, and as jazz from dance bands to bebop hit a low ebb in its commercial potency by the late 1940s, the magazine needed to rethink its own strategy for survival.

Conclusion

The history of jazz in the first half of the twentieth century has been heavily researched, and it is clear that it was a vital music that prefigured many of the characteristics of subsequent popular music culture in America. It is also evident that jazz generated an amount of press coverage that was previously unparalleled in popular music, which included the creation of specialist music periodicals such as *Down Beat*; the music press simultaneously chronicled and contributed to the construction of a jazz tradition and helped to shape the key terms of debate over the value of jazz as both a popular music and a serious art music.

However, it is also clear that key critics in the mid-1940s began to tip the discourse of jazz increasingly toward framing the music as serious art and away from concerns about the importance of jazz as a popular music. As Scott DeVeaux has argued, with this shift, the whole narrative of jazz history becomes adjusted accordingly: "for if bebop is the juncture at which jazz becomes art music, then earlier styles are once again in a precarious position—unless it can be demonstrated that in some important sense they had always been art music, and that status was simply unacknowledged."[88] This shift had implications not only for the place of jazz in art music history, but for the absence of jazz in *popular* music history. Any jazz-oriented music after bebop that could be argued to fit the model of serious, complex art music would remain identified as jazz, but if it featured elements that did not easily fit the new model, such as humor, vocals, or a strong dance beat, it risked being marginalized from the emerging jazz tradition. This is why, despite embodying the standard hallmarks of jazz—blues roots, improvised solos, and swing feel—1940s artists like Louis Jordan, Slim Gaillard, and others occupy a marginal place in jazz history but a prominent one in rhythm and blues.

The American jazz press becomes an interesting focus of study to explore alternative ways of representing jazz and its relationship with other forms of popular music and to reconsider the potential relevance of jazz to seemingly unrelated genres such as rhythm and blues, rock 'n' roll, and rock. The music press is also interesting because we are able to see how an anti-commercial musical discourse develops within a music publication even when the very existence of the publication is predicated upon the mass appeal of the music. On the one hand, jazz critics were concerned about the dwindling commercial sales of jazz, and on the other, they were in the process of reconstructing jazz into an art music that ideally worked unfettered by commercial concerns; critics complained that no one bought jazz without fully acknowledging that they routinely excluded popular race records and rhythm and blues—and performers of which who often had links to jazz—from the jazz canon. Within a few short decades, then, jazz had gone from being a subversive form of dance-floor filling popular music that was dismissed as commercially driven mass culture, an agent of moral corruption, and an aesthetically primitive form of music, and transformed itself into a genre vying for (and increasingly winning) status as an art music.

2

The Dismissal of Rock 'n' Roll by Jazz Critics at Down Beat

As any of you who have looked at Down Beat know, the more detail, the more problems. It's not a matter of what to leave in, but what to leave out. History is storytelling. Naturally, any story is a matter of exclusion—deciding what to leave out. It's a matter of drawing boundaries.

SCOTT DEVEAUX, 2005[1]

Nobody likes rock and roll but the public.

BILL HALEY, 1956[2]
QUOTED IN *DOWN BEAT*, MAY 30, 1956

By 1950, *Down Beat* was suffering a financial crisis. Its success was built on the popularity of big band culture, and the swing era had clearly passed. The sounds of bebop had found favor with influential jazz critics but had not caught on with a mass audience. Meanwhile, big bands were expensive ensembles to keep on the road, and with changing audience tastes, even the best bands struggled to survive: two of the top three big band winners in *Down Beat*'s 1949 poll broke up before the poll results were published—an ominous sign for both the remaining bands and the music press that covered them. *Down Beat*'s editor and owner, Glenn Burrs, found it increasingly difficult to keep the magazine afloat, and in May 1950, he sold it to the John Maher

Printing Company.[3] John Maher, *Down Beat*'s new owner, had no particular interest in jazz but was determined to reinvigorate the magazine. In 1952, he lured Hal Webman and Norm Weiser from *Billboard* magazine to become the new editor and publisher of *Down Beat*, respectively, in an effort to ensure that the magazine would be directed by staff who were in touch with the commercial music of the time. Jack Tracy replaced Webman as editor in 1953, but continued the policy of covering new forms of popular music. As David Brackett has noted, by the end of the 1940s, *Billboard* "had re-christened race music and old-time music (which by the early 1940s was being referred to as 'hillbilly' or 'folk' music) 'Rhythm and Blues' and 'Country and Western.'"[4] This change could also be felt at *Down Beat*, where there was a conscious effort to expand coverage outside the big band field, and over the next few years the magazine would cover styles as diverse as jazz, country, rhythm and blues (hereafter R&B), pop, classical, and rock 'n' roll.[5] Jazz coverage always predominated, especially in the columns of mainstays like Leonard Feather, Ralph Gleason, and Nat Hentoff, but the staff were also clearly attempting to live up to the genre-spanning slogan that began appearing on the magazine's cover: "Everything in the World About the World of Music."

This chapter examines one of the most turbulent periods in the history of *Down Beat*, when the magazine persevered by reinventing itself as a general popular music periodical. It focuses in particular on the way jazz critics reacted to the emergence of rock 'n' roll and R&B. In his book on genre formation, Fabian Holt remarks that "jazz people paid little attention to rock and roll in the 1950s."[6] However, while this view may be widely held, I contend that there is more to the story than this statement implies, and certainly when it comes to *Down Beat*. Indeed, there is a neglected, seldom referred to period in the history of the magazine when a largely forgotten female music journalist named Ruth Cage defended R&B from critical attacks, which were coming not only from the usual suspects in trade papers and the middlebrow press but also from established jazz critics and musicians.

What can we learn from the dismissal of R&B and rock 'n' roll by jazz critics, and what did it mean for jazz musicians and critics to dismiss R&B by replicating arguments used to dismiss jazz fans decades earlier? To what extent do the commercial considerations of a music magazine's publisher affect the aesthetic discourses printed in its pages? To answer these questions, we must explore how music journalism works as a commercial institution. Music magazines are not staffed by disinterested observers objectively reporting events in a music scene, and in order to understand the history of popular music we must understand how music magazines work *as magazines* and how the peculiarities of personal and professional relationships in the world of music journalism—not least the daily considerations of a specialist music periodical trying to compete and thrive as a commercial publication—shape the way music genres are written about.

Corn of plenty

The music we now refer to as "country and western" first made headlines in *Down Beat* in 1949. The trade press at that time was reporting a state of crisis in the music industry: the stability achieved with swing music and dance bands at the turn of the 1940s was being challenged by the declining demand for live performance and the increasing popularity of records. As Richard Peterson explains:

> By 1947 "canned music," that is recorded music played on jukeboxes, at "sock hop" dances, by disc jockeys over the radio, and at social occasions in the home, was seriously eroding the employment of musicians and the sale of sheet music. The growth of recorded music was dramatic. In 1941 total record sales of all types of music amounted to $41 million dollars, but by 1947 sales had reached almost a quarter of a billion dollars. Then even record sales turned down—17 percent in 1948 and another 8 percent in 1949.[7]

The public preference for recorded music over live performance was perceived to have contributed to the demise of many a professional dance band, and when record sales themselves began to slide, no one knew quite who to blame for the downturn. Country music proved to be an easy target: as Peterson notes, country tunes began selling well around 1948, and stood out "as the most conspicuous members of a barrage of songs created outside Tin Pan Alley and a threat to the standard way of making hit songs."[8] Fiddle and guitar songs began to carve out a significant share of the market (between 4 and 7 percent), signaling the start of a process that would gradually push big band orchestra arrangements and Tin Pan Alley off the charts over the next decade.

Since its inception in 1934, *Down Beat* had covered popular music, developing its own discourse and critical conventions. For the first few years the record reviews were not divided into genres; instead, the reviewer's choice of language would position the music somewhere among the intermingling currents of hot jazz (the swinging, improvised-soloing, authentic stuff), sweet music (the stuff that didn't necessarily swing or feature improvisation and followed European ballroom music styles more than African-American influences), and pop (the music of Tin Pan Alley). By the late 1940s, however, the record reviews section was neatly divided into five genres—hot jazz, swing, dance, vocal, and novelty—and each was judged slightly differently according to its own genre-specific criteria.

Country music didn't fit into any of the molds above. While hot jazz fans may have bickered in the past with pop fans over issues of taste, both parties were hurting from the instability of a changing music industry, and they found a common enemy in country music. Tin Pan Alley was losing its hold on consumers and swing music was barely hanging on; meanwhile, musical genres once considered to be on the fringes of popular taste, notably so-called "race" music on the one hand and "hillbilly" music on the other, were beginning to sell in increasingly large numbers. At the end of the 1940s, country music was sufficiently different from the worlds of pop and jazz to be an obvious target for derision. As Bernard Gendron has documented, when big bands began to suffer at the end of the 1940s, *Down Beat* writers sometimes pointed the finger at the relative success of country music, running headlines including "Music, Where Is Thy Swing? Cowboys, Barn Dancers Romping and Stomping," "Hillbilly Boom Can Spread Like the Plague," and "That Hillbilly Threat Is Real."[9] The language used was clearly derogatory: the word "hillbilly" was derived from the slang term "billy," meaning a rough, unschooled, and simple-minded person, and a "hillbilly" was such a person from the remote backwoods of the Appalachian Mountains.[10] Country performers understandably considered the term to be offensive, and indeed, most of the national coverage of their commercial success was condescending. *Newsweek* referred to country music records as coming from the "twang-wail-and-howl division of the electronics industry," and couched the commercial success of country in terms such as "corn of plenty."[11] Even the word "corny," a popular term among jazz musicians for describing bad or outmoded musical taste, suggested a connection between the fields of corn associated with Southern farms and culture that was deemed old-fashioned, backward, and trite.

Nevertheless, country music's growing popularity was undeniable. Peterson demonstrates that alongside the negative coverage came more enthusiastic articles in trade papers like *Billboard* and *Variety* that praised the potential of the music as a source of profit for the industry, suggesting with increasing frequency that "it would be more profitable to incorporate country music into the larger commercial music business than to ridicule and suppress it."[12] Less than a year after *Down Beat* ran the derogatory headlines quoted above, it too changed its tack: advertisements with a distinct country flavor began to appear in the magazine, indicating that its editorial aesthetic and commercial imperatives were not always aligned. One advertisement for Premier Multivox amplifiers, for instance, features a photo of a guitarist decked out in full cowboy regalia, smiling proudly beside his Premier Multivox amplifier.[13] Advertisers for musical instruments would no doubt have been aware that the readership of *Down Beat* included a significant demographic of instrument-buying professional musicians who gigged performing a range of genres out of commercial necessity, and its circulation was still larger than that of *Cowboy Songs*, *Country Song Roundup*, and other country-friendly fan publications.

By January 1953, a new "country" heading had appeared in *Down Beat's* record review section, while a new country news column contained industry information, features on new artists, and announcements of live performances. The country music column would go through a range of incarnations in the following eighteen months and would be titled at various times "Folksy Music," "Country & Western," "Nashville Notes," and "Sashayin' Around."

Country music insiders—radio DJs, managers, and small-time performers such as Bill Bailey—were hired to write these columns, and it appears that *Down Beat's* editors were agreeable to the eclecticism of musical opinion that resulted, where a column written by a country music promoter could appear on the same page as a jazz column written by a long-established *Down Beat* critic. The strategy to attract a new kind of readership to the magazine was transparent, and new subscribers were actively recruited in the country music columns: "C&W FAN CLUBS: There are constant regional reports in this mag on all c&w activity. Advise your members in your fan magazines that one-year subscriptions [to *Down Beat*] (26 issues) is a five spot… or you can be billed later."[14]

The country music coverage in *Down Beat* was full of contradictions. Record reviews placed a strict emphasis on a country record's commercial potential in its reviews section and seems to downplay the skill involved in writing, performing, and recording country repertoire (marking a stark contrast to the magazine's jazz record reviews). The country reviews were generally much shorter than jazz reviews—usually fifty words or less—providing a brief description of the music and then, strikingly, a verdict on the song's commercial potential. Jazz reviews, which often appeared on the same page, rarely concerned themselves with whether or not the song might be a hit, which left more room to discuss the record's artistic merit.

Feature articles on country artists, on the other hand, tended to emphasize the trained musicianship of country musicians as performers. Instead of promoting his cowboy image as authentic, for instance, a feature on singer Ferlin Huskey emphasized his versatility as a professional entertainer: "in addition to straight vocal work, Ferlin also does novelties, comedy, and impressions. His catalogue of impressions runs to some thirty ranking country and western, as well as pop, singers."[15] Another article on performer Rex Allen notes that "the Republic Pictures star almost became a classical singer at one point. He was offered a music scholarship to the University of Arizona after working in high school music groups."[16] Neither article pretends to depict the performers according to their stage persona: instead they focus on the credibility of the performers as skilled professionals rather than romanticizing them as untrained, "authentic" folk artists. This kind of coverage made sense for a jazz-oriented publication like *Down Beat* and also highlights the importance of vaudeville and variety entertainment conventions in the country music scene of the 1950s.

Country and western coverage in *Down Beat* reached saturation in June 1954, a month that also saw the magazine celebrate its twentieth anniversary. The anniversary issue included a retrospective account of the history of *Down Beat*, featuring a collection of clippings and headlines from the previous twenty years; but what stands out from the jazz coverage is a full-page article justifying the inclusion of country music. Written by James Denny, the manager of WSM Radio in Nashville, "Why the Upsurge in Country Music?" made the case for country coverage in *Down Beat*:

> For many years, the experts on musical history believed and taught that true folk music consisted solely of old songs. Now they are revising their books in this respect. Modern country-and-western performers have added several chapters to the history of the nation's music in recent years, and compositions by these latter-day exponents have become as much a part of the national scene as the hamburger and the jukebox.[17]

According to Denny, there were four factors that contributed to the success of country music. First, the career trajectory of fiddler-turned singer Roy Acuff, the biggest star of the Grand Ole Opry in the late 1930s and early 1940s, was explained as part of the wider shift across all dance bands away from instrumentalist bandleaders as stars and toward the crooning singer star with band accompaniment. The next two factors at play were the migration from the rural south to cities around the United States coupled with the growth of radio, allowing country to spread to a wider audience. However, the fourth factor—and Denny's most provocative argument—regarded an alleged decline in the quality of Tin Pan Alley songwriting:

> All of this reflects the fourth element responsible for the vast appeal of country music—the decline of popular music that took place as the country ballads were growing into their own. Popular music grew out of a phase of folk music, too—jazz and the blues. True, this was urban folk music, but folk music just the same. It began with the Negro groups

in Memphis and New Orleans and spread across the nation. But the spread of popular music tended to damage the quality of its product. Commercialization resulted in stereotyped forms and weak lyrics. The public lost interest and subconsciously began to look for sincerity and freshness of expression, This, they found in country music both old and new.[18]

Here Denny suggests an alignment between seemingly disparate genres—country, jazz, and blues—through their shared status as sincere "folk music." No doubt Denny saw the purpose of his article, at least in part, was to convince a core audience of jazz-oriented *Down Beat* readers that country coverage belonged in the magazine. However, like jazz and blues before it, country music was not some pure folk expression untouched by the forces of commerce. The myth told in "Why the Upsurge in Country Music?" has been recycled in country music journalism ever since the country record boom of the early 1950s. However, as country music scholar Joli Jensen explains,

> What this narrative does *not* allow us to understand is that country music has always been commercially constructed.... The "legends" of country music were commercially produced and disseminated; the "traditional" sound of country music is a sound designed to *seem* authentic. But country music is no more (or less) "real" than pop or rock or jazz or blues or folk.[19]

Nor does the narrative explain Denny's confusing attempt to welcome the "freshness" of country music into the world of commercial pop charts, while simultaneously condemning the pop world as one that corrupts and dilutes musical quality. Indeed, Denny concludes his article by praising the trend that "pop tunes and pop lists from the past few years have consisted of country and western recordings" while predicting that "this new era of national music tastes may see the field of country and popular become one and the same," without any apparent fear that country might suffer the same fate which, according to him, fell upon jazz and blues.

The editorial team at *Down Beat*, along with the rest of the music industry, was clearly having difficulty in understanding how to write convincingly about the country music scene. The assumptions behind its inclusion in the magazine clearly stem from commercial concerns of expanding its readership rather than considerations of country music's aesthetic or cultural worth. By the middle of 1954, *Down Beat's* editorial shake-ups were seemingly beginning to pay off. Publisher Norm Weiser wrote that "we are happy to report that our 'new look,' which started some twelve months ago, has resulted in the largest readership ever enjoyed by any consumer music publication."[20] However, the magazine's new flexible approach to editorial scope meant its support for new genres could prove fickle: just after James Denny predicted that the "new era of national music tastes may see the field of country and popular become one and the same," *Down Beat* started reporting that the country craze might be on its way out, and meanwhile devoted increasing coverage to another formerly marginalized genre: rhythm and blues. This change in policy is not likely down to chance: keeping in mind that publisher Norm Weiser was a former *Billboard* staffer, it is worth noting the close relation between *Down Beat's* editorial policy changes and the fortunes of the *Billboard* record charts. Phillip Ennis has shown that both country and R&B songs began crossing over to the *Billboard* pop charts in increasing numbers in the 1950s.[21] Country songs were the first to make a significant crossover impact, but in 1954 there was a 50 percent increase in the total number of crossover hits, and of these, "almost twice as many records moved from R&B to pop than from country to pop—the exact reverse of the previous year."[22] Compare this with *Down Beat* headlines: a mere four months after the magazine optimistically announced "The Upsurge in Country Music," another article appeared bearing the headline "Who's to Blame for Dip in Country Music Field?" According to country disc jockey Nelson King, the cause for the downturn was the growing "fad" of rhythm and blues:[23]

> When the r&b men became aware of the growing acceptance of c&w music a few years back, they DIDN'T try to hook onto our wagon by getting r&b artists to record country tunes. They DIDN'T try to influence their r&b writers toward penning r&b songs with a Tennessee mountain flavor, but they DID try to improve the r&b field by seeking better rhythm and

blues material and producing better rhythm and blues records.... Now look at us, and ain't we a sorry sight. When a few rhythm and blues records began to gain widespread recognition, we DID become greatly alarmed, decrying a trend that might ruin country music. For years we have loudly proclaimed the clean, family type entertainment to be found in country and western music, but when the r&b trend started, did we, as an industry, try to find better, cleaner country type songs? We DID not. While all the time whining of an outside invasion of our field we were writing, publishing, and recording country songs with a definite rhythm and blues flavor.[24]

King lamented in another article that the distinctive features of country music were also being eroded by the influence of pop music and that country artists were now being pressured to select songs based on their cross-over appeal: "country music for pop's sake; not country music for country music's sake."[25] The fear of mixing genres expressed here is reminiscent of wider fears of cultural miscegenation in the United States, and King urged a more rigid policing of genre boundaries to protect country music's aesthetic and commercial identity; the only solution, he felt, was to return to "country music artists using true, country material."[26] (Interestingly, King's claims that R&B musicians refused to allow a country flavor to seep into their music do not bear up to scrutiny; as Chuck Berry recalled in his autobiography, "curiosity provoked me to lay a lot of the country stuff on our predominantly black audience and some of the club goers started whispering, 'Who is that black hillbilly at the Cosmo?'"[27] Berry likewise claimed that his 1955 debut single "Maybellene" was "my effort to sing country-western, which I had always liked.")[28]

Nelson King was one of several voices in *Down Beat* to express concern that country music songwriters and performers were becoming too influenced by the musical conventions of R&B and pop. One article described how country DJs rallied against unwholesome R&B lyrics,[29] while another argued that pop disc jockeys discriminated against country music.[30] The last issue of *Down Beat* to feature country music coverage of any kind contained a front-page article that was almost desperate in its tone; written by Chicago DJ Randy Blake, the title ran "Disc Jockey Urges Return to Spinning Only Country Music," as he emphasized the importance of keeping genre boundaries separate:

This is the music of the people, people who represent the family...the backbone of a country—people whose emotions are honestly simple, direct, and wholesome....Country music is country music, period. Rhythm and blues is a field unto itself. Pop, likewise. So is grand opera. Each has enjoyed the fullest extent of its own prosperity by, and only by, catering to its own established audience. Things were all right in these fields–until somebody yelled panic. One day everything was normal. The next day it wasn't. Overnight, somebody had said rhythm and blues was on the upbeat. Somebody believed that. And somebody had yelled, "Oh my gosh, we are in the wrong end of the music business!" The news spread. The panic—call it a trend if you like—was on.[31]

Blake's worries, of course, turned out to be unfounded: what was initially labeled as a decline for country can retrospectively be seen as a period of transition in the sound and style of country music. Over the 1950s country recordings incorporated musical elements from pop recordings such as lush string orchestrations and arranged background vocals, giving way to the rise of what later became known as the "Nashville Sound." All the while both country and R&B music were continuing to make significant inroads to the pop charts. While it was true that country music coverage gradually declined in *Down Beat*, Maher Publications clearly seemed to have more faith in the commercial longevity of country music than some of its writers who were sounding the alarm. In January 1955, Maher Publications ran an advertisement in *Down Beat* publicizing the launch of a new magazine, *Country & Western Jamboree*, proudly claiming it to be "the first major monthly publication designed exclusively for all country and western fans, complete with by-line articles by the top stars, picture stories, current news reports from all sections of the U.S. and Canada, complete route list of all major C&W road shows, and many other exciting features."[32] Printed out of the same Chicago headquarters as *Down Beat*, *C & W Jamboree* launched in March 1955. With country now excluded from the magazine, it remained to be seen whether R&B music could survive comfortably alongside *Down Beat*'s mainstays of jazz and dance band coverage.

The rhythm and blues debate in *Down Beat*

Down Beat had covered performers like Louis Jordan and Joe Turner since the 1940s, and some of these would later be recognized as founding fathers of rhythm and blues. But the term "R&B" first began to regularly appear in the magazine in 1952, with the introduction of an "R&B Notes" column written by Ace Mitchell and the addition of a rhythm and blues category to *Down Beat*'s record review section. The transition was not a smooth one, however, and the introduction of a "rhythm and blues" category next to the existing headings of "jazz" and "popular" records coincided with the appearance of a peculiar disclaimer at the outset of the section:

> Records in the popular and rhythm-and-blues sections are reviewed and rated in terms of broad general appeal. Records in the jazz section are reviewed and rated in terms of their popular musical merit. Records in the popular and rhythm-and-blues sections of interest from the musical standpoint are marked with a sharp (#), or, if exceptionally interesting, a double sharp (##).[33]

The disclaimer contains some interesting assumptions: as a rule, it would appear that popular and rhythm and blues records were apparently so lacking in musical value that they could only be discussed in terms of "broad general appeal," or to put it less charitably, in terms of how they might appeal to the lowest common denominator of the music-listening audience. By contrast, any record that purported to be "jazz" could be scrutinized on its musical (read "artistic") merit. Whoever wrote the disclaimer stopped short of saying that records in the popular and rhythm and blues categories were completely worthless, so instead they use the vague criterion of "broad general appeal," but there is a definite sense of confusion in how to reconcile judging the music of Tin Pan Alley and rhythm and blues in a review section developed with a strong jazz aesthetic, without continually evaluating the former categories as some kind of sub-standard jazz.

Down Beat's R&B coverage was sporadic in the early 1950s, before being taken over by Ruth Cage in September 1954. It may be contentious to call Cage the world's first rock critic, but she is certainly a unique and mostly forgotten figure in what one might call the pre-history of rock criticism; moreover, she was one of the earliest apologists for R&B writing for a predominantly white consumer audience. Although she was never a featured journalist in the magazine—there was maybe one page of R&B coverage for every twenty pages of jazz and tin pan alley—what she did write now reads as a treasure trove of insights, as she tried to make sense of the R&B phenomenon for *Down Beat's* jazz-oriented readership.

The term "rhythm and blues" gained currency in 1949 when *Billboard* used it to rename what had previously been their "race music" charts. But by the mid-1950s new substitute labels were being volunteered, as the industry began to perceive a change in the relationship between the music and its market, as R&B acquired a growing white youth audience. As Cage noted, several of the labels borrowed from the lexicon of jazz culture: one record label used the term "cat music" to describe R&B,[34] and in 1955 interviewers occasionally referred to Elvis Presley as a bebop artist.[35] Cage also acknowledged the influence of the deejay, Alan Freed, who, she reported, had "decided that the kind of music he spins will have a new and broader connotation under a new name. On his shows it's 'rock and roll' not 'rhythm and blues.'"[36] Although rock 'n' roll and rhythm and blues have since come to be perceived as different genres, in the mid-1950s *Down Beat* tended to use the terms "rhythm and blues," "R&B," and "rock 'n' roll" interchangeably.

Cage was one of the earliest journalists to write insightful articles about the aesthetic and social debates surrounding the R&B phenomenon. In one column, for instance, she offered a perceptive critique of the relationship between genre divisions in trade papers and racial discrimination in the music industry and beyond:

A New York radio commentator, Buddy Bowser, got us off on an unhappy train of thought the other day when he said to his listeners, "Rhythm and blues is just another form of segregation." Perhaps we wouldn't have got so interested in this line of thought if we hadn't noticed a short time later that Sammy Davis Jr.'s record of *Hey, There* is being listed by a top trade paper in its r&b standings. Maybe there is some other explanation of why a ballad, sung like a ballad in conventional pop style, gets in the lineup with the tunes with a blues beat. However, neither Rosemary Clooney nor Johnnie Rae's versions of this hit got so classified. What made Sammy's different?.... If hits are determined by sales, how can Ruth Brown's *Oh, What A Dream* be No. 1 on r&b charts and then nowhere on pop charts (especially since Patti Page's version is somewhere in the 30s in such listings)? Just what is it that makes Joe Turner's *Shake, Rattle, and Roll* a thing different from the carbon copy version by Bill Haley's Comets? Not many of us have forgot that r&b is simply the latter-day name for race records.... We pursue Bowser's thought in the interest of the performers who don't get a fair shake.[37]

Throughout the time she wrote for *Down Beat*, Cage examined the racial assumptions about the R&B audience as the music grew in popularity with a mass audience of both white and black teenagers. In early 1955, R&B came under attack in several American music publications. Some of the more colorful critiques appeared in *Variety* which, along with *Billboard* and *Cashbox*, was one of the main trade papers for the music industry at the time. One article expressed concerns that major record labels were losing their market to small independent labels, noting that "the major diskers are not finding it easy to crack the r&b formula."[38] Another article, titled "A Warning to the Music Business" followed, condemning record labels for trying to make a "filthy fast buck" from sexually suggestive R&B songs:

Music "leer-ics" are touching new lows.... We're talking about "rock and roll," about "hug," and "squeeze," and kindred euphemisms which are attempting a total breakdown of reticences about sex. In the past such material was common enough but restricted to special places and out-and-out barrelhouses. Today "leer-ics" are offered as standard popular music for general consumption, including consumption by teenagers.... Before it's too late for the welfare of the industry—forgetting for the moment the welfare of young Americans—VARIETY urges a strong self-examination of the record business by its most responsible chief executive officers.[39]

David Brackett suggests these articles were "driven by fears about aspects of the music style, the threat to the established structure of the music industry, and the breakdown of extant social barriers that would accompany an unprecedented integration of African American performers into white society."[40] With hindsight Brackett's conclusion reads as common sense, but surprisingly few journalists came to similar conclusions at the time; instead much of the middle-brow press followed *Variety's* lead and expressed similar concerns.[41]

One of the few sane voices in the press at this time was none other than Ruth Cage. Unlike her contemporaries, Cage pointed out that R&B's transition from being almost totally ignored to suddenly becoming "the greatest threat ever to the nation's morals in two issues of *Variety* is certainly as quick a climb as show business ever has recorded."[42] She quickly dismantled the arguments against sexually suggestive lyrics in R&B songs:

> They want us to believe that until r&b came along, romance in songs was all a matter of hearts and flowers and walking along shady lanes. For their information, we may suggest a perusal of some notions which were, and are, promulgated by such sophisticated (as opposed to "primitive") sources as Cole Porter, Lorenz Hart, Harold Arlen, and others. If they want a quick example, may we point to a line in a presumably acceptable current hit which goes "I'd love to make a tour of you" and defy them to point out a bluer line in an r&b hit.[43]

Cage prefigured arguments now common in popular music studies by maintaining that the real reason R&B was causing such a stir was that it was mobilizing the purchasing power of the teenage market. She also suggested the R&B "leer-ic" story in *Variety* was fueled by discontented major labels losing their control of the record charts to independent labels, bolstering her case by pointing out that *Variety* had a history of loyalty to the performance-rights organization ASCAP, which was taking a financial hit due to many R&B hits belonging to its rival, BMI, for rights licenses. Formed in 1914, ASCAP had traditionally represented the interests of long-established music writers and publishers of Tin Pan Alley. Meanwhile, BMI had been formed in 1939 by radio networks as a rival licensing agency to ASCAP and was associated with publishers and writers who had tended to be excluded from membership in ASCAP, including those working in genres such as Latin, R&B, and country music. As Cage put it:

> At first it seems inconsequential that in the same publication seven of the top 10 tunes are licensed by BMI while only three are potential coin grabbers for ASCAP. But then an editorial points out that r&b is mostly BMI and this statement rather jogs a memory which recalls this publication's being terribly pro-ASCAP when BMI was in the throes of birth…. The fact is that new talents and new writers are producing the stuff the public is buying. This fact is not likely to delight the fellow whose annual stipend depends on the tastes of yesteryear and who apparently can't readjust their skills.[44]

Sensible as these arguments were, not long after the *Variety* articles many of the key jazz critics at *Down Beat* also began dismissing R&B. Ralph Gleason (who would, of course, later become co-founder of *Rolling Stone* in the late 1960s) took something of a moderate stance, arguing that "if [kids] listen to enough r&b long enough, the elemental rhythm and vocal won't be enough for them. They're going to want music, too. And you know what just might happen? They might turn to bands again," by which Gleason meant jazz-based big bands.[45] According to Gleason, R&B was a positive influence as long as it motivated kids to dance, but it would only be a matter of time before R&B lost its appeal and tastes would revert toward trained musicians playing music that married dance beats and "musical sophistication." Dance bandleader Les Elgart shared this view in another *Down Beat* feature, arguing that the teenage audience might well turn to big bands after they became bored with the "limitations" of the R&B form:

Figure 2.1 *Bill Haley cover issue of* Down Beat, *May 30, 1956. Copyright 1956 © by Maher Publications. All Rights Reserved. Used by Permission.*

I think the kids have gone wild over the rhythm & blues stuff as a kind of reaction to bands that have gone too far out in the cool school direction. The average teenager isn't emotionally moved by the modern sounds—progressive jazz, or whatever you want to call it. They have turned to

rhythm & blues...because that's where they feel that driving excitement
that was so much a part of the great bands of the swing era. But the rhythm
& blues form is so limited that they get over it in a hurry....Meantime, it
has stimulated their sense of rhythm—they learn to dance to it—and that's
where we come in.[46]

A segment of the jazz community, then, was dismissing R&B for aesthetic
rather than moral reasons. Although Gleason and Elgart stopped just short
of calling R&B "primitive," Ruth Cage quoted a DJ as explaining that R&B's
"crude primitiveness has an appeal,"[47] while James Ferguson, Bill Haley's
manager, was quoted as saying "rock 'n' roll is the savage beat of the tomtom
come to us through the ages."[48]

In another column, Cage suggested that the relationship between R&B and
jazz was closer than most jazz critics wanted to admit:

A recent argument that lasted through a dozen cups of coffee here began
with speculation as to what finally would result as rhythm and blues gained
"respectability." The comparisons between the development of r&b and
similar events in jazz not so long ago are pretty obvious. The question is will
there be as much distillation, as much bastardization (as r&b itself may well
be considered), and will there be as great a variety of by-products musically.[49]

Cage also declared that in arguments concerning the genealogy of R&B,
she tended to lean toward "the cousin-in-the-jazz-family version."[50] The
comparisons between the development of R&B and jazz do seem obvious,
but Cage was the first writer at *Down Beat* to explicitly voice them, and once
she exposed them she tried to legitimize R&B using the same methods that
early jazz critics used to legitimize jazz. She used her columns to showcase
R&B artists coming from professional musical backgrounds, and especially
artists versed in the jazz idiom. Charles Brown was praised for performing his
own compositions and described as "handsome, educated, talented, and well-
schooled in show business."[51] After noting that Wild Bill Davis studied music
on a scholarship at college, Cage emphasized that he "created an important
new jazz sound with the Hammond organ" while playing with Louis Jordan,
created an arrangement for the Count Basie band, and played Birdland leading

his own band, where he "killed the customers with everything from *Shake, Rattle, and Roll* to *April in Paris.*"[52] She drew attention to how vocalist and trumpeter Joe Morris paid his dues playing in bands for Lionel Hampton and Buddy Rich before moving into R&B.[53] In her later columns, Cage became even more explicit in championing of the musical professionalism among such R&B artists as Jimmy Brown and Dakota Staton:

> [Jimmy Brown] hired no musician who could not read music. He will allow no movement, no gesture that doesn't belong in the arrangement. His guys will play in public only those things they've rehearse [*sic*] hard and well. Brown is a fine trumpeter and a terrific showman.... We watched him rehearse and chose to use his story here, hoping that it would add to our theory that we were witnessing growth [in R&B], not decay.[54]

> [Dakota Staton] brings to every record, every performance a background of musical training. She has studied harmony, music, theory, and has taken vocal training in the classics and semiclassics .... She's another example of a fact which seems to be news to those who've just discovered the field— she's got *trained talent.*[55]

Such arguments seemed to have little impact on the magazine's longstanding jazz critics. Leonard Feather, perhaps the most well-known jazz critic of his time, and certainly the most influential writer at *Down Beat*, addressed Ruth Cage and the R&B debate directly, acknowledging that while "there may be something to her theory" about the campaign against R&B being rooted in ASCAP-BMI tensions, "what concerns me ... is not simply the lyrical content but the overall musical level of this phase of the arts."[56] Noting that "rhythm and blues" was simply an updated name adopted by *Billboard* in 1949 to replace the politically incorrect genre of "race records," Feather contrasted early "race" music with the R&B of 1955:

> Back in the 1920s and '30s the biggest sellers included such singers as Bessie Smith, Ethel Waters, Ma Rainey and scores of others in the same general class. Instrumentally there were Louis Armstrong, Fletcher Henderson, even Duke Ellington.... There was no real borderline

between jazz and r&b music. All right, let's look at the r&b picture today .... With rare exceptions such as Joe Turner and Ruth Brown ... the entire r&b market today is dominated by three factors:

- Vocal groups that seem to have issued a challenge to one another boasting: "We can sing out-of-tuner than you can."
- Tortured, tortuous ballad singers who would lose all their appeal if they were fitted with spines.
- Instrumentalists who made names for themselves on personal appearances by playing a solo and simultaneously removing their jacket, pants, shirt, and teeth while suspended from a chandelier.

These artists are suitably served by two kinds of material:

- Love songs whose lyrics literally (and I mean *literally*) could have been written by any reasonably bright third-grader in grammar school.
- Novelty jump tunes written by the younger brothers of those who wrote the love songs.[57]

Feather's critique of R&B reveals how R&B coverage was situated quite differently than country in the context of a jazz publication. Like country music, R&B was being covered by *Down Beat* because it was quickly becoming a commercially significant music division from which musicians could earn a living and would, therefore, be of interest to *Down Beat*'s target readers; but unlike country, R&B was clearly related to the jazz tradition and when maverick critics like Ruth Cage drew connections between R&B and jazz, Feather therefore felt this might tarnish jazz's new reputation as a "respectable" music. Whereas Feather had never paid attention to country music in his columns, he clearly felt he had the authority to dismiss R&B. Feather did not explicitly take up the topic of R&B again, but continued to undermine the genre via his famous "Blindfold Tests," where a guest artist was blindfolded and asked to listen and provide comment to a selection of records. Feather would occasionally throw an R&B record into an otherwise jazz-oriented listening session, resulting in tests like one with Carmen McRae carrying the headline "Carmen Blanches on Hearing R&B," where McRae was given extended space to criticize the Lola Dee record "Ooky Ook":

if it's possible for me to give it no stars, can I do that? All right, well, no stars!... To begin with, usually with rhythm and blues you can't understand anything they're doing, and that's one of the main reasons I'm against it ....I don't think it takes any talent to sing [an R&B song like] *Sh'Boom*, but it takes talent to sing things by Cole Porter and Gershwin and Rodgers and Hart.[58]

Ruth Cage's R&B columns became less frequent throughout the remainder of 1955, but when they did appear Cage used them to champion the musical professionalism of R&B musicians to the *Down Beat* readership. On one occasion she invited arranger Quincy Jones to share his thoughts on R&B and was quick to emphasize his credibility as an arranger of jazz as well as R&B. Jones himself attempts to link R&B and jazz together: "it used to be that r&b and jazz were pretty closely related ... and we seem to be moving right back to that state .... As far as rhythm and blues is concerned, the words are really just for the sake of commercial convenience. The basic element of r&b is, in a sense, the basic emotional element in jazz."[59] Both Jones and Cage were keen to celebrate the rising R&B performer Ray Charles as an example of a trend toward increasing musical professionalism in the R&B genre. For Jones, it was not "just a matter of chance that Ray Charles is the top r&b musician in the country today as well as a very fine jazzman. If you think playing the blues has hurt his feeling for jazz, don't get caught in a session with him."[60] The status of jazz had also been boosted over the years by watershed performances at legitimate concert halls. It was no wonder, therefore, that Cage felt the debut of R&B music at Carnegie Hall was of great significance, which she hoped might pave the way to "a more respectful attitude toward this music with a beat and the artists who perform it with professional skill."[61]

Cage mined the intersections between jazz, R&B, and rock 'n' roll, and in so doing pointed toward an alternative way of conceiving the relationship between these genres. There are other significant artists that Cage could have covered which support this view and fit into a wider trend of genre-crossing in the 1950s. Eric Porter has argued that Dinah Washington, for instance, took a similar path with her career, making jazz, R&B, and pop records on a range of different record label imprints, while her "booking agents and record company simultaneously presented her as a blues, R&B, jazz, and, later, crossover artist."[62] Porter notes how Washington performed not just at jazz festivals and clubs but also at R&B venues and concerts that juxtaposed artists who were perceived to work in different genres, including a March 1956 concert sharing the stage with Thelonious Monk, Miles Davis, Terry Gibbs, T-Bone Walker, Little Willie John, and the Clovers in a gig billed as "Jazz vs. Rock 'n' Roll," and another concert in January 1957 alongside Ray Charles, Charlie Ventura, and Sil Austin. Interestingly, both of these concerts took place in Detroit around the same time a young entrepreneur named Berry Gordy had recently opened the 3-D Record Mart, a record store specializing in jazz. By 1959 Gordy had created Tamla Records with a house band of talented jazz musicians who were also comfortable crossing over into playing R&B music—by 1960 he had renamed it Motown Records. Porter argues that studying such moments has the power to "move us beyond simply expanding the parameters of what constitutes a jazz moment or a jazz genre":

> They might encourage us instead to explore musical phenomena that cannot be contained within a paradigm of jazz studies but whose analysis could still be significantly informed by jazz studies. In other words, rather than placing jazz and invocations of jazz into a larger framework of something like "jazz culture" or expanding the circle of what counts of jazz or who counts as a jazz musician, we might identify and write about various spheres of musical activity that intersect with but are not coterminous with jazz but whose existences are still determined, at least in part, by the idea of jazz and the political economy of the jazz world.[63]

Throughout her columns, it is clear that Cage was involved in this project decades ahead of her time. She doggedly searched for evidence and ideas to legitimize the genre of R&B; as in the case of Ray Charles, R&B musicians tended to be judged as credible musicians not based on how well they played R&B, but rather on whether they had jazz credentials. Unfortunately, Cage ceased to write for *Down Beat* after 1955 for unknown reasons, but her departure may have been linked to other significant changes in the editorial strategy of the magazine, which I will now explore.

Down Beat finds a market in jazz education

The strategy at Maher Publications to diversify its coverage had produced mixed results. Meanwhile jazz had moved beyond the big band era and was beginning to experience both an economic resurgence and signs of growing cultural legitimation. The former was due in part to the rise of independent labels, which benefited the jazz music industry in the same way they had done for R&B. As Lopes has argued, by the mid-1950s new independent jazz labels such as Prestige, Blue Note, Verve, and Riverside were having success recording previously marginalized genres and catering to niche markets. These labels untapped a new market of jazz record buyers that major labels had ignored, with independent labels representing around three-quarters or more of recorded jazz issues.[64] The rise of independent labels was also partly due to the rise of new recording formats, with the 45 rotations-per-minute single being important for labels focusing on youth-oriented music such as R&B, and the long-playing record (LP) being significant for the growth of adult niche markets such as jazz. Keir Keightley has argued that LPs were consciously used by labels to target an adult record-buying market who had more money to spend on music than the teen market; therefore the 1950s saw an increase in the production and sales of packaged albums geared toward presumed adult tastes, such as classical music, jazz, and "adult pop."[65] There were also noticeable shifts in jazz concert promotion in the United States, first with the creation and success of the Newport Jazz Festival in 1954, and also with a more gradual change in venues for jazz performance, away from commercial clubs and toward concert halls and college campuses.

These broader changes did not go unnoticed by the editors of *Down Beat*. In the spring of 1956, *Down Beat* reported that for the first time ever, jazz music would be discussed at the Music Educators National Conference.[66]

Conference president Robert Choate of Boston University said that the organization, which represented 30,000 of the nation's music educators, had "never discussed jazz in any phase before....We cannot stay within the little tower of the classroom....Any good schoolteacher must know something about jazz. It's the idiom of our youth."[67] It is not clear from his statement whether Choate meant that jazz was the idiom of the youth he was teaching or the idiom of his own youth. The introduction of jazz education into schools reflected an influx of new schoolteachers who had grown up with jazz rather than the contemporary tastes of young students (if Choate *did* intend to mean that jazz was the idiom of the nation's students, press headlines across the middlebrow press contradicted him as they declared rock 'n' roll to be the new youth craze).[68] This shift in attitude was being keenly observed by Charles Suber, who had been hired as the advertising manager at *Down Beat* in early 1953 by Norm Weiser. According to McDonough, the pivotal moment came in the spring of 1956, when Suber was invited to attend a spring festival of high-school jazz bands in Brownsville:

> He went down to cover it as a story, and came back extremely excited by its implications....Jazz education turned out to be the strategy both *Down Beat* and its advertisers needed. The business justification was straight and clear. The best way *Down Beat* could survive as a magazine was to serve musicians, particularly learning musicians. And jazz education provided the magazine an opportunity not only to write about music, but to help build it as well. "We had this burgeoning school jazz movement", says Suber, "with several hundred thousand kids and a generation of educators who came out of the swing band period. It was not only a growing audience. Most of our best circulation that the advertisers wanted to pay for came directly from this market."[69]

On May 2, 1956, *Down Beat* dropped the subtitle "Everything in the World About the World of Music," which had been printed on its cover for the years while it was actively covering music outside the worlds of jazz and Tin Pan Alley. Several issues later the usually diplomatic Ralph Gleason ranted about the television performances of rock 'n' roll's biggest star, Elvis Presley, describing them as "the newest phenomenon in the strange, perverted taste of the American public....His physical gyrations...[are] frankly, sickening....It's bad enough that he scratches himself when and where he itches and picks his nose, but it's really disgusting to watch the rest of it."[70] Nat Hentoff, for his part, penned a feature article titled "Musicians Argue Values of Rock and Roll," which included contributions from jazz pianist Billy Taylor, R&B sax player Sam Taylor, and jazz and session bassist Milt Hinton. As with Leonard Feather and his Blindfold Tests, Hentoff's article demonstrates that attacks on R&B were not simply a matter of white critics dismissing African-American culture; black jazz musicians were also critical. Billy Taylor does not mince his words in expressing his disgust for the current youth tastes in music and dance, but also attacks what he perceives to be the manufacturing of R&B's popularity:

It's a formula they've sold people on, and they make everything fit into the formula.... This r&b taste was created; it didn't come spontaneously from the teenagers. It grew out of the race records and since has been getting progressively worse musically. They took the worse parts of that music— monotonous rhythm, bad harmonies, double-meaning lyrics—and capitalized on them.... But remember, none of the things that are rhythm and blues hits or manufactured pop hits ever come back. They're dead in six weeks, and when they're dead, they're forever dead.[71]

Milt Hinton is not as harsh in his indictment of R&B, and in fact worked as a session player on several R&B recordings. His view was that musicians had "a responsibility to educate people to a better class of rhythm and blues":

We can put in some good things so that each session is a little better than the one before. We can gradually clean rhythm and blues up and improve them. In that way, we can salvage something out of this. The kids accept rhythm and blues as music, but actually it's a lower stage of music. Most of the guys playing it are good musicians [but] know it's not good music. But we can improve it, and since this new trend has brought the kids back to listening to music, we can bring them from their present tastes to listen to and appreciate better music.[72]

If Taylor and Hinton's arguments fall short of recycling the moral arguments made against jazz in the early twentieth century, they certainly echo the aesthetic and mass cultural arguments from earlier decades. In this case, however, rather than arguing for the "elevation" of jazz to a Euro-classical informed musical aesthetic, they are hoping to elevate R&B to the higher realms of jazz.

These views clearly fit well with the newly adopted educational agenda of *Down Beat*. Later in the year, a supplement in the magazine called *Record Whirl* appeared and employed a similar kind of argument regarding rock 'n' roll: "If with regret, we've no choice but to admit rock 'n' roll is part of our national culture, for the present, anyway. To disclaim it is futile; to deny its existence, unrealistic. To eradicate it, or at least to demote it, seems to be a matter of urgency."[73] The unprecedented sales of Elvis Presley were also perceived as a sign of an uneducated record-buying public:

> Can 50,000,000 Americans possibly be wrong? The answer it seems to us, is that it's not really a problem of right and wrong. Except in clear-cut matters of fact and morality, it's presumptuous for any man to declare another right or wrong. It can be said, however, that 50,000,000 Americans have shallow or undeveloped tastes. And indeed, it should be said.[74]

The last shots fired against rock 'n' roll in the *Down Beat* of the 1950s came from the jazz critic Barry Ulanov. For Ulanov, rock 'n' roll and Elvis Presley stood as convenient symbols of mass culture and its corrupting effect on society. Like Billy Taylor, Ulanov laments the easily manipulated tastes of a public raised on mass culture:

> It is part of a vast industrial civilization like ours, a basic part, to be frantic to be amused, amused all the time ... to be easily taken in by any novelty and overwhelmed by anything really unfamiliar if it is on a large enough scale, if it is sufficiently ostentatious, pretentious, and empty.... These crazes, these fashions, these figures—whether out of New York or Hollywood or Chicago, on a strip of motion-picture film, a phonograph record, or a television screen—these are the entertainments demanded by a society that much of the time at least is distinguished only by its massiveness.[75]

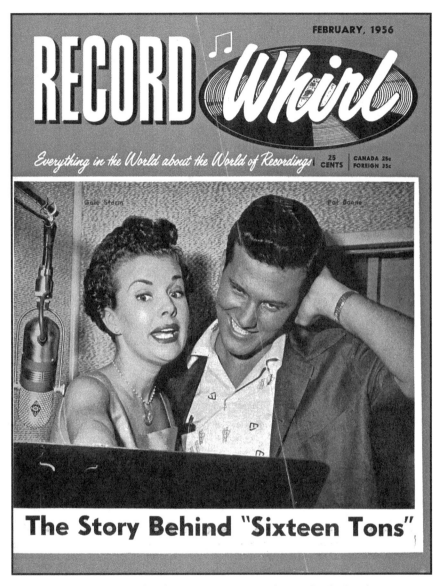

Figure 2.2 *Pat Boone and Gale Storm cover issue of* Record Whirl, *February 1956. Copyright 1956 © by Maher Publications. All Rights Reserved. Used by Permission.*

Ulanov was worried that the economics of mass culture were eroding artistic standards, that the "debacle of taste and deluge of barbarians" were replacing "men and women of quality … as standards collapse and it becomes harder and harder for the average ear to distinguish between the good and the bad, between the true and the false."[76] Not unlike mass culture theorists such as Dwight McDonald, Ulanov also makes a connection between the public's apparent passivity in musical taste to passivity in the political sphere: "if a whole country can be such a pushover for a song and a dance, what does that suggest about that same nation's political susceptibilities?"[77] Ulanov's criticisms are also reminiscent of early accounts of the "primitivism" and "barbarism" of jazz eroding high culture, though in his case it is Presley leading the barbarians out of the jungle. Jazz is now high culture:

> It's an attack from all sides on popular music of quality, on jazz, an inevitable attack, one which had to come as soon as it became apparent that jazz was back in favor once again, that popular music could have quality.... No, it's not just Presley. It's a whole army of savages. And if we're not careful, we're going to lose a lot more than we ever have lost before under the pressure of these mass attacks.[78]

Conclusion

The issue of *Down Beat* in which Hentoff's article with Billy Taylor and Milt Hinton appeared was actually a special issue purporting to consider the merits of rock 'n' roll. Bill Haley was featured on the cover and in an interview, in which he took a populist stance in an effort to defend rock 'n' roll from its critics: "you can't fool the American public. There has been a lot of bad music recorded, but the public buys what they like—they don't buy bad music ... nobody likes rock and roll but the public."[79] The idea that "nobody but the public" liked rock 'n' roll resonates with a comment that Raymond Williams would make two years later in *Culture and Society*:

> The masses are always others, whom we don't know, and can't know. There are in fact no masses; there are only ways of seeing people as masses .... In practice, we mass, and interpret them, according to some convenient formula. It is the formula, not the mass, which is our real business to examine.[80]

Comparing the critical debates surrounding jazz and R&B in music criticism helps us to do exactly that. Having sampled some of the R&B and rock 'n' roll coverage in *Down Beat*, we may note a few key issues.

One aspect of this "formula" is that if one looks at three common arguments used to dismiss jazz in the early twentieth century—namely jazz as mass culture appealing to the lowest common denominator of public taste, jazz as an agent of moral corruption, and jazz as an aesthetically primitive form of music—all of these arguments were employed by jazz critics and musicians only a few decades later to dismiss R&B and rock 'n' roll. The 1940s marked a turning point in the history of jazz discourse, as jazz was reconceptualized as a serious, complex art music. Any jazz-oriented music that fits this model remained jazz, but anything that featured vocals and a strong dance beat, for instance, was cast away. When jazz critics attacked R&B in *Down Beat*, it was not simply a case of white critics dismissing R&B and recycling a racist reading of music (although there are, embarrassingly for Gleason, Feather, and Hentoff, obvious similarities between the two discourses). With the terms "R&B" and "rock and roll" being used interchangeably during this period, there was no clear distinction being drawn between music made by black or white musicians.

Some of the writers who were brought in to cover these new musical trends felt that their impact was being underestimated. In one of her columns Ruth Cage noted, tongue firmly in cheek, that "the latest prediction from the pundits of show business' cash register informs us that rhythm and blues will have had it by June. So we figured we'd better get those things into print which some day might interest historians who choose to document this 'temporary' influence on American tastes."[81] R&B and rock 'n' roll were consistently represented as fads whose appeal was destined to be short-lived. Perhaps this accounts for why jazz critics found it so easy to label these emerging genres as manufactured, juvenile, and musically lacking, rather than noticing the similarities between reactions to the birth of rock 'n' roll and to jazz in its heyday as a popular music.

Throughout the 1950s, *Down Beat* was a highly reactive commercial music magazine, chopping and changing the breadth of its coverage in an effort to reflect changing trends in American popular music. In the end, the commercial crisis that *Down Beat* had faced at the beginning of the 1950s was resolved by reinforcing an ideology of jazz as a high art instead of a popular art. When R&B began to draw comparisons to jazz, critics engaged in promoting jazz as a legitimate art music had two options: they could either argue that rock 'n' roll and R&B were also legitimate or they could attempt to distinguish jazz as something different, severing it from any association with those genres. Critics like Ulanov and Feather saw that R&B and rock 'n' roll could be constructed as oppositional genres to jazz—an illustrative tool for explaining what jazz was not. Jazz could be categorized as swinging, improvised sometimes blues-inflected, sometimes harmonically progressive music that was also clearly *not* a passing fad, *not* commercially driven, and *definitely not* R&B or rock 'n' roll. Such a definition pushed jazz further on the path toward cultural legitimacy while simultaneously constructing a boundary between jazz and genres with which it might otherwise have much in common. And yet as we have also seen in this chapter, jazz critics simultaneously seemed to mourn jazz losing its status as popular music even though they had actively helped to shape its new status as art. Gleason hoped that if "kids listen to R&B enough" they would get tired and turn to big bands, while Ulanov similarly dreamt of a moment when the tastes of youth would return to jazz and "popular music could have quality" again. Not only does it betray the slipperiness of the term "popular music" as deployed by critics at the time, but it also marks the beginning of what would become a longstanding resentment on the part of certain jazz critics who viewed rock 'n' roll—by having supplanted the historical role of jazz as the most vital music genre in American popular culture—as consigning jazz to occupy a place halfway between the worlds of art music and popular music, and not wholly accepted by either.

3

The American Jazz
Press Covers Rock

*Yeah, you know, that's what Ralph would preach to me all the time.
'You young people, you just don't pay enough attention to history!'
Ralph was always saying that.*

JANN WENNER, 1990[1]

*Rock groups are supposed to be something other than jazz.
But like so many other things in our world, what seems
to be turns out not to really be at all.*

RALPH GLEASON, 1967[2]

Historians seem to agree that 1967 was a pivotal year in rock music's bid to be taken seriously as an art. It was the year of the Monterey Pop Festival, an event which, apart from showcasing the musicians involved, brought striking images of the rock audience as both a significant culture and commercial market to the attention of the mainstream press and record companies. It was the year that the Beatles released *Sgt. Pepper's Lonely Hearts Club Band*, which received unprecedented analysis in the highbrow press and, more than any other album, provoked music critics across the board to reconsider rock as something more than mere entertainment. Finally, it was the year of the birth of *Rolling Stone*, which would grow to become the single most important and authoritative rock periodical in the world, establishing a canon of music, writers, and aesthetic criteria for rock music, the legacy of which would still be in evidence half a century later.

But if 1967 marked the emergence of new ways of thinking about rock, it also marked the point at which other preexisting musical discourses were found to be lacking when applied to rock music. The success of *Rolling Stone* rests on top of another, much less-discussed story, namely the failure of the existing music press in 1967 to address rock culture in a way that brought together the two key audiences necessary for any profitable periodical: advertisers and a mass readership. And it was not for lack of trying: in addition to well-known rock predecessors to *Rolling Stone* like *Crawdaddy!* and *Mojo-Navigator*, there were also several established American jazz magazines, such as *Down Beat* and *Jazz & Pop*, that publicly changed their editorial policies to include rock coverage that summer, months before the first issue of *Rolling Stone* hit the newsstands in November.

"*Down Beat*, as the world's leading publication dedicated to America's only original art form, has watched musical fads come and go, but has never overlooked significant trends or changes in our music," wrote editor Dan Morgenstern in June 1967, as he announced the magazine's new policy of including rock music in its coverage.[3] He had just taken over as editor-in-chief from his friend Don DeMichael, who had held the position for the previous six years. Morgenstern continued:

> The fact that many of the most gifted young rock musicians are showing an increasing awareness of jazz (from the bedrock of the blues to the "new thing"), as well as the growing sophistication of [rock] music itself, are significant trends of great potential. *Down Beat*, without reducing its coverage of jazz, will expand its editorial perspective to include the musically valid aspects of the rock scene. Jazz, itself the result of the convergence of many different strains and influences, has survived as an art because it has remained capable of change and expansion. Rock-and-roll, an offspring of rhythm-and-blues, partakes of the same process … There are straws in the wind that the future paths of jazz and rock may converge— already, there is much interaction—but whatever the future may hold, the music of today's young America is vital and provocative. There is no better

medium for creative reportage and commentary on these fascinating happenings than *Down Beat*, whose staff and contributors are uniquely qualified observers of... the contemporary music scene and represent a broad spectrum of opinion. As is our coverage of jazz in all its aspects, our selective approach to rock will be stimulating, informative, and always concerned with encouraging high musical standards. It will be interesting, we predict, even to those of our readers who have yet to be convinced that this new music has artistic merit and is related to jazz. Of them, we only ask an open mind.[4]

Only a month later, another American jazz publication, *Jazz*, would follow suit, changing not only its coverage but the very title of the magazine from *Jazz* to *Jazz & Pop*. What was happening in the jazz press to prompt these amendments in editorial scope? Did they see themselves as trying to fill the gap for a magazine that took rock seriously? Were jazz critics becoming overwhelmed by the aesthetic significance of rock music, or were there commercial concerns fueling the change? Morgenstern wrote that *Down Beat* was "uniquely qualified" to report on these events, and it certainly was: the publisher boasted that "music enthusiasts spend more money to read [*Down Beat*] than the total spent to read all other music publications published in the US," making *Down Beat* by far the biggest music-focused magazine in America.[5] The fledgling *Rolling Stone* also claimed to be intent on covering the rock scene, but its first issue sold a measly 6,000 copies; *Down Beat* dwarfed that circulation twelve times over.[6]

Much as we now tend to think of jazz and rock as separate musical traditions, it by no means follows that their listening audiences are mutually exclusive, and this is no less true today than it was in the 1960s. As we saw in the previous chapter, several key figures in the jazz community had a negative reaction to the birth of rock 'n' roll in the mid-1950s, dismissing it as simplistic, vulgar, and crassly commercial youth music, unwittingly echoing critiques of jazz earlier in the century. Jazz critics at *Down Beat* and *Metronome* constructed a discourse that championed jazz as a new kind of modernist art and dismissed music genres that they felt were passing commercial fads, including rock 'n' roll. However, rock 'n' roll—and music falling under the related labels of rhythm and blues and rock—had survived beyond the 1950s and could no longer be easily dismissed as a forgettable novelty. Moreover, both jazz audiences and critics had been polarized and fragmented by the emergence of free, avant-garde, and "new thing" jazz in the late 1950s and early 1960s. The focus of this chapter is why and how the American jazz press began to cover rock in 1967 and the problems that the inclusion of rock in the jazz press presented to jazz critics. First, however, I will summarize some of the key changes in the categorization of jazz, rock 'n' roll, and rock in the first half of the decade.

Jazz, rock and race in the 1960s

The late 1950s and early 1960s saw both jazz audiences and critics polarized and fragmented by two distinctly different and politically heated new jazz styles: "soul jazz" on the one hand, and "free jazz" on the other. Soul jazz emerged in the late 1950s when East Coast musicians such as Cannonball Adderley, Art Blakey, and Horace Silver, began writing and performing songs with a strong black gospel blues feel. It coincided with the Civil Rights Movement, which was a key moment in African-American history not just for its struggle toward a future without racial segregation and discrimination, but also for the blossoming of racial pride in African-American cultural heritage. David Brackett has convincingly argued elsewhere how "the term 'soul' had circulated in conjunction with certain forms of African American music since the late 1950s, but this was not music riding high on the R&B charts, for the most part, but rather 'soul jazz.'"[7] As Lerone Bennett Jr. explained in a 1962 article published in *Ebony* magazine, the development of soul jazz was intimately linked not only to this wider context but also to a keen sense of dissatisfaction among black jazz musicians who were tired of earning less than their white counterparts:

> The emergence of soul as a movement kicked up racial issues which have been simmering in jazz for years. Jazz is and has been, at least partially, a music of protest. During the last 15 years, it has mirrored rather accurately the strains and tensions of the "angry ghetto." Soul music is the latest and

perhaps most accurate reflection of the state of mind or soul, if you wish, of the young urban Negro. There is in the music a new note of racial pride, a celebration of the honky-tonky, the house-rent party and people who say "dis here" and "dat dere"—an embrace, in short, of all that middle-class American condemns.[8]

Part of the anger Bennett mentions was seemingly directed at proponents of the West Coast jazz style, a commercially successful sub-genre led mainly by white jazz musicians such as Dave Brubeck and Chet Baker. As such, soul jazz was not just a new style but the "outgrowth of a bitter musical war with muted racial undertones":

Outraged by the growth of classical-oriented jazz and inspired by the success of artists like Mahalia Jackson and Ray Charles, the young New York musicians began in the late Fifties to reassess the Negro folk idiom—the cries, chants, shouts, work songs and pulsating rhythmic vitality of gospel singers and shouting choirs. Then, in one of the most astounding about-faces in jazz history, the fundamentalist (most of them are conservatory-trained liberals) abandoned Bartok, Schönberg and "all that jazz" and immersed themselves in the music of Thomas A. Dorsey, Roberta Martin and Howlin' Wolf. Jazz, which had been rolling merrily along on a fugue kick, turned from the academy and faced the store front church.[9]

On the one hand, soul jazz was a new style of danceable and commercially viable jazz that connected with both black and white audiences, with John S. Wilson remarking in the *New York Times* that it appeared "to have drawn many of the fugitives from rock 'n' roll into the jazz market."[10] On the other hand, however, the racial subtext of soul jazz exacerbated a tension between black and white jazz musicians. "Soul" was not so much a set of musical characteristics as a signifier of a racial difference. Writing in a 1961 *Down Beat* article on Les McCann and Ray Charles titled "FunkGrooveSoul," critic John Tynan observed that "the word 'soul' itself has become synonymous with the truth, honesty, and yes, even social justice among Negro musicians. In some quarters, if one hears someone referred to as a 'soul brother' or even just a plain unadorned 'soul,' the reference is clear—the individual is Negro."[11] While leading soul jazz musicians such as Horace Silver repeatedly claimed that "soul is not a racial attribute, that it is, in part, environmental and that some white musicians definitely have it," Bennett observed that such answers "have not quieted the fears of some white musicians who believe that Negro musicians by returning to the church have at last entered a never-never land from which they are barred."[12]

Although they might initially seem to come from opposite ends of the musical spectrum, another new style called free jazz (sometimes also labeled "avant-garde" or "new thing" jazz) emerged at the same time as soul jazz and was not unrelated from an ideological perspective, particularly with regard to its racial politics. As Kevin Fellezs has convincingly argued, the jazz tradition had become deracinated through the construction of a jazz art discourse by (predominantly white) critics: jazz was purported to be an art music which, while having roots in African-American culture, had transcended racial boundaries to become a "universal" art form.[13] At the same time, however, musicians such as Sonny Rollins (with his 1958 album *Freedom Suite*) and Charles Mingus (with compositions like "Fables of Faubus") were making deliberately political jazz that commented on the injustices of racial discrimination in the United States. But it was not until Ornette Coleman and Cecil Taylor began to experiment with dissonant free improvisation in the late 1950s and early 1960s that free jazz began to cohere as a genre. The reaction from critics was polarized to an unprecedented extent: when Ornette Coleman released his seminal album Free Jazz in 1961, responses were so split that *Down Beat* editor Don DeMichael commissioned a double review of the album. Pete Welding gave the album the maximum rating of five stars, calling it "a forceful, impassioned work that might stand as the ultimate manifesto of the new wave of young jazz expressionists."[14] John Tynan, by contrast, awarded the album zero stars, condemning Coleman's experiments with collective free improvisation and going so far as it labels it as a threat to jazz as a whole: "the only semblance of collectivity lies in the fact that these eight nihilists were collected together in one studio at one time and with one common cause: to destroy the music that gave them birth. Give them top marks for the attempt."[15]

The politics of free jazz were articulated most clearly by a new wave of African-American critics, particularly Amiri Baraka (writing as Leroi Jones) and A.B. Spellman. *Down Beat* was the often the forum where such debates were played out: Baraka's polemical essay "Jazz and the White Critic," for example, which first appeared in *Down Beat* in 1963, declared that "usually the critic's commitment was first to his appreciation of the music rather than to his understanding of the attitude which produced it.... The major flaw in this approach to Negro music is that it strips the music too ingenuously of its social and cultural intent." As Fellezs observed, Baraka reacted "strongly against the idea that bebop and the blues represented a broadly American, rather than a specifically black American, cultural perspective."[16] Although Baraka was more of an advocate of free jazz than soul jazz, he connected the radical politics underlying both styles to a broader ideological project of black cultural nationalism in his seminal 1963 book, *Blues People*:

> The step from cool to soul is a form of social aggression. It is an attempt to place upon a meaningless social order an order which would give value to terms of existence that were once considered not only valueless but shameful. Cool meant non-participation; soul means a new establishment. It is an attempt to reverse the social roles within the society by redefining the canons of value. In the same way the "New Negroes" of the twenties began, though quite defensively, to canonize the attributes of their "Negroness," so the "soul brother" means to recast the social order in his own image. White is then not "right," as the old blues had it, but a liability, since the culture of White precludes the possession of the Negro.[17]

To their credit, the editors of *Down Beat* continued to publish Baraka's writing even though they were often the explicit targets of his polemics. Following *Blues People*, Baraka published a regular column for *Down Beat* called "Apple Cores" between 1964 and 1966, all of which were later anthologized in his second book, *Black Music*.

While divisive new sub-genres were causing the jazz community to fragment, the categorization of rock 'n' roll also went through important changes in the first half of the 1960s. Bernard Gendron has argued that the impact of the Beatles and Bob Dylan forced the middlebrow press to take the aesthetic and cultural significance of rock 'n' roll (at least in its 1960s incarnation) seriously—not least because "to continue to vilify rock 'n' roll in the traditional manner would be to alienate the young adult market that it was courting assiduously with subscription offers and that was now growing rapidly because of the first infusions of the baby boom."[18] The widespread influence of the Beatles and Dylan on youth culture—but also recognition (albeit reluctant at times) of the talent involved in the songwriting of the former and the lyric-writing of the latter—coincided with the use of hyphenated genre labels to described particularly the musical trends of the mid-1960s. From 1965, classical musicians began to cash in on the popularity of the Beatles by recording orchestral arrangements of their songs, while the Beatles and other bands began experimenting with the use of harpsichords and strings in their own original recordings—a trend that was described by critics as "baroque rock."[19] Likewise, bands that capitalized on the vogue for Indian classical music during this period by grafting sitar or sitar-inspired riffs onto their records were described as playing "raga rock"—notable examples include the 1965 releases of the Kinks' "See My Friends" and The Beatles' "Norwegian Wood." During the same period, bands like the Byrds arranged the acoustic folk music of Bob Dylan using rock instrumentation (as with their June 1965 hit recording of "Mr. Tambourine Man"), while Dylan himself famously "went electric" at his legendary Newport Folk Festival appearance that same summer, ushering in the "folk rock" movement. According to Gendron, the combination of these events prompted a broader change in genre categories:

> Along with this newfound respectability came a new streamlined label, "rock," to challenge the somewhat disreputable old term "rock 'n' roll." No doubt, this terminological change was triggered by the entry of abbreviate, composite names like "folk rock" and "baroque rock." "Rock" connoted a certain added maturity, seriousness, depth, aesthetic self-consciousness, craftsmanship, and transgressive power, in contrast to the connotations of adolescence—innocent and silly fun, dancing and shrieking—evoked by the term "rock 'n' roll."[20]

The change from "rock 'n' roll" to "rock" was actually more complex than Gendron suggests. Rather than being directly triggered by the introduction of hyphenated genre labels like "folk rock," it is clear that trade papers such as *Variety* and *Billboard*—and particularly British music papers such as the *Melody Maker, Disc,* and the *New Musical Express*—used the terms "rock," "rock bands," "rock fans," and "rock stars" (as well as alternative labels such as "beat music" and "beat groups") periodically as a short hand to describe rock 'n' roll from the mid-1950s to the mid-1960s. The widespread adoption of the shortened term "rock" should, therefore, be seen as the culmination of long-standing use of variations on the term "rock 'n' roll." However, Gendron is right about the important consequences for the subsequent cultural accreditation of popular music once the transition had been cemented, particularly when it came to issues of race. As he notes, whereas rock 'n' roll had designated both black and white music, "rock" became associated predominantly with white music by white artists, By contrast, music made by black artists of the same period tended to be described using terms like "soul" or "funk" (language that had migrated wholesale from soul jazz culture), or was otherwise designated as "rhythm and blues" (which, lest we forget, was the term introduced to replace "race music" in the late 1940s). As Gendron incisively observes, these designations mattered because "the accolades that came in torrents in the late 1960s were directed almost exclusively at contemporary white 'rock' music, with only occasional nods to 'soul' music. White 'rock' became paradigmatically the 'art' music of this divided musical field, with 'soul' relegated to the old 'rock 'n' roll' function of 'fun' and 'dance.'"[21]

Amid the vibrant mid-1960s period of flirting with sounds drawn from the worlds of classical and raga music, rock musicians were also borrowing ideas from jazz. Members of Cream, the Jimi Hendrix Experience, the Byrds, the Blues Project, the Grateful Dead, and Big Brother and the Holding Company were all interested in jazz music and used jazz elements in their own music.[22] Meanwhile, a young generation of jazz musicians such as Gary Burton, Charles Lloyd, and Larry Coryell were embracing rock music and incorporating it into their jazz output. Coryell described his early days in New York in 1965 as follows:

> We were saying, we love Wes [Montgomery], but we also love Bob Dylan. We love Coltrane but we also love the Beatles. We love Miles but we also love the Rolling Stones. We wanted people to know we are very much part

of the contemporary scene, but at the same time we had worked our butts off to learn this other music [called jazz].[23]

By 1967, musicians from jazz and rock backgrounds were beginning to get together to jam and form large ensembles like Blood, Sweat, and Tears, and Chicago; although these two bands would not release their debut albums until 1968, they were merely the most visible signs of growing relations between certain parts of jazz and rock cultures.

Motivations for the American jazz press to cover rock

The interactions between rock and jazz musicians described above were representative of similar interactions at the level of amateur musicians and audiences, and this had an important impact on *Down Beat* magazine. Contrary to popular belief, the readership of *Down Beat* in the 1960s was not primarily an older generation that had grown up with jazz, but young males in their late teens and twenties—very much the same age and gender demographic that *Rolling Stone* would appeal to in the near future. According to Dan Morgenstern, *Down Beat's* editor from 1967 to 1973, research showed that the magazine's readership was primarily male high school and college students, who stopped reading the magazine once they left education and entered the work force.[24] There were also a number of veteran subscribers, of course, who had maintained an interest in jazz throughout their lives, but the mainstay of the readership had been young students from the mid-1950s onward.

As discussed in the previous chapter, *Down Beat* survived the decline of the swing era by re-inventing itself as a consumer publication for serious fans, and crucially, young learning musicians—a move championed largely by advertising manager Charles Suber. The rise of the stage band movement in America meant that significant numbers of high-school students were being turned onto jazz music, and since *Down Beat's* main advertising revenue came from instrument manufacturers during its days as a magazine for working musicians, it was a relatively easy transition for manufacturers to turn their marketing efforts toward younger, learning musicians looking to buy instruments.[25]

This advertising base remained largely unchanged through the 1960s, and by 1967 *Down Beat* was clearly trying to capture and expand the market of student musicians. Since the 1950s, special issues dedicated to a particular instrument had been an important strategy for the magazine, and the publisher could be seen boasting in the magazine's pages to both readers and advertisers that according to surveys, "DB readers each own 2.1 instruments."[26] For a biweekly publication, the number of annual special issues was at risk of overwhelming the regular issues: brass, big band, drums, guitar, education, readers poll, and critics poll editions of *Down Beat* were all published on an annual basis. However, a key difference between the 1950s and late 1960s was that young amateur musicians were now buying far more electric six-string guitars, bass guitars, and drums than they were trumpets, trombones, or saxophones. *Down Beat* had a potentially high-spending readership of learning musicians who were listening to at least as much rock as jazz, and instrument manufacturers were eager to exploit that market. The signs were there as early as 1965, when there were advertisements in *Down Beat* for Vox guitars and amps that featured pictures of the Beatles and used the slogan "The Sound of the Longhairs."[27] But these ads were totally at odds with the content and editorial direction of the magazine.

Most of the staff at *Down Beat* rarely listened to rock, but the magazine's advertisers urged its owner, John Maher, to put pressure on editors to openly include rock coverage. As editor Dan Morgenstern recalled:

> The advertisers had been pressuring the old man [Maher] about including rock because they were saying 'these young musicians you're talking about, of course most of them today are playing or listening to rock 'n' roll and not jazz.' The line was that there were threats or veiled threats of reducing or withholding advertising if this wasn't going to be done.[28]

Ordinarily Maher appreciated the need to separate advertising from editorial, but at the time the decision to include rock coverage was argued to be a matter of "the survival of the magazine."[29]

To make this decision more palatable for any jazz purists who subscribed to the magazine, Morgenstern softened the blow by citing the increasing sophistication in rock music and the growing interactions between jazz and rock as the reasons for the magazine's new editorial policy. This was all true, of course, but the third reason remained unwritten: advertisers believed there was an untapped market of young people buying rock records and musical instruments, and since *Down Beat* was the most obvious vehicle to market and promote these products, they wanted the content of the magazine to better reflect and attract this new kind of readership. "There wasn't ever enough space to cover everything we would have liked to cover in the jazz world itself, let alone rock" Morgenstern recalled, concluding that the decision to include rock coverage would never have happened without pressure from the advertisers.[30]

But *Down Beat* was not alone in beginning to include rock in its musical scope. As noted earlier, in August 1967 the New-York based *Jazz* magazine changed both its editorial policy and its title to *Jazz & Pop*. *Jazz* began in 1962 as a venture subsidized by record producer Bob Thiele and operated by his partner Pauline Rivelli. Dan Morgenstern was hired as editor at the outset and Rivelli, who was initially designated managing editor, learned from him the fundamentals of running a music magazine. By 1967, Rivelli had been editor-in-chief for several years and in August she wrote an editorial explaining the change:

> With this issue, *JAZZ* magazine moves in a new direction, with a new name. By increasing coverage to the most musically vital aspects of popular music, we hope to bring serious attention to the revitalization now occurring in American music ... 1967 has witnessed the birth of a serious American pop music which encompasses jazz, rock, folk and blues ... Jazz, pop, classical, folk ... these are crude descriptive categories at best, and they better apply to the in-group exclusiveness of their audiences than to musical sounds. At least so far as the music is concerned, there are no neat boundaries.[31]

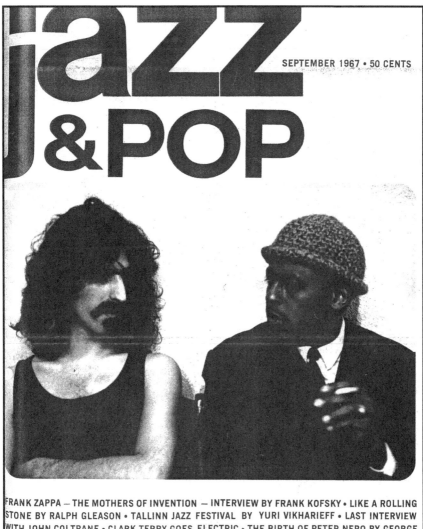

SEPTEMBER 1967 • 50 CENTS

FRANK ZAPPA — THE MOTHERS OF INVENTION — INTERVIEW BY FRANK KOFSKY • LIKE A ROLLING STONE BY RALPH GLEASON • TALLINN JAZZ FESTIVAL BY YURI VIKHARIEFF • LAST INTERVIEW WITH JOHN COLTRANE • CLARK TERRY GOES ELECTRIC • THE BIRTH OF PETER NERO BY GEORGE HOEFER • WHAT'S HAPPENIN' • JAZZ AND POP TOP 20 • POP TALK • JAZZ & POP/EDUCATION • RECORD REVIEWS

Figure 3.1 *Frank Zappa and Archie Shepp cover issue of* Jazz & Pop, *September 1967.*

Jazz magazine was founded on many of the same principles as *Down Beat*, including an effort to appeal to young musicians. A notice soliciting advertisers in the magazine read: "*Jazz & Pop* continues to help in the development of the Stage Band Movement. The majority of our readers are

Student Musicians ... For its advertisers, *Jazz & Pop* provides the most direct access to the buying musician and the things of quality he needs ... top line instruments and accessories, equipment, materials and recordings."[32] The tendency to construct its readers as musicians rather than record buyers or general consumers was perhaps partly due to the influence of Charles Suber, the same man who had originally developed this strategy for *Down Beat*. Suber had been fired by *Down Beat* owner John Maher in April 1962; according to John McDonough, "the two men had differences on a range of issues, and when Suber began saying publicly that he was thinking of starting a new magazine, Maher replaced him."[33] Suber went on to work as the educational consultant for the newly founded *Jazz* magazine, and then in 1968 Maher suffered a heart attack and asked Suber to rejoin the *Down Beat* staff, where he would once again work as the publisher as well as the primary staff member in charge of advertising. Suber was heavily invested in jazz education, and by the late 1960s he had become very excited by the possibility of a jazz renaissance fueled by the big band rock of groups like Chase, Chicago, and Blood, Sweat, and Tears. Suber felt that these new attempts to fuse jazz with rock would hold an obvious appeal for students in high-school stage bands, and further might bridge the gap between rock and jazz for many young rock fans who would not otherwise have listened to jazz.

As Pauline Rivelli put it in her editorial, "let's face it. Jazz needs popular music ... economically as well as aesthetically."[34] There were clearly commercial considerations influencing the decision of jazz magazines like *Down Beat* and *Jazz* to start including rock coverage. But it was not quite so simple: both *Down Beat* and *Jazz* were experiencing all-time circulation highs *before* they made their announcements to cover rock, and there *were* signs of increasing interactions between jazz and rock music. Instrument manufacturers, and to a lesser extent, record companies, saw *Down Beat* as a reliable way of reaching their target market of young consumers. As a magazine that claimed to be the biggest consumer music periodical in America with an established distribution system and steady advertising income, *Down Beat* especially had much to gain by including rock music in its coverage. There was a significant demographic of school band students in this era who not only listened to the Beatles, but to stage band versions of

Beatles songs performed by the likes of Buddy Rich and Maynard Ferguson. This element of youth culture is not necessarily what comes to mind when historians and documentaries conjure images of a subversive rock listening audience of the late 1960s, but clearly there were significant numbers of high-school students who were avid listeners of music, learned instruments through school band programs, and listened to at least as much rock as jazz.

Down Beat rock coverage in practice

There was initial concern among the *Down Beat* staff that the editorial change might provoke a backlash from readers and result in subscription cancellations; but despite a few nasty letters complaining about the "banal chord pounding and two syllable phrasing" of most rock 'n' roll, Morgenstern recalled there was far less reaction from readers than expected, and the number of subscription cancellations were "absolutely insignificant."[35] There were also numerous letters praising the decision to include rock: a fifteen-year-old reader, Michael Alvino, epitomized the ideal type of consumer that *Down Beat* was trying to attract with the change: "I dig jazz and dig rock also. But no one published stories on rock.... I have plenty of records both rock and jazz and now that *DB* will report rock I think that I will become a steady reader and may subscribe."[36] Another rock fan wrote that with "so many teenie-bopper fan magazines around now," she was "surprised and pleased to find a magazine like yours on the stands," which covered rock and pop music.[37] Some readers clearly perceived an absence of rock journalism and saw *Down Beat* as filling that void—after all, the magazine introduced rock coverage a full four months before the first poorly distributed issue of *Rolling Stone* ever appeared. *Down Beat* would also have been more likely to appear on a variety of newsstands throughout cities in North America and even elsewhere in the world, and it was not uncommon for school libraries to subscribe to it; *Down Beat* would, therefore, have reached an audience of young readers who might have been interested in rock coverage but been quite unaware of other early sources of rock criticism, such as *Crawdaddy!* magazine or Richard Goldstein's "Pop Eye" column in the *Village Voice*.

Once the staff decided that they would include rock coverage, they encountered the problem of *how* it should be covered. It was important that the rock coverage appeal to rock fans without alienating the existing jazz readership. Morgenstern wanted to get writers who were conversant with jazz to the extent that they could make references or comparisons and put rock into a context which made sense to jazz fans. He also thought it was a good idea to encourage jazz fans to read the rock coverage: "we thought if there was some sort of equilibrium established it would be good for both jazz and rock."[38] But none of the staff at *Down Beat* were interested in rock music themselves. Cost-cutting had meant that former editor Don DeMichael was forced to close down the magazine's LA office earlier in the sixties, and Dan Morgenstern's move from New York to Chicago effectively closed down the New York office as well. The Chicago headquarters held the core team of Morgenstern and his associate editor, Bill Quinn, a capable jazz editor but with no interest in rock music.

Morgenstern got in touch with James Gabree after reading an article about rock culture that Gabree had written for *Playboy* and hired him to write a series of articles for *Down Beat* called "The World of Rock," providing a critical overview of the contemporary rock scene.[39] Gabree wrote his first article with a disclaimer that pointed out the lack of serious, professional criticism devoted to rock music:

It is hard to believe that a music this vital needs an "introduction" at all. And yet, despite a spate of articles on rock in the press in such ordinarily snooty journals as *Esquire* and *The National Review*, it is clear that among lovers of "legitimate" music, rock is still held in high disrepute. Serious criticism of popular music other than jazz and folk has been sparse, so much so that much of our attention over the next few issues will have to be devoted to developing a method of analysis. Many of the concepts used in discussing jazz and folk can be applied to rock as well. But since rock is less clearly "art," it is more difficult to assess. The pop music press is of no help: from prepubescent *16* magazine to megacephalic *Crawdaddy*, pop critics seem to feel compelled either to trivialize the music or to smother it under a blanket of pedestrianism.[40]

Gabree's most controversial article appeared in *Down Beat* a few months later—a cover story titled "The Beatles in Perspective." Here he challenged the artistic significance of the band only a few short months after they had released their breakthrough *Sgt. Pepper's Lonely Hearts Club Band*. Gabree argued that "the Beatles never have been in the vanguard of pop music," and that "very few are willing to take the foursome's work for what it is: an introduction to a world of creative adventure, of which the Beatles are merely the popularizers, not the creators."[41] The number of letters received condemning Gabree's article was unprecedented in the history of the magazine, and articles appeared in future issues of both *Down Beat* and the short-lived *Cheetah* rock magazine that debated Gabree's claims.[42]

Reviews of rock albums also started to appear in a discourse that might have appealed to the jazz reader unfamiliar with rock music. The first rock review was a five-star rave about the Grateful Dead's debut, written by Edward A. Spring, who felt that "jazz fans should find this LP a good introduction to some of the better rock music," and went on to recommend that "along with the recent Beatles albums, the Byrds, the Lovin' Spoonful, Paul Butterfield, and Bob Dylan, I find the Grateful Dead outstanding, and I especially recommend them to jazz fans."[43] Reviewer Mark Wolf also awarded five stars to *Their Satanic Majesties Request* by the Rolling Stones, but struggled to connect the album to jazz music, vaguely remarking that *Satanic Majesties* was comparable to Ornette Coleman's *Free Jazz* because they were both "exceptional" albums and "revolutionary events" in the respective worlds of jazz and rock, or noting that "this music is not unlike Coltrane's, in that the listener can't be left unaffected by the message presented."[44] Such reviews were poorly written and conceived, but Morgenstern felt unable to effectively exercise editorial control since he did not listen to rock himself. As he put it, the rock coverage in *Down Beat* "probably could have been done better if we had been a little more knowledgeable about rock, but we were not."[45]

It would have been a confusing time to be reading *Down Beat* in the year following its decision to include rock coverage in the magazine, since its writers were clearly straining to cover contrasting ideologies. The April 4, 1968 issue, for instance, featured Janis Joplin on the cover and an interview with Jimi Hendrix inside, as well as a "Guide to Jazz for Flower People." *Rolling*

Figure 3.2 *The Beatles and Cannonball Adderley cover issue of* Down Beat, *November 16, 1967. Copyright 1967 © by Maher Publications. All Rights Reserved. Used by Permission.*

Stone may have been offering the controversial free gift of a roach clip to new subscribers during this time, but *Down Beat* was not far behind, offering a free copy of the Grateful Dead's debut album as their subscription gift in that issue. But the record and live concert review sections bore no indication of an interest in rock culture: in fact, no rock albums whatsoever were reviewed in the issue—instead, the leading reviews were releases from Stan Getz, Herbie Mann, and Cal Tjader. This inconsistency was typical: a "rock and pop" heading would appear in the record reviews section only to disappear in the following issue. The tension was also reflected in feature stories. In the issue following Janis Joplin's cover story, the main features were a story on Count Basie and an extended discussion of a Woody Herman big band concert.[46]

However, some *Down Beat* writers took a more positive approach to rock and to its relationship with jazz. Critics were certainly noticing the interactions. Harvey Pekar (who later gained a cult following as the writer of the realist comic strip *American Splendor*) devoted an entire feature article to examining what the present experiments in rock music meant for the future of popular music as a whole. "What we may be witnessing," he ventured, "is the creation of a new, as yet unlabelled form of music, as America around the turn of the century saw the development of jazz … Jazz grew from the synthesis of several forms: European popular and Afro-American folk musics; marches; ragtime, etc. A similar synthesis is now taking place in 'popular' music."[47] Another critic, Bob Perlongo, wrote about the "kinship" the Beatles had with jazz, which to him became especially evident on the *Sgt. Pepper* album:

> Lovely Rita … is a wild-away affair that, oddly enough, is very much like something Woody Herman and Chubby Jackson might once have done. And stranger still are the ghostly echoes of Pres [saxophonist Lester Young] of the Kansas City Six days in the clarinet in the background on When I'm Sixty-Four … That the Beatles are apt students of the jazz idiom is well illustrated by this exceptional album.[48]

Rock coverage in *Down Beat* was problematic for two reasons: first, the lack of expertise and interest among the editorial staff resulted in rock coverage often occupying only 10 percent of the magazine's content and frequently being of low quality; second, rock was often covered in a way that would appeal to jazz fans, using criteria originally designed for jazz music, and such connections were often far from credible—Perlongo's *Sgt. Pepper* review above is one example. In practice, then, *Down Beat* critics were writing about rock for an audience that they assumed were also jazz fans, even though it was entirely possible that *Down Beat* readers listened to rock for different reasons than they listened to jazz. There did not appear to be any sustained attempt on the part of *Down Beat* editors to grow a rock readership and give it an identity on its own terms. Despite these problems, *Down Beat's* circulation figures in 1967 were at their highest ever and would increase over the next several years. *Rolling Stone* may have been seen as more influential and representative of the counterculture according to the history books,[49] but its circulation was still less than *Down Beat's* rising circulation by the end of 1969, and it could be argued that that *Down Beat's* readership represented a different but equally significant segment of the new rock audience.

Feather and Gleason's clashing attitudes to the jazz-rock rapprochement

Although writers alluded to the growing similarities between jazz and rock on numerous occasions in *Down Beat* during 1967, there had not yet been a sustained, developed discussion comparing the two genres: was it possible to review jazz alongside rock in the same publication and could the two really be judged according to the same criteria? How were they similar and how were they different? And finally, were jazz and rock merging as some writers and musicians had suggested that year?

Leonard Feather, *Down Beat's* most prominent critic at that time, wrote an extended essay at the beginning of 1968 that addressed exactly these questions. The piece was titled "Pop=Rock=Jazz: A False Musical Equation Dissected," and in it Feather tried to pinpoint the precise differences between jazz, rock, and pop. As he put it, "it is too easy to resort to such glib clichés as 'what sounds like jazz to me may not be jazz to you.'"[50] He took issue particularly with the critic Ralph Gleason, who had recently begun to devote the majority of his attention to contemporary rock music, at one point writing that the new "rock bands are really jazz bands; the guitar soloists … are really jazz players."[51] Such a statement was ludicrous to Feather, who argued there was "an undertone of defensiveness in the claim that rock is really jazz, as though this were an attempt to upgrade a young, growing, but often maligned form by identifying it with one that has been established for a half century and has achieved a belated modicum of recognition as a genuine art."[52]

Feather argued that there were clear genre boundaries in American popular music and wanted in particular to separate three traditions that he felt were being conflated and confused with harmful consequences. These were *current teen pop* (performers broadly fitting under the labels of rock and rhythm and blues, such as the Beatles and the Rolling Stones, but also including "hyphenated rock manifestations" such as folk-rock and performers like Bob Dylan and Paul Simon), *traditional pop* (American Songbook composers such as Rodgers and Hammerstein, George and Ira Gershwin, Duke Ellington and Billy Strayhorn, and Cole Porter), and *jazz* (Louis Armstrong, Billie Holiday, Charlie Parker, Miles Davis, etc.). While Feather appeared to allow for some overlap between the categories of traditional pop and jazz—presumably Ellington would also be considered a jazz musician and Holiday a traditional pop singer, Feather contended that "there is massive evidence that rock and jazz musicians for the most part consider their worlds mutually exclusive."[53]

For Feather, one of the key differences between rock and jazz was that rock's value lay in the lyrics of songs rather than the level of musicianship in groups. This stood in contrast with jazz, which Feather argued

> has yet to produce a lyricist with the perception, the intellectual insight, or the gift for imagery of a Bob Dylan or a Paul Simon. By the same token, rock has yet to come up with an Art Tatum ... Pop, in the main, is as far behind jazz in technical virtuosity and improvisational fluency as jazz is behind rock in verbal creativity.[54]

Feather also pointed to the evidence that many rock musicians had begun taking jazz lessons to expand their musical vocabulary, but jazz musicians had no trouble assimilating the instrumental qualities of rock music, playing Beatles' covers and rock rhythms out of commercial necessity rather than aesthetic uplift; by contrast, he had "yet to hear of a jazz guitarist who has turned to Jimi Hendrix in order to bone up on the technique of setting fire to a guitar."[55] Feather's choice of Hendrix as a guitarist with little to offer jazz musicians is odd in retrospect, as Hendrix has since been recognized almost universally as an unrivaled technical master of the electric guitar, and has heavily influenced countless jazz musicians, whether guitarists or not.[56]

But Feather's key argument was that the slackening of genre distinctions posed a threat to jazz music, which he felt was losing what little media coverage it used to get by the growing interest in contemporary pop; Feather was probably thinking in particular of the few jazz critics like Gleason who were increasingly devoting their columns to pop instead of jazz. Feather called for a reform in press coverage that treated what he felt were the three valuable genres of American music as separate, but all deserving of attention:

> It is to be hoped that the trade and music press, as well as newspapers and general interest magazines, radio and television, will move toward a more complete, honest, and critical coverage of all three branches of music. Jazz needs this attention because, except in a couple of areas (festivals and sometimes concerts), it has run into an economic crisis … Rock deserves attention, for … [i]t is attempting lyrically and musically to establish itself as an art form no less vital and durable than jazz … Pop, the traditional brand of pop, needs help particularly, since in the past few years it has suffered desperately from lack of adequate press coverage … What we need now is a regulation of publicity that accords reasonable treatment to all three idioms, without any attempts to obfuscate the issues by pretending that one form is the same as another.[57]

Feather's concern about dwindling press coverage for jazz was shared by Martin Williams, who criticized both Gleason and *Village Voice* jazz critic Mike Zwerin for their recent approaches to music writing. He focused in particular on Zwerin:

> [I]f people keep telling Zwerin that jazz is in the doldrums, or whatever, it may be because Zwerin spends quite a bit on his column space discussing rock—enthusing about this that or the other rock group which has learned more than three or four chords, or which has been influenced by jazz … And it is also, I might guess, because Zwerin has lately been promoting the idea

that some kind of amalgam of rock and jazz is going to produce a new style, or even new music. Zwerin doesn't say it in so many words, but I get the idea that after this great coming-together takes place, jazz as such may disappear.[58]

Feather and Williams shared two central concerns. First, they worried about what they saw as the beginning of a trend, where jazz critics would embrace rock and consequently abandon jazz. Writing about rock was a waste, of course, because it already got the lion's share of radio, record, and ticket sales, whereas jazz was a music in economic decline, and needed all the publicity it could get. Second, the fact that Gleason, Zwerin, and others were making noises about the rapprochement between jazz and rock would only confuse the matter further. The critical consensus on the jazz tradition was already being fractured by the avant-garde jazz movement, and arguing for similarities between jazz and rock further destabilized the definitions of jazz they had worked so hard to construct.

Ralph Gleason, on the other hand, had a very different assessment of the relationship between the jazz and rock of the late 1960s. Gleason was one of Leonard Feather's few rivals for the title of most widely read jazz critic in America. Both lived on the west coast, Gleason in San Francisco and Feather in Los Angeles, and both had music columns syndicated to newspapers across the country. But Gleason had become heavily interested in rock and was excited by the links he saw between jazz and rock music. He was especially excited about the San Francisco music scene, and wrote about it not only in his syndicated newspaper column but also in a monthly column for *Jazz & Pop*. It was this column that Feather was likely referring to when he paraphrased Gleason's pronouncement that the boundaries between jazz and rock musicians were dissolving. As the new title of the magazine indicated, many of the key staff members at *Jazz & Pop*—particularly editor Pauline Rivelli and associate editor Frank Kofsky—tried to distinguish the magazine from its competitors by promoting an aesthetic that bridged the gap between jazz, rock, and pop music. As an established jazz critic who had undergone a near-religious conversion to contemporary pop music, Gleason was the perfect writer to lend authority to the magazine's new agenda. From his very first column, Gleason frequently argued for the links between jazz and rock, as in the cases of bands like the Grateful Dead and Cream:

> Rock groups are supposed to be something other than jazz. But like so many other things in our world, what seems to be turns out not to really be at all … The point, of course, is that good music is good music regardless of labels. The music that Garcia's group, The Grateful Dead, plays is really jazz even though the sound of the electric guitars at first inhibits you from saying that. The Dead have a deep, driving swing that is irresistible and the solos played by Garcia are pure jazz solos.[59]
>
> What [Cream] plays is a kind of music that really seems to me to qualify as jazz. It doesn't sound like Ben Webster, but then neither does Sonny Murray or Cecil Taylor and we accept them as jazz … It has the irreverence of jazz, the edge of jazz and the feeling of spontaneity always involved with jazz. And it is exciting music. The time will come, in the not too distant future, when concerts will present groups like the Cream and jazz groups like Albert Ayler.[60]

Gleason looked to his musical surroundings in San Francisco for evidence as he argued for a blurring of boundaries between jazz and rock. The improvised, feedback-heavy "freak-outs" of west coast psychedelic bands—which were an important part of live performances but often excised from recorded versions of songs—reminded him of the dissonant explorations of avant-garde jazz musicians. This would not have endeared him any further to Leonard Feather, who had made public his reservations about the avant-garde jazz movement. In fact, what is often forgotten about Gleason in discussions of his decision to embrace rock music is that, far from abandoning jazz, he was one of the most vocal champions of the avant-garde movement. An example of this crucial difference between Feather's and Gleason's aesthetic agendas can be found in the transcript of a panel discussion on the future of jazz they had that included pianist Bill Evans. Hosted by the University of California in Berkeley, it was reported in *Down Beat* that the discussion featured an especially heated debate over the merits of avant-garde jazz, in which Gleason was the only one to praise the avant-garde scene without reservation:

Figure 3.3 *James Brown cover issue of* Jazz & Pop, *June 1968.*

"I think today standards are being discarded," [said Feather]. "The rules of harmony, for example. Some musicians today say, 'It's just feeling.' They forget the rules one learns in school and that have been developed in 500 years of music."... Feather asked Gleason how he felt about the future of standards and rules. "I'm horrified to think there'll be rules or standards," Gleason replied, going on to say there have always been unanticipated changes in jazz. "If they're going to abandon [musical standards], then I want them to abandon instruments," Evans said wryly. "Just let 'em slam a door!"

"I don't care if they slam a door so long as they knock me out," was Gleason's rejoinder.[61]

Gleason may have lacked Feather's precision in articulating musical ideas, but by examining his *Jazz & Pop* columns, it becomes clear that Gleason maintained a remarkably consistent and coherent aesthetic in his writing throughout the late 1960s. This aesthetic rested on his twin enthusiasms for avant-garde jazz and psychedelic rock, and his belief in the musical overlap between the jazz explorations of Pharoah Sanders, Albert Ayler, and Archie Shepp, and the rock experiments of the Californian (and to a lesser extent British) rock bands. Gleason may have sometimes equated certain kinds of jazz with rock, but if he wrote that "the drive to pin labels on things in this country, to categorize and to bag them for easy disposal, is a great handicap," it was not so much because he felt there was no difference between jazz and rock as the fact that the clash between the two traditions was hindering the growth and acceptance of a new music that was arising out of interactions between them.[62] He was especially excited by the mixing of jazz and rock groups on concert bills at the Fillmore in San Francisco and by the positive reactions of young rock audiences and musicians to avant-garde jazz. "Sooner than we think," wrote Gleason, "jazz will burst forth in a great revival":

> The seeds are sprouting. There are hundreds of kids in Berkeley who are into the free-form jazz thing. The same is true, I am told, in other centers of social confrontation and cross-fertilization. What will come out of it is impossible to predict except to say that it will be a music of great strength, closer to the people than any music has been yet in this country, aside from the blues.[63]

With such a radical aesthetic vision, it is little wonder that Gleason repeatedly suggested that the categories of "jazz" and "rock" were becoming problematic. Quoting Charlie Parker, Gleason felt that in the musical climate of the jazz and rock scenes in San Francisco, there truly was "no dividing line in art," that "all the labels [were] changing," and that a new genre of music was emerging to bridge the gap between jazz and rock.[64]

Conclusion

Two established magazines in the American jazz press, *Down Beat* and *Jazz*, announced editorial changes to include rock coverage months before the first issue of *Rolling Stone* was published; both ultimately failed to capture the untapped mass readership for rock music, and yet in the late 1960s they rivaled *Rolling Stone* in circulation and reach. On the surface, the message at *Down Beat* was one of inclusivity. Jazz critics and musicians had been split throughout the 1960s into two opposing camps: avant-garde and free jazz on the one hand versus the more established forms of jazz on the other. The split was fragmenting an already small jazz community, and in his year-end editorial summarizing the events of 1967, Dan Morgenstern expressed the hope that "the factionalism that has split the jazz community for so long showed signs of waning."[65] The economic renaissance jazz had enjoyed in the mid-1950s was over, and sales had slipped back into a path of decline by the late 1960s, partly due to rock music taking up an increasing share of the market.[66] Morgenstern was, therefore, ready to encourage any prospects of a revitalization, even if they were at odds with one another: on the one hand, he encouraged solidarity among jazz listeners and musicians and advocated lobbying for government funding of jazz, just as supporters of symphony orchestras had done for classical music; on the other, he expressed the incompatible hope that jazz might survive as a commercially viable music by embracing its interactions with rock and its mass audience:

> There is, of course, the potent question of the future relationship between jazz and rock (or pop, or what have you). Some strong voices herald the rapprochement, while others issue strident nays ... Whatever the prognosis, a particularist, exclusive, and non-proselytizing attitude ill behooves jazz in its present predicament, which, briefly stated, is the crying need for a bigger audience. If rock offers a bridge, jazz would be foolish not to cross it.[67]

If some members of the jazz community had historically relished their outsider status, Morgenstern was the ultimate inclusive supporter, advocating any avenue that promised survival for jazz even at the risk of contradicting himself—constructing jazz as an art in need of state support while simultaneously refusing to let go of the dream that jazz might again become popular through an association with rock.

However, rock was a problematic subject for the jazz press. The staff at *Down Beat* was, for the most part, both uninterested in and unknowledgeable about rock music, and this was reflected in the magazine's coverage. Morgenstern's editorial philosophy ensured that rock would always be represented in *Down Beat* in relation to jazz—not as an outsider music rebelling against authority and taken on its own terms, but as the youngest member of a musical family, forever looking up to its wiser jazz parent. Almost without exception, jazz was presented as a music to which rock musicians ought to aspire; while rock musicians were praised for developing more "sophisticated" music, it was usually according to the criteria of jazz music. In his categorization of popular music, Leonard Feather did not create a distinct category for rock music but instead put bands like the Beatles and the Rolling Stones under his created category of "current teen pop" music; the problem was that unlike bands like Cream and Chicago, the Beatles and the Stones did not aspire to jazz as many commercial musicians had in the past. *Jazz* became *Jazz & Pop*, and in contrast to *Down Beat* its key staff members were rock fans: and the difference in editorial outlook between *Down Beat* and *Jazz & Pop* could be partly revealed by comparing the arguments of the respective star critics for each magazine, Leonard Feather and Ralph Gleason. But neither magazine was attempting to construct a readership from scratch, and it would take the birth of a new magazine to successfully grow a mass rock readership and give it a distinct identity by taking rock seriously on new terms.

4

The Birth of Rolling Stone

*Down Beat is so unfailingly pompous about popular music
because it knows jazz is "better." It's more complex, more subtle,
and requires more skill and attention in performance and enjoyment,
so it has to be. But it doesn't.*

ROBERT CHRISTGAU, *DOWN BEAT* LETTER TO THE EDITOR, SEPTEMBER 19, 1968[1]

*Popular music criticism has had few guidelines. Jazz men
developed some, but rock and roll critics, finally descending upon us
circa 1967, were mere babes in the woods.*

JANN WENNER, *ROLLING STONE RECORD REVIEW,* 1971[2]

As we have seen, *Down Beat* was a key part of the American popular music press up until the late 1960s. As the longest surviving periodical of record for jazz, *Down Beat* and its staff selectively reported and interpreted musical events over the decades, helping to construct a jazz tradition with its own lexicon, themes, and canon. However, *Down Beat* and the American jazz press failed to absorb rock music into their discourse in a way that appealed to rock fans, and where they failed, *Rolling Stone* enjoyed spectacular success, overtaking the circulation of the jazz press in a few short years to become the largest and most influential popular music periodical in America.

There have been numerous accounts of the birth of *Rolling Stone*, ranging from the journalistic to the academic.[3] My account will have a different emphasis, since my aim is to explore how jazz and rock criticism operate in relation to one another. In this chapter I intend to examine the emergence of a rock-centered American music press, surveying the most important outlets for early rock coverage and the precursors to *Rolling Stone*. I will then examine the two most important figures in the creation of *Rolling Stone* as a rock authority in its crucial first year of publication: co-founders Jann Wenner and Ralph Gleason. Finally, I will consider the two most important and influential critics who worked for the magazine in its early years, Jon Landau and Greil Marcus, and how they contributed to the creation of *Rolling Stone's* distinctive rock discourse. The combination of these people and their choices distinguished *Rolling Stone* from its competitors as an authoritative rock journal from early on in its history, ultimately leading to it overtaking *Down Beat* as the largest circulating popular music periodical in America by the end of the 1960s.

Contextualizing the emergence of an American rock press

In one of the earliest scholarly assessments of the history of the American music press, Simon Frith alleged that "in the 1950s and early 1960s, the USA had no music papers between the trade press on the one hand...and the teeny-bop magazines on the other."[4] As for the development of the rock press, Frith argued that it emerged from two other sources: first, the underground press, such as the *LA Free Press* and the *Berkeley Barb* beginning in 1964, and second, new specialist music magazines, with *Crawdaddy!* beginning in 1966, followed by papers such as *Mojo-Navigator*, *Creem*, and most importantly, *Rolling Stone*.[5] Subsequent accounts of the music press have largely followed this line of argument, historicizing rock journalism in a way that disregards the numerous American jazz, folk, and blues publications in existence during that period, as well as the appearance of rock and pop coverage in other areas of the American press.[6] This is despite the fact that these other print media discussed rock 'n' roll at key moments in its history, formed the context out of which rock magazines would eventually emerge, and clearly had an impact on how young rock critics conceptualized rock discourse.

All of these sources were important, not necessarily because their styles of rock writing were imitated by those in the rock press (though this happened in some cases), but more often because the creators of the rock press could define their own ideology *against* the existing context of rock coverage. According to numerous accounts, almost all of the significant young rock critics in the late 1960s—Paul Williams, Greg Shaw, Jann Wenner, Jon Landau, Robert Christgau, Greil Marcus, to name only the most prominent— grew up eagerly seeking out rock and pop writing wherever they could find it prior to the rise of the specialist rock press.[7] As Marcus put it, "you just read what you could get your hands on."[8] In this section I will briefly sketch an outline of American rock music coverage prior to the birth of *Rolling Stone*. There are at least six significant sources of coverage to discuss: the trade press, specialist music press, teen press, mainstream newspapers and magazines, underground press, and international press. I will conclude by briefly examining the pre-*Rolling Stone* rock press, focusing on the cases of *Crawdaddy!* and *Mojo-Navigator*.

Rock 'n' roll had been covered in the music trade press ever since it was identified as a marketable musical commodity. An appropriate starting point is the year 1949, when R&B producer Jerry Wexler famously coined the term "rhythm and blues" in the pages of *Billboard*. Wexler got his start in the music business working as a journalist for the paper, and came up with "rhythm and blues" to replace the chart known until that point as "race records," on the grounds that the former label was embarrassing: "'race records' didn't sit well. Maybe 'race' was too close to 'racist' … I liked the sound of 'rhythm and blues'—it sung and swung like the music itself."[9] Others obviously agreed, as the market formerly known as "race records" became increasingly discussed as "rhythm and blues" not only in *Billboard* but in other trade papers like *Variety* and *Cash Box*. *Down Beat*, which had never previously covered "race records," began to introduce rhythm and blues coverage as a regular feature. Later, as rhythm and blues and rock 'n' roll began to dominate the charts, trade paper coverage of R&B and rock 'n' roll continued to discuss the music in terms of its commercial value, but still dismissed its musical worth on the grounds that it was instrumentally primitive, lyrically embarrassing, and a transitory teen fad. This dismissive attitude toward rock and pop would remain as an undercurrent in the trade press throughout the 1950s and 60s despite the music's growing commercial and cultural significance.

The oldest and most important of the specialist music publications were jazz publications. I have already discussed how the jazz press reacted to rock 'n' roll; here I want to note again that jazz critics and publications had written significantly about rock 'n' roll and pop at key moments in their histories. The other important specialist music publications were the folk press, particularly *Sing Out!* and the *Little Sandy Review*. As Lindberg et al. explained,

> Whereas jazz criticism was specifically concerned with "competence" and "quality" and to some extent influenced by "high art" values and classical music criticism, folklore discourses were consolidated almost solely by the idea of "authenticity" ... in this discourse, jazz conceptions of musician and skill ... were contrasted by metaphors referring to expression, such as "lived experience" and "feeling."[10]

First published in 1950, *Sing Out!* was a response to the first wave of the American folk music revival led by figures such as Alan Lomax and Pete Seeger with his group the Weavers. The publication promoted not just folk music, but a very explicit folk ideology valuing authenticity, lived experience, and feeling that could be applied to any kind of music; as the first editorial explained, "no form—folk song, concert song, dance, symphony, jazz—is alien to it."[11] In 1961, the second wave of the folk revival was heralded by the creation of the *Little Sandy Review*, published by Paul Nelson and his friend John Pankake out of Minnesota. Both the jazz and folk press and their ideologies would prove to be important early influences on rock critics in the late 1960s.[12]

On the cusp between the specialist music press and the teen press were song lyric magazines such as *Song Hits* and *Hit Parader*. The focus of these publications was on reprinted lyrics of popular songs, but they also provided biographical information on pop performers. They were cheap to produce and therefore readily affordable, and despite the fact that they were marketed at the teenage market, these magazines were sometimes picked out by individual writers and editors who attempted to take pop music more seriously. As Greg Shaw, co-founder of *Mojo-Navigator*, recalled, this was especially true of *Hit Parader*:

> *Hit Parader* really set the tone for the music press in America, because it was written intelligently, taking music away from the teenyboppers and putting it in a more serious context. In the early '60s, when I started reading it, the editorship was taken over by a guy called Jim Delahant … all of us who got into the music press were inspired by him because, besides celebrity interviews and so on, he'd have features on unknown, esoteric bands. Weird folk singers, jazz no one cared about—he'd put it in there. He was a great writer, and he had the power to do it.[13]

Other rock critics, such as Lenny Kaye and Jon Landau, also cited *Hit Parader* as an influential early source of information, with Landau commenting that Jim Delehant was one of the first writers he could remember asking musicians questions about the production and engineering of their records.[14]

Alongside song lyric magazines were teen magazines with a broader editorial scope, such as *Tiger Beat* and *16*, where content not only included musical performers but also articles on film stars, personal advice columns, "real life" stories, and so on. *16* was particularly important, founded in 1957 and then turned into a publishing success by editor Gloria Stavers, who joined the magazine in 1958. As Dave Marsh explained, "the reasons for Gloria's stature have to do with the way she used every issue of *16*, month after month, from 1958 to 1975, to express her absolute loyalty to a specific vision of teen culture."[15] Teen magazines have been routinely neglected or dismissed in accounts of popular music criticism on the grounds they did not take music seriously (see, for instance, the quotes from Frith, Shaw, and Williams in this chapter); but this ignores the fact that the teen press industry was substantial in both size and content, developing a discourse that valued pop music (especially in the case of *16*) and appealed to a large market of young female music fans. Furthermore, according to Paul Gorman's oral history of the music press, many of the young men who would later grow up to be rock critics also purchased and read these magazines for information on pop musicians.[16]

The mainstream press, including broadsheet newspapers and general interest magazines, also covered rock 'n' roll to the extent that they felt it was relevant to their readership, first for its social significance and later to consider its artistic merit. As we saw in Chapter 3, Bernard Gendron has argued that by the summer of 1965, a decisive discursive shift had occurred where the music of the Beatles and other rock groups began to receive serious consideration in several articles published by middlebrow newspapers and general interest magazines such as the *New York Times* and *Life*.[17] Entertainment reporters such as Jane Scott of the *Cleveland Plain Dealer* were also important in critically analyzing teenage culture rather than dismissing it out of hand. During the mid-1960s the label "rock" came to distinguish not just musical differences from 1950s "rock 'n' roll" but also ideological differences—for some, rock was music to be taken seriously. However, most of the writers who devoted attention to rock music during this time were older critics who remained outsiders to rock culture; as Gendron argued, "their own cultural capital was not invested in the future of rock, which could die without affecting their authority or their interests. In effect, rock would not finally achieve full and secure cultural accreditation until it acquired its own critics and its own publications, altogether committed to its cultural enhancement."[18] Some of the men's interest magazines, notably *Esquire* and *Playboy*, would later feature columns and articles by critics such as Robert Christgau and John Gabree, but these would not appear until after the formation of the specialist rock press. Likewise, Ellen Willis was hired by the *New Yorker* to cover rock in 1968, but the magazine did not feature regular rock coverage prior to the advent of American rock magazines in 1966–67.

The term "underground press" is a slippery category (potentially it could include regularly published newspapers with paid staff, campus newspapers, and homespun operations such as short-run mimeographed newsletters), but the two most influential American underground newspapers in the 1960s were the *Village Voice* and the *LA Free Press*. The *Voice*, which began in 1955, was the first newspaper to venture into serious rock criticism by hiring Richard Goldstein to cover the music in 1966. It also served as a model for the creation of the *LA Free Press* in 1964, which grew to have a circulation of

90,000 by the end of the decade.[19] Other publications, such as the *Berkeley Barb* and campus newspapers, provided an important early forum for critics writing about rock.

The last influence on American rock magazines founders to note is the foreign music press, and in particular music papers published in the UK. As noted in earlier chapters, the British *Melody Maker* was a key forum for early jazz criticism, but from the mid-1950s onward it also published coverage of the music falling under the labels "rock 'n' roll," "rock," "rhythm and blues," "beat music," and "pop," and gradually became more sympathetic to the aforementioned genres as the 1960s progressed. Other important early British music publications of the era included the *New Musical Express* (*NME*), *Disc*, and the *Record Mirror*, as well as teen-oriented papers including *Marilyn, Boyfriend, Marty, Jackie, Fabulous*, and *Rave*. (A full account of popular music writing in other countries is well beyond the scope of this book—for a global overview of music journalism, see Simon Warner's account in *The Sage Handbook of Popular Music*.)[20]

These six sources of rock coverage provided the context out of which the specialist rock press emerged in the 1966–67 period. Four rock magazines from that period were particularly significant: Paul Williams launched *Crawdaddy!* magazine in February 1966; this is now generally acknowledged to be the first American rock magazine. Six months later the team of David Harris and Greg Shaw created *Mojo-Navigator* magazine, a San Francisco-oriented publication now cited as a prototypical example of the fanzine, especially because Shaw would go on to create several more important music publications. Gerald Rothberg published the first issue of the New York–based *Hullabaloo* shortly afterward in October 1966 (*Hullabaloo* later changed its name to *Circus* in 1969), while back in San Francisco Jann Wenner and Ralph Gleason launched *Rolling Stone* in November 1967. In their overview of the history of rock criticism, Lindberg et al. describe how rock critics also began to appear in other non-music-specific publications, such as the underground press, daily newspapers, weeklies, and monthlies; but they concluded that it was the specialist music magazine press in particular that formed the nexus of rock criticism: "it was the profile of these magazines and the positions developed by their main writers that drew the contours of the field."[21]

Paul Williams made it clear from the first issue of *Crawdaddy!* that rock was the primary focus of his publication and that it differed from other writing about rock because it took the music seriously:

> You are looking at the first issue of a magazine of rock and roll criticism. *Crawdaddy* will feature neither pin-ups nor news-briefs; the specialty of the magazine is intelligent writing about pop music. *Billboard, Cash Box*, etc., serve very well as trade magazines; but their idea of a review is: "a hard-driving rhythm number that should spiral rapidly up the charts just as (previous hit by the same group) slides." And the teen magazines are devoted to rock and roll, but their idea of discussion is a string of superlatives below a fold out photograph. *Crawdaddy* believes that someone might be interested in what others might have to say about the music they like.[22]

Williams argued that his magazine fulfilled a need for serious, intelligent criticism of rock music that was not being met elsewhere. He was also clearly aware of a tension between jazz and rock criticism, and indicated in the second issue of *Crawdaddy!* that a feature in a forthcoming issue would be the contrasting critiques of a Ramsey Lewis album by a jazz critic and rock critic, illustrating what happened when conflicting criteria were used to evaluate the same music.[23] *Mojo-Navigator* editor David Harris also wrote explicitly about the problem of jazz critics judging rock, commenting how a San Francisco critic's article about rock music using the aesthetic criteria of jazz constituted "an attack by a jazz buff on a music which he doesn't understand…one cannot write a criticism of a music which alienates one from the outset; it is absurd for someone who doesn't seem to like rock 'n' roll to try to evaluate the merits of various bands."[24]

The founders of the early rock magazines explicitly claimed that they would provide something different from existing rock coverage. Unlike the trade papers, they were interested in discussing the cultural and aesthetic significance of the music. Unlike teen magazine writers, the creators of the rock press were almost exclusively male, and in reacting against coverage of rock in the teen press constructed rock criticism as not only serious, but

Figure 4.1 *Bob Dylan cover issue of* Crawdaddy!, *August 1966. Copyright 1966 © by Wolfgang's Vault. All Rights Reserved. Used by Permission.*

as a primarily male pursuit.[25] Unlike the journalists writing for mainstream newspapers or general interest magazines, the new rock writers were insiders to rock culture—fans of rock rather than outsiders commenting on it as a curiosity. The rock press was produced in a larger press context, and even if it defined itself in opposition to certain existing rock coverage, "square" publications were influential in providing rock coverage *against* which the bulk of new rock critics would react.

The founders of *Rolling Stone* create a rock authority

The period between 1966 and 1969 saw the birth of a plethora of specialist rock magazines—*Crawdaddy!*, *Mojo-Navigator*, *Hullabaloo*, *Cheetah*, *Eye*, and *Creem*, to name a few. Some would not make it past a handful of issues, while others managed to survive for years. But one magazine eclipsed them all in longevity, influence, and profitability: as Lindberg et al. put it, "within a year or two of its start in November 1967, *Rolling Stone*, with its in-depth articles, substantial interviews and reviews, had succeeded in becoming *the* authoritative voice on popular music for most of the Western world."[26] In this section, I will examine how two figures, Jann Wenner and Ralph Gleason, endowed *Rolling Stone* with an impressive authority during its crucial first year.

If one person is to be singled out as being responsible for the success of *Rolling Stone*, it is clearly co-founder and editor Jann Wenner. Born in New York City and raised in California, Wenner recalls having an early interest in journalism: "when I was seven years old I had a neighbourhood newspaper called the *Weekly Trumpet*. ... We reported on things like I'd listen to my parents at the dinner table and I'd hear that neighbours were getting divorced and so I'd rush that into print."[27] As a freshman at the University of California in Berkeley in 1963, he worked as a radio affiliate for NBC—couriering studio tapes, reading traffic reports over the radio, and reporting on the student movement that was gaining momentum on campus.[28] However, by 1965 Wenner had discovered a greater passion, becoming infatuated with the music of the Beatles, Dylan, and the Stones, as well as the growing countercultural scene in San Francisco; he also found a kindred spirit in Ralph Gleason, the jazz critic for the *San Francisco Chronicle*, who had also been profoundly affected by rock music and culture. As Wenner recalled,

[Ralph and I] were both just in love with rock and roll and took it very seriously, I mean enjoyed it enormously but also took it very seriously. I mean we could see what was happening when you saw what the Beatles stood for and the Stones and what Dylan was writing and these are serious people. They're serious artists.[29]

According to Robert Draper, in 1966 Wenner tried numerous ways to establish himself as a music writer: contributing a music column to the Berkeley campus paper, the *Daily Californian*; spending the summer in London, England, attempting unsuccessfully to freelance for the British music weekly *Melody Maker*; returning to San Francisco after being recommended by Gleason for a job as the entertainment editor of the short-lived Sunday edition of Warren Hinckle's *Ramparts* magazine.[30] When *Sunday Ramparts* folded in May 1967, it wasn't long before Wenner decided to create his own music magazine. In the following months he researched the existing music press and media landscape, absorbing and opposing various ideas and influences before synthesizing them into his own vision of what a successful music magazine should be. Paul Williams at *Crawdaddy!* and Greg Shaw at *Mojo-Navigator* both recalled Wenner asking them for advice on how they ran their music magazines. Williams remembered that "Wenner got together with me and asked a lot of questions before he started *Rolling Stone*," while Shaw, who lived in San Francisco, claimed to have been regularly questioned by Wenner:

I'd known Jann Wenner for a year or so in San Francisco. He used to come over to my flat and sit there and watch me turn the crank and ask me questions: "Why do you do this? How does this work? How do you know to put interviews in the front and record reviews in the back?" I kind of gave him a basic course in putting magazines out. I mean, that's a bit of an exaggeration, but he did hang out and he did ask all those questions.[31]

According to Draper, Wenner also quizzed the production staff of his former employer, *Sunday Ramparts*, to learn about producing a professional-looking paper. He managed to persuade Dugald Stermer, the *Ramparts* art director, to allow him to copy and use the professional *Ramparts* design (itself based on

The Times of London and the *New York Herald Tribune* Sunday magazine) for *Rolling Stone*, and then lured *Ramparts* production director John Williams to moonlight as the producer for Wenner's magazine. Finally, he hired Baron Wolman, a professional photographer in the Bay area, to become the official photographer for *Rolling Stone*.[32] As Wenner later recalled, "I had a sensibility about doing things clean and neat and orderly and well designed and presentable ... the look of these underground papers didn't appeal to me at all."[33] From the first issue, *Rolling Stone* was far more professional looking than *Crawdaddy!* or *Mojo-Navigator* had ever been.

In the inaugural issue of *Rolling Stone*, Wenner wrote a mission statement outlining his concept for the magazine:

> We have begun a new publication reflecting what we see are the changes in rock and roll and the changes related to rock and roll. Because the trade papers have become so inaccurate and irrelevant, and because the fan magazines are an anachronism, fashioned in the mold of myth and nonsense, we hope that we have something here for the artists and the industry, and every person who "believes in the magic that can set you free."[34]

Wenner's key idea was to produce professional reportage of the music he loved; *Rolling Stone* would be like a news magazine, such as *Newsweek* or *Time*, but aimed at a youth audience and with rock 'n' roll as its primary focus. As Wenner put it years later in an interview with Charlie Rose,

> My feeling was that, when I started at that time, no mainstream media, whether television, newspapers, or magazines, or movies even spoke to young people, or spoke for young people, or to young people, or they didn't take music seriously, or they weren't aware of the generational change that was about to shape up. Rock and roll music was the medium of communication among young people.[35]

At that summer's Monterey Pop Festival in California, Wenner met a *Newsweek* reporter, Michael Lydon, who was covering the event in the press

Figure 4.2 *Cover of first issue of* Rolling Stone, *November 9, 1967. Copyright 1967*
© *by Rolling Stone LLC. All Rights Reserved. Used by Permission.*

section. Soon after, Wenner had convinced him to become *Rolling Stone*'s first managing editor. According to Lydon, "I had numerous years of reporting and fully professional journalism experience under my belt, which was relatively rare ... He wanted somebody to be his sort of anchor."[36] Lydon eventually left the magazine to pursue a freelance career, but not before putting Wenner in touch with John Burks, another *Newsweek* correspondent whom Wenner would hire as *Rolling Stone*'s managing editor in its second year. Burks remembered that:

> We were definitely following out a news magazine concept. The original news magazine idea, the way *Time* did it, would be you read newspapers from over the U.S. and the world and condense them for next week. And at the start we did relatively more of that and relatively less original reporting. And then by the time I'd left the staff was big enough that ... we had sources we just didn't have in the first place, so a lot of it became original stuff. But in the beginning there was a lot more cadging, I say without shame.[37]

In addition to researching the practices of *Crawdaddy!* and *Mojo-Navigator*, Wenner was allegedly also influenced by the British music paper *Melody Maker* after spending the summer of 1966 in London, according to Draper.[38] In their study of the rock press, Lindberg et al. explain that "the long tradition of jazz criticism [was] a central influence on the emerging pop and rock criticism at *Melody Maker* in this period" with four major consequences. First, many of the aesthetic criteria that jazz critics had developed began to be applied to rock criticism. Second, the new rock critics hired at Melody Maker were influenced by both the professional standard of jazz writing and the musical knowledge of the jazz critics already working at the paper. Third, the authors described how "a new sensibility regarding of individual musical skills and expressive abilities among beat, rock and R & B musicians was adopted from a jazz listener and critic's point of view—an approach unforeseen in earlier 'fan' or 'trade' magazines." And finally, the notion of treating rock as "serious" rather than simply "commercial" music was also influenced by the way jazz had long been treated in *Melody Maker*.[39]

According to John Burks, some of this influence could also be felt in the early issues of *Rolling Stone*, not least because the magazine sometimes reproduced entire articles from *Melody Maker* and continued to use it as a key source for content and story ideas throughout the early years of the magazine; indeed, Burks remembered that the *Rolling Stone* office subscribed to both *Melody Maker* and *New Musical Express*, "and stole from them liberally—'stole' meaning rewrite and freshen up a little bit."[40] Draper also noted that "Ralph Gleason suggested contacting *Melody Maker* with an offer to trade copy. Thus came an up-to-date column on the London scene by *Melody Maker* writer Nick Jones, whom Jann promptly dubbed *Rolling Stone*'s 'London correspondent.'"[41] Interestingly, *Down Beat* editor Dan Morgenstern similarly remembered that Wenner initially approached him to do an ad exchange; Morgenstern thought this was a great idea, but *Down Beat* owner John Maher was against it, and Morgenstern never heard from Wenner again.[42] The magazine reflected Wenner's rock 'n' roll tastes, but he was also evidently aware of the practices of certain longstanding jazz publications.

Overall, Wenner had a vision for a rock magazine that operated, read, and looked like a credible news source. As Wenner later put it,

> I was a rock and roll fan and there was no publication for me, of any kind, that would treat it with the respect and dignity and joy that it really represented and deserved. It was either shut out from the mainstream media, or they ridiculed it. They put it down, like it was screaming teenage girls, what will they do when they grow up, etc. It was really looked down on. So what they were missing was one of stories of our times.[43]

Trade papers like *Billboard* wrote on rock culture as outsiders, yet rock had come to rival adult popular music as the most commercially significant music on the market. *Time* and *Newsweek* provided models of magazines that compiled and presented an authoritative account of relevant news with every issue. The design of the sophisticated, elegant-looking *Sunday Ramparts* was directly copied to produce a professional-looking rock magazine that bore more resemblance in visual style to the London *Times* than to its counterparts in the underground press. Early staff members like Williams, Lydon, and Wolman were all important in giving the magazine its professional appearance, but it was Wenner who was able to bring them on board and direct them on a meager budget. Or in Wenner's words, the success of *Rolling Stone* "depends a great deal on and is shaped by the talent you bring into it … The management of talent, which I think I am good at, is knowing what somebody is good at, getting them to do what they're good at, or matching them with a good idea."[44]

The second important figure in distinguishing *Rolling Stone* as a rock authority in its early days was Ralph Gleason, co-founder and consulting editor of the magazine. Gleason had earned his reputation as one of America's most important jazz critics, writing for a wide range of publications including *Down Beat* and contributing a regular column to the *San Francisco Chronicle* which was syndicated to over sixty other newspapers. But the rise of rock culture, and the San Francisco rock scene in particular, had a profound impact on him. When Jann Wenner had approached him about producing a rock magazine, Gleason did not need much convincing. Apart from coming up with the name "*Rolling Stone*," Gleason brought both a wealth of experience and his considerable reputation to the new magazine. As Draper noted, Gleason was crucial to the successful start of *Rolling Stone* for several reasons: first, he had experience starting up new publications—notably the production of his own magazines, *Jazz Information* and *Jazz*—and therefore had a sense of how to avoid the pitfalls that routinely sank new press ventures. Second, Gleason's status as a well-known critic meant that he was armed with contacts for record labels and publicists, meaning it would be easier to secure advertising and access to artists based on his reputation. In short, as Draper put it, "Gleason would mean instant cachet for Jann's venture."[45]

Gleason was also able to consider contemporary issues in the rock scene, like the problem of musicians being exploited by their recording and publishing contracts, and give them an historical perspective by relating them to similar events in jazz history. *Rolling Stone* contributor Ben Fong-Torres reflected on Gleason's role at the magazine in its early years:

For having next to no physical presence in the office … he was a *great* presence. He was the patriarch, though he didn't come across as that old, and we looked to him for guidance. If I were to smell a payola story, I could always send it past Ralph and he would just say, "Look, this is garbage—here, these are some editorials from five years ago, copy'em for your files, what you're talking about is part of a typical six-year cycle, and what you guys really ought to be is studying the jukebox industry, now that's where the scandal leads." He could put you back in your place, or up on a higher level, whichever the situation called for. He was our encyclopedia.[46]

Gleason contributed a column to *Rolling Stone* called "Perspectives"—a title he had originally used for his regular music column in *Down Beat* in the 1950s—and he occasionally drew on his wealth of experience as a jazz critic to consider how the psychedelic San Francisco scene fitted into the long history of American popular music. For instance, if he was advocating that young bands should understand how music publishing worked, he would bring in an example of Louis Armstrong selling his early hits;[47] if he discussed the explosive growth of the record industry in the 1960s, he would compare it to what it would have meant for Benny Goodman to have a hit record in the swing era.[48] As John Burks recalled, most of all,

> *Rolling Stone* writers respected Gleason as representing outsider culture whether or not they listened to jazz … Jazz guys have always been outsiders, underdogs, and what they were doing, jazz, was making a commentary on American life … Now here comes rock 'n' roll, Jefferson Airplane and Bob Dylan, and they have an outsider message which is not mainstream, it's not the establishment version, nor was jazz—so they had these things in common.[49]

Gleason was a mentor figure not just to Wenner, but also to most of the early staff at the magazine. Furthermore, he was a peer to many of the music industry executives who were struggling to make sense of rock and recognized him as an established, credible critic. Acting as a bridge between the two generations, Gleason endowed *Rolling Stone* with authority for both rock audiences and the music industry.

Rolling Stone critics and the construction of a rock aesthetic

The third figure to augment the status of *Rolling Stone* as a rock authority in its first year was rock critic Jon Landau. Wenner's editorial, entrepreneurial, and interpersonal talents made him the driving force of *Rolling Stone*, and Gleason's name was crucial for giving the magazine early credibility, but Landau managed to develop a distinct rock aesthetic that had an impressive influence on rock artists and producers. After writing an article praising Aretha Franklin's new recordings on Atlantic, Landau received a call from R&B producer and vice-president of Atlantic Records, Jerry Wexler, who was clearly impressed with Landau and asked for his advice on which song to release as Aretha's next single.[50] When Landau panned the Rolling Stones' *Their Satanic Majesties Request*, Charlie Watts contacted Landau a few weeks later and "promised that the band would try harder next time around."[51] When Landau dismissed a Cream concert as boring and repetitious, Eric Clapton recalled reading the article only to realize that "it was true…I immediately decided that that was the end of the band."[52] These events all took place within the first year of the magazine's publication and helped to establish the status of *Rolling Stone* as a magazine that was taken seriously by artists as well as the industry.

Landau was raised in New York City and later Cambridge, Massachusetts, by two music-loving parents and was exposed to popular music criticism from an early age. Although he did not share his father's love of jazz, throughout his childhood he read the jazz magazines to which his father subscribed, namely *Down Beat* and *Metronome*. His favorite feature was Leonard Feather's "Blindfold Test": "I was fascinated…they'd get somebody in there and play them five or six records, not tell them what they were playing, and just have them talk about the music, whether they recognized the artist or not, and I always found that discussion was my favorite part."[53] In fact, Landau was drawn more to the discussions and arguments than he was to the music itself: "I probably related to those magazines more than I related to jazz as something for me personally. There was a lot of vitality in them, people staking out territory, defending their tastes."[54]

From an early age, Landau's own tastes leaned more toward folk, R&B, and rock 'n' roll. His first published music writing appeared in a locally produced mimeograph called *Boston Broadside*, which covered the local folk scene.[55] Landau wrote several folk music reviews for the paper while he was still in high school, but it would not be until his sophomore year at Brandeis University that his music-writing career would truly take off. During his early university years he worked at the local music store Briggs and Briggs, and it was there that he met eighteen-year-old Paul Williams, who had begun dropping off the first issues of his rock mimeograph, *Crawdaddy!* to sell at the store. Landau was the youngest person working at the store, and the two hit it off; as Landau recalled, "in due course, I told him his magazine was awful, that no one writing for it knew anything about music, and that I knew just the man he needed: me."[56]

Unlike many of his peers in rock criticism, Landau was a serious student of the guitar throughout his childhood and had become an accomplished amateur guitarist by the time he started writing for *Crawdaddy!* His musician's perspective set him apart from his peers from his very first review—a mixed reaction to Mitch Ryder and the Detroit Wheels—which he wrote with a surprising authority, giving detailed, specific critiques of guitarists' playing styles, vocal tone, and the engineering and production of the record.[57] He was highly critical and rarely found a record to be without flaws, but he always supported his strong opinions with specific musical examples, and it was this style that distinguished him from other writers. Wenner offered him a featured full-page column in *Rolling Stone*, making him the principal rock critic for the magazine. Landau later remembered: "I was impressed [by Wenner]. I mean, I never had anybody write me a letter asking me to start with the first issue. Totally professional—he's gonna pay me—right away got the flash that he was serious. I was being treated professionally. It was a whole new thing for me."[58]

While at *Rolling Stone*, Landau wrote many influential columns and carved out a distinct and recognizable rock 'n' roll aesthetic. Lindberg et al. summarize how Landau's critical stance contrasted with the general editorial policy at the magazine, especially with regard to the psychedelic bands from San Francisco versus music with stronger roots in 1950s rhythm and blues:

Jann Wenner, Ralph Gleason and many of their writers had a heavy San Francisco bias. For them a new era in rock music had begun with Jefferson Airplane's *Takes Off* (or perhaps with Buffalo Springfield's "For What It's Worth") in late 1966. They tended to see the Beatles (with *Sgt. Pepper*), Jimi Hendrix and Pink Floyd as more or less gifted disciples of the San Franciscans...Landau on the other hand was not only placed on the East Coast, in Boston, but he was always skeptical about the San Franciscan gospel. Especially Gleason announced the birth of new rock aesthetics, close to the aesthetics of avant-garde jazz, while Landau stressed that rock aesthetics really had their foundations in 1950s body music.[59]

In July 1968, Landau tried to explicitly articulate his aesthetic in an essay column titled "What's Wrong with Rock 'Art.'" He was especially concerned by the perceived shift in rock 'n' roll from its "honkey-tonk atmosphere" to the "atmosphere of an art exhibit." For Landau, this trend represented "a misunderstanding of what rock and roll is, and what listening to and playing rock entails." He argued that the aesthetic values at the heart of rock music extended back to its roots in the 1950s, when it had emerged as a synthesis of blues, country and western, and pop: "it was, at its best, unpretentious, hard, simple, body music. Nobody had to tell you to get up and dance." According to Landau, the best rock continued to maintain these core values, but in the months leading up to his essay musicians had taken steps away from the essence of rock, evidenced in the recent work of the two most important rock groups of the 1960s: the Beatles' "Fool on the Hill" and the Rolling Stones' *Their Satanic Majesties Request*. This new rock "art" was "pious, subtly self-righteous, humorless and totally unphysical ... The joyfulness and uninhibited straight-forwardness which is such an essential side to all rock and roll was often lost in the shuffle. Rock became cerebral."[60]

Additional insight into Landau's rock aesthetic could be found in his other reviews from this period, such as his pan of *Satanic Majesties* and his praise of Otis Redding and soul music:

The Rolling Stones have been the best of all possible worlds: they have the lack of pretension and sentimentality associated with the blues, the rawness and toughness of hard rock, and the depth which always makes you feel that they are in the midst of saying something. They have never impressed me as being kitsch. *Their Satanic Majesties Request*, despite moments of unquestionable brilliance, put the status of the Rolling Stones in jeopardy... they try too hard to prove that they too are innovators, and that they too can say something new... Unfortunately they have been caught up in the familiar dilemma of mistaking the new for the advanced. In the process they have sacrificed most of the virtues which made their music so powerful in the first place: the tightness, the franticness, the directness, the primitiveness... In rock there seems to be an inverse ratio between the amount of striving there is to make art and the quality of the art that results. For there was far more art in the Rolling Stones who were just trying to make rock than there is in the Rolling Stones who are trying to create art.[61]

The lack of intellectuality and detachment [in soul music] which is necessarily a part of this expression is responsible for the resultant intimacy of the music. Soul music approaches folk music in its lack of self-consciousness. And it is art, even though the artist may not seek to do anything beyond entertain.[62]

If one were to compile a list of the terms and adjectives Landau used to describe good rock and soul music in this period—and these two genres were clearly related for Landau, who described Otis Redding as both rock and soul in another essay[63]—it becomes clear that his aesthetic was remarkably similar to hot jazz critics earlier in the century. For Landau, the best rock and soul was unpretentious, raw, direct, primitive, lacking in self-consciousness and intellectuality; it was folk music and, therefore, great art precisely because the musicians did not self-consciously aspire to make art. Although he did not consciously draw from early jazz discourse in his arguments, Landau's rock aesthetic was nevertheless strongly reminiscent of the "primitivist" folk aesthetic celebrated by early jazz critics; however, such arguments had largely been abandoned in jazz discourse ever since the rise of bebop and the reconstruction of jazz as a modernist art. Landau's rock discourse starkly opposed contemporary jazz discourse, unwittingly producing a similar tension to that which had originally occurred between "moldy fig" and modernist jazz fans in the 1940s.

Landau's most famous piece of writing from this period was his aforementioned review of a Cream concert, which took place on March 23, 1968, at Brandeis University where Landau was studying as a history major; interestingly, *Down Beat* critic Alan Heineman was also studying at Brandeis for his doctoral degree and happened to attend and review the same concert, making it possible to contrast the approaches of the two critics.[64] Whereas Heineman felt that the concert confirmed that Cream was a band producing "a moving, powerful, original sound," Landau gave an opposite verdict, reserving particularly harsh criticism for Clapton and concluding that the guitarist was "a master of the blues clichés … [and] a virtuoso at performing other people's ideas."[65]

In order to interpret these two reviews, each needs to be taken in their proper context. Heineman started out writing as a jazz critic for *Down Beat*, but when the magazine changed its editorial policy he also started writing about rock and quickly became one of the magazine's most prominent rock critics. Heineman was encouraged to write about rock in a way that might appeal to jazz listeners, but this mandate suited his own musical tastes. In his review of Cream, Heineman begins by outlining some of the differences between jazz and rock: rock lacked the rhythmic complexity of jazz, and as a mostly electric, amplified music was inevitably far louder than most jazz, producing sounds in live performance that were "just this side of physically tangible."[66] Yet Heineman also clearly believed there was a certain overlap in the criteria of the two genres, as he devoted a significant portion of his review to analyzing the rhythmic complexity of Cream's performance; he also felt it was significant that Ginger Baker had "jazz roots" and pronounced that Eric Clapton had "few or no technical equals, in jazz or rock."[67]

Landau, on the other hand, flatly denounced the possibility that Cream had anything to do with jazz. "Cream have been called a jazz group," he wrote, but "they are not. They are a blues band and a rock band."[68] And as such, they failed to meet his standards of good blues and rock. Landau felt no need to qualify such a statement, especially given that the magazine he was writing was targeted explicitly at a rock readership. Landau and Heineman were individual critics, and one cannot interpret from their Cream concert reviews the fundamental differences between jazz discourse and the emerging rock discourse of the late 1960s. But it *is* possible to say that Heineman considered himself to be primarily a jazz critic who was also a rock fan, whereas Landau was primarily a rock critic, that *Down Beat* and *Rolling Stone* were primarily jazz and rock magazines, respectively, and that they consequently fostered different ways of writing about rock music, even when dealing with the same concert.

A revealing postscript to this analysis is that Robert Christgau, then writing the rock column for *Esquire* magazine, wrote a letter to *Down Beat* complaining about Heineman's review:

> I'll believe Alan Heineman knows a damn about rock when he stops treating it as a debased form of jazz … *Down Beat* is so unfailingly pompous about popular music because it knows jazz is "better." It's more complex, more subtle, and requires more skill and attention in performance and enjoyment, so it has to be. But it doesn't, unless one's esthetic assumptions adhere to a mold that seems to me academic, snobbish, and moribund … Obviously, many of the musicians in rock disagree with me, including those in Cream. I think they are making a mistake. By abandoning the rigid structural framework that is a hallmark of rock, they enter a half-world that pleases only those (and there are many, some of them young) who want rock to turn into something more artistically respectable, namely jazz, and are willing to undergo all kinds of slop in the meantime. Cream's live performances are interminable and uneven, mediocre jazz and mediocre rock rather than a successful compound. The reason Heineman and other jazz writers dig them so much is that they now feel needed.[69]

Landau and Christgau were very different critics whose attitudes diverged on many issues, but they clearly agreed on the issue of Cream. In fact, just as Christgau's letter echoed several of the arguments made by Landau a few months earlier, so too did Landau echo parts of Christgau's letter a few months later in his *Rolling Stone* review of the second Blood, Sweat, and Tears album, when he complained that "styles exist in tangent on their record, but never merge into one … The listener responds to the illusion that he is hearing something new when in fact he is hearing mediocre rock, OK jazz, etc., thrown together in a contrived and purposeless way."[70] Despite their differences, both Landau and Christgau were *rock* critics, contributing to the development of a rock discourse that would soon displace jazz as the dominant popular music discourse in the music press.

In hindsight, Christgau's letter to Heineman seems a little unfair: one could make the argument that rather than digging the music because he now felt needed, he felt needed because a significant number of fans were similarly enthralled by Cream and its experimentations in merging jazz and rock. But it is also a prescient letter: Christgau and Landau's conviction that the jazz-rock merger of Cream was a mistake proved to resonate with the members of the band, and Heineman's argument was forgotten. Christgau would say this is not a matter of different discourses, but about one aesthetic being more valid than another, and moreover about the weakness of the jazz-rock fusion aesthetic.

Wenner, Gleason, and Landau each endowed their own kind of authority to *Rolling Stone* in its first year, and the magazine attracted more influential staff as it grew during the end of the 1960s. The most influential figure in this second wave of staff was Greil Marcus, who worked only just over a year as the magazine's first record review editor but professionalized the section, as well as exerting a tremendous influence on the thoughts and writing of rock critics under his helm and those who followed after he left. Marcus is perhaps now best known for books like the highly influential *Mystery Train* (a book which paved the way for the recognition of rock as a significant part of the history of American arts and letters), but these can be seen as the culmination of a rock ideology that was already evident in his early writing for *Rolling Stone*.

Marcus grew up in the Bay area reading Ralph Gleason, not so much for his coverage of jazz (in which Marcus had no interest), but for his other more occasional writings and interviews with popular musicians such as Fats Domino, Big Joe Turner, Ray Charles, Hank Williams, and Elvis Presley, as well as his reports of the Beat movement and popular culture rebels like Lenny Bruce.[71] Marcus met Jann Wenner in the spring of 1964 while they were both students at Berkeley, but the two would not strike up a professional relationship until 1968, by which time Marcus had become a graduate student of American political thought at Berkeley. He began contributing reviews to *Rolling Stone* not long after in response to a solicitation published in the magazine, and soon after started writing rock criticism for other publications such as the San Francisco *Express-Times*.

By 1969, Marcus was well known within the burgeoning clique of American rock critics, and solidified his reputation as a serious critic by editing *Rock and Roll Will Stand*, a collection of criticism that managed to blend irreverence and intellect and became widely read by writers and fans alike. His own essays in the book stand out in their seriousness of purpose, as Marcus tried to claim that rock 'n' roll simply could not be understood by older generations:

> [R]ock 'n' roll has existed only since about 1954, and thus it's a sad fact that most of those over thirty cannot be part of it, and it cannot be a part of them. I don't want to talk about the ability of adults to "enjoy the Beatles" or to "think Dylan has something to say," but about the rock 'n' roll era as the exclusive possession of our generation, about what our love for it and our immersion in it might imply for our consciousness and vision.[72]

Marcus also became friendly with Ralph Gleason during this time, and at one point complained to Gleason that the record review section was awful. According to Draper, Gleason passed on the complaint to Jann Wenner, who in turn called Marcus to offer him the job of editing the review section.[73] Marcus went on to recruit acquaintances and friends such as Barry Franklin, Bruce Miroff, Langdon Winner, and John Morthland to write reviews. He also began corresponding with writers who had responded to the reviewer solicitation advertisement in the magazine, such as Lester Bangs and Ed Ward. Marcus began editing the section in July 1969 and appeared on the masthead as the record review editor for the first time on August 8, 1969. Marcus felt that "Most of the people I was working with couldn't write.... So because I was a control fetishist I'd sit down and completely rewrite them. They didn't know enough to be pissed off."[74] Sometimes the quality of the writing was a greater criterion for publication than the actual music in question. As Marcus put it, "I would run reviews of stuff I'd never heard of or that seemed totally weird, just based on the quality of the writing or the humor."[75] However, it was Marcus who was influential in getting people to write about rock with a certain sort of seriousness and in establishing a sense of professionalism and purpose to the section; Marcus felt that rock 'n' roll was an art and an important part of American culture, and as Lindberg et al. suggest, he functioned "as a sort of ideological guru for most of the writers."[76]

Marcus was influential at *Rolling Stone* not only as an editor, but as a writer. He was a key contributor to some of the most important articles to appear in the magazine, such as the coverage of the Woodstock festival and the Altamont concert. As a scholar of political science and American studies, Marcus was able to analyze the social significance of such events, and yet he applied the same scope to his analysis of individual records. Lindberg et al. argue that an excerpt from his most famous record review, a four-page analysis of Bob Dylan's *Self-Portrait*, can serve as a key to his overall approach to rock criticism:

> Dylan's songs can serve as metaphors, enriching our lives, giving us random insight into the myths we carry and the present we live, intensifying what we've known and leading us toward what we never looked for, while at the same time enforcing an emotional strength upon those perceptions by the power of the music that moves with his words.[77]

Marcus would later argue in *Mystery Train* (1974) that the same could be said of all the best rock 'n' roll. However, Marcus ultimately condemned *Self-Portrait* in this review, which according to Draper led to a conflict with editor Wenner resulting in Marcus leaving his position as record review editor on August 9, 1970.[78] He was replaced at the magazine by Ed Ward, but through his later writing, particularly his book *Mystery Train*, Marcus's distinct approach to rock writing continued to influence both readers and critics.

A final key element in the rock aesthetic promoted by *Rolling Stone* was not one represented by any particular individual critic, but rather by the absence of demographic diversity across its writing staff: as with jazz criticism in previous decades, the writers for *Rolling Stone*—especially in its early years— were almost exclusively male. In her excellent critique of the representation of women in the 1960s rock press, Norma Coates argues that *Rolling Stone* in particular "played an important role in creating and circulating the masculine mythologies that held rock culture together, and in placing women in specific roles on its margins."[79] The magazine not only covered rock culture, "but in large part helped to define and characterize it... [it] limned out the boundaries of rock culture and sorted out its insiders and outsiders." Not only were women writers absent from its pages, but female artists tended to be represented as belonging to folk and singer-songwriter traditions and therefore outside the realms of "authentic" rock. Although a short article in 1968 "questioned the absence of women in rock," even those women who were undeniably participating in rock rather than folk—such as Grace Slick and Janis Joplin—"were sometimes judged more for their lack of sex appeal than for their artistry."[80] Worse off were female fans, who were represented as either tasteless teenyboppers (the opposite of the authentic rock fan) or disposable sex objects, also known as "groupies." One of the earliest *Rolling Stone* feature stories to capture the attention of the national press was its 1969 article on groupie culture, which was "for a long time the definitive statement on the relationship of women to rock and to rock stars," according to Coates:

> That relationship, of course, was sexually and socially subservient. Under the cover of objective reporting and observation, but under the sway of traditional gender politics, Rolling Stone neglected to consider the truly transgressive aspects of groupiedom, or that groupies' aggressive sexuality could be subversive statements about gender roles in rock as well as mainstream culture. Moreover, Rolling Stone's writers passed on the opportunity to envision a role for women in rock culture that was not tied to the normative gender roles they grew up with, a move that could have been truly countercultural, if not revolutionary.[81]

Neither was the content of *Rolling Stone* nor the makeup of its writing staff simply a matter that could be dismissed as a reflection of the gender roles of American counterculture—after all, the 1960s was also the era of second-wave feminism. Nor was it the case that women were simply not interested in the profession of popular music journalism. Not only were Ellen Willis (through her writing for the *New Yorker*) and Lillian Roxon (who published her influential *Rock Encyclopedia* in 1969) producing influential rock writing at the time, but also other magazines, notably *Jazz & Pop*, had a significantly higher number of female staff in editorial roles. In what is arguably the earliest essay calling out sexism in rock culture, editor Patricia Kennealy-Morrison (who succeeded Pauline Rivelli in the role) noted in a 1970 *Jazz & Pop* article that despite the rock audience being largely female in the Beatlemania era, not only was the post-1967 live music audience and record-buying public for rock predominantly male, but "it takes only a quick glance at J&P's rate card demographic breakdown to see that for a music magazine put together *entirely by women*, the readership is some 92% male." Foreshadowing later critiques by scholars such as Coates, Kennealy-Morrison also criticized the subservient roles that men in rock culture expected women to perform, before concluding that "rock is just another dismal male chauvinist trip, with one important difference: it's got the power and the looseness with which to change itself. It better happen quick."[82]

Conclusion

I want to conclude by briefly examining three characteristics of 1960s rock discourse exemplified in *Rolling Stone,* which are especially relevant when considering how it usurped *Down Beat* to become the dominant American periodical specializing in popular music—crucially, the roots of all three characteristics could be found in the history of jazz criticism, but had become untenable in jazz discourse by the end of the 1960s. The first was the establishment of *rock as a youth music*. Rock was largely dismissed by music critics at its inception, and as Gendron points out, the older music critics who had warmed to it had not grown up with it. As Greil Marcus put it, "most of those over thirty cannot be a part of [rock 'n' roll], and it cannot be a part of them."[83] As Wenner recalled, "music was the method in which young people were talking to each other. [*Rolling Stone*] was kind of a tribal telegraph and it was just beyond something any of the established media paid attention to and left us this enormous opening."[84] However, even though the readership of *Down Beat* at the end of the 1960s was demographically similar to that of *Rolling Stone* at the end of the 1960s (young middle-class males), jazz itself was represented as a mature, respectable music with a longstanding artistic lineage—a trait which had been hard won, but nonetheless marked jazz as the music of a past and not current generation. The second characteristic was the celebration of *rock as fun*. Whereas jazz recordings with a simple, repetitive tune and danceable beat were frequently spurned by jazz critics as selling out, good rock songs with identical characteristics were praised by rock critics. Jon Landau, the chief critic at *Rolling Stone* and arguably the most influential rock critic of his time, was the most ardent proponent of this aesthetic: for him, rock 'n' roll was, "at its best, unpretentious, hard, simple, body music. Nobody had to tell you to get up and dance."[85] Finally, a third distinct characteristic was *rock as an anti-commercial music despite its mass culture status*. By 1968, the recording industry had become a billion dollar business, thanks in large part to the commercial success of rock music—a mass culture on a scale that jazz had never known even at the height of its popularity. This directly informed the aesthetic of rock critics, most notably Robert Christgau, who when reflecting on his music writing of the late 1960s suggested that "popular art achieved a vitality of both integrity and outreach that high art had unfortunately abandoned," prompting him to formulate his own rock sensibility by melding "the communitarian rhetoric of the counterculture and the populist possibilities of pop into a sort of improvised democratic radicalism."[86] Jazz, on the other hand, was once a part of mass culture but that moment in history had long since passed. Jazz was not simply anti-commercial—it was struggling to be commercially viable at all.

These three characteristics were not necessarily the three definitive elements of rock discourse, but they were particularly important in positioning it in opposition to jazz discourse of that time. The same characteristics were, of course, present in jazz discourse at earlier points in its history, but had largely been abandoned by jazz critics of the late 1960s. Therefore, even though rock critics such as Marcus, Landau, and Christgau were formulating a rock discourse that stood in opposition to contemporary jazz discourse, in many cases they were unwittingly reproducing similar tensions and arguments to the discursive conflict that occurred decades earlier between traditionalist and modernist jazz fans.

It should be noted that despite the generalizations above, both *Down Beat* and *Rolling Stone* published a plurality of critical views and arguments. Neither had consistent "house styles" in this period and frequently published conflicting opinions about the merits of jazz, rock, their various sub-genres, and the nature of the relationship between the two. It was clear, however, that a tension existed both between *and* within jazz and rock discourses at this point. I will now examine what happened when the players in this emerging conflict came face to face at music festivals.

5

Newport 1969 and the Uneasy Coupling of Jazz and Rock

It goes against the intellectual's grain, no doubt, but isn't it one of the great achievements of jazz that it has been an intrinsic part of popular music, first in this country and soon elsewhere as well, for five decades or more? Despite the fact that it is an art, or because it is? .... And who the hell says that "art" must always be pure and holy and profound? Me, I'd rather tap my foot to some soul jazz, organs, electric bass, and all, than be hectored by some no-blowing poseur's naked ego trip. One may be a commercial cop-out, the other serious art—but don't bet on it. These are ambiguous times.

DAN MORGENSTERN, 1970[1]

By 1969, George Wein remembered, even the Newport Jazz Festival was in trouble. "It was slipping in the eyes of the press because at that time, if you were over forty, you were finished. This was when corporations were hiring twenty-two-year-old kids to tell them about what the youth market was." Rock had taken over so completely that Wein finally decided he had to include it on the program and called friends to find out which rock musicians could actually play. "Well," they told him, "Jethro Tull plays the flute and Frank Zappa plays good guitar, and Jimmy Page with Led Zeppelin plays good blues."

> *"So I hired all these groups. I had a rock festival, but I also had some good jazz. On the last night I had poor Stephane Grappelli playing with the World's Greatest Jazz Band with Yank Lawson, and right after them, I had Sly and the Family Stone, so you can see what a mess it was."*
>
> GEOFFREY C. WARD AND GEORGE WEIN, 2000[2]

The George Wein quote above is taken from the Geoffrey C. Ward book, *Jazz: A History of America's Music*, based on the Ken Burns documentary of the same name, and serves as an example of the important role festivals play in popular music mythology. Through their organizational practices, programming, and press coverage, festivals and their outcomes contribute to the narratives that give order to music history. This is especially true for festivals that occurred in the year 1969, when Woodstock and Altamont suddenly became the twin microcosms out of which critics tried to interpret the sociocultural significance and paradoxes of rock culture. Earlier in the year, the Newport Jazz Festival helped to shape debates about the prospects of mixing jazz with rock and has since become represented in dominant jazz discourse as one of the events heralding the end of jazz (indeed, the Ward and Burns quote serves as an introduction to a section titled "Jazz Is Dead").

In reality, Stephane Grappelli and the World's Greatest Jazz Band played after Sly and the Family Stone rather than before, and the concert in question took place on the Saturday night, rather than the final evening on Sunday as Wein remembered. But these are the least of the distortions contained in Ward and Burns version of events. In the "Jazz Is Dead" narrative, jazz critics writing in 1969 like Leonard Feather and Martin Williams are cited in an effort to demonstrate that the rapprochement between jazz and rock was judged as misguided even in its early stages; yet this selective sampling of critics ignores the many voices in the music press who encouraged the increasing interactions between jazz and rock in 1969, including Wein himself. Furthermore, it is an exaggeration to describe the Newport Jazz Festival as being in trouble, especially with a subtext implying that the incorporation of rock in its program was an act of desperation; while it is true that the festival had sometimes been criticized for being too commercial (a criticism leveled at Newport throughout its history), the festival bore no signs of hardship leading up to 1969. In fact, according to Dan Morgenstern, Wein had his hands full throughout 1968 expanding the scope of the successful Newport Jazz brand: "deaf to all talk of the impending death of jazz, Wein in '68 drew record crowds to Newport (54,000 admissions); conducted a 20-city U.S. jazz tour for the Schlitz Brewing Co., making important inroads for jazz in the south and southwest... made a second annual jazz tour of Mexico," and produced "the year's most notable festival tour—*Newport Jazz Festival in Europe.*"[3] At the beginning of 1969, Morgenstern held up Wein as a shining example of success in an otherwise lean year for jazz. It was true that critics in the music press were encouraging Wein to bring rock to Newport, but it was equally clear that Wein was doing just fine without them.

In approaching the significance of the 1969 Newport Jazz Festival in jazz and rock history, I will begin by examining the frequently ignored jazz-rock sympathizers writing for *Down Beat*, *Rolling Stone*, and *Jazz & Pop* during the late 1960s. I will then examine press coverage of the buildup to the festival, including criticisms of previous Monterey and Newport jazz festivals, coverage of the jazz concert series that George Wein co-produced with Bill Graham at the Fillmore, and the publicity generated by the upcoming Newport festival. I will then consider how press reactions after the festival provide an early snapshot of the larger culture war that would erupt between jazz and rock, driving a wedge between audiences, critics, and musicians. I intend to demonstrate that the seeds of this culture war were sown earlier than present-day jazz discourse would lead us to believe—certainly before the word "fusion" became an established term in the jazz lexicon, but also before Miles Davis released the benchmark jazz-rock album *Bitches Brew*—and that the 1969 Newport Jazz Festival was pivotal in exposing the fault lines of the conflict.

The jazz-rock misfit critics of the late 1960s

In the two preceding chapters, I described how the American jazz press began covering rock music in the late 1960s and how a rock-centered music press simultaneously emerged and defined itself in opposition to existing music discourses, including jazz discourse. On the whole, most jazz critics were not interested in discussing rock and most rock critics had very little interest in jazz; but there were important exceptions to this rule, and in this section I will examine a group of critics whom I will call the "jazz-rock misfits"—those who encouraged a blending of jazz and rock genres, and consequently found their aesthetic values literally misfitting both the established dominant jazz discourse and the emerging dominant rock discourse of the late 1960s.

From the beginning, *Rolling Stone* editor Jann Wenner saw rock criticism as a different project than jazz criticism; an indication of this viewpoint can be found in his introduction to *The Rolling Stone Record Review*, which compiled album reviews published in the magazine between 1967 and 1970:

> [P]opular music criticism has had few guidelines. Jazz men developed some, but rock and roll critics, finally descending upon us circa 1967, were mere babes in the woods... although we frequently reviewed and recommended great classics in contemporary jazz and blues, we have decided not to include that here, as a vast body of literature already exists in these areas which we could barely improve on.[4]

Wenner no doubt excluded early *Rolling Stone* jazz and blues reviews from the record guide for exactly the reason he stated, and yet the result was that a part of *Rolling Stone*'s early identity—its jazz coverage—was invisible in the magazine's record review anthology. In fact, several *Down Beat* critics contributed to *Rolling Stone* in its early years, and two of its most significant early staff members—consulting editor Ralph Gleason and managing editor John Burks—were serious jazz fans.

As I have already discussed Ralph Gleason at length in Chapter 4, I will focus my attention here on John Burks, who was arguably the most important figure to join the *Rolling Stone* staff in its second year, leaving his position at *Newsweek* to become the managing editor of *Rolling Stone* in October 1968. Burks was nine years older than his new editor-in-chief, and unlike Wenner, Burks was an avid jazz fan. He was hired to increase the standards of *Rolling Stone*'s reporting, but his personal tastes in music also contributed to the music coverage of the magazine to an extent. Given Burks' interests combined with the fact that the end of the 1960s was a time of great cross-pollination between jazz and rock genres and the emerging jazz-rock scene, it is not entirely surprising that 1969 marks a high point for the amount of jazz coverage in the magazine.

Burks was a skilled amateur drummer, playing in rhythm and blues and bebop bands throughout high school and sharing the stage with musicians ranging from rock 'n' roller Bill Haley to jazz trumpeter Lee Morgan. He was also an avid reader of the jazz press, with subscriptions to both *Down Beat* and *Metronome* as a teenager, and wrote briefly for *Metronome* as a campus correspondent. When Burks moved to San Francisco to study at the state university, he helped organize a regular university jazz festival, and sat in on drums with an experimental group called The Jazz Mice, led by multi-instrumentalist Ian Underwood (Underwood would later become a key sideman for Frank Zappa). Burks became increasingly interested in journalism and edited the San Francisco State campus newspaper; at one point he penned an editorial on Charlie Parker and caught the attention of Ralph Gleason, who praised the article in his *Chronicle* column. Gleason and Burks became friends from that point on, but it would still be several years before Gleason would recommend Burks to Jann Wenner for the position of managing editor.

Burks endured a transition time between working for *Newsweek* and *Rolling Stone* when he was writing for both magazines, and in fact the first significant articles that Burks contributed to *Rolling Stone* were actually expanded versions of stories he had previously written for *Newsweek*. As he recalled, "you did a 5000-word piece that got cut to 600 words, so the way it worked back then was they encouraged you to freelance with people. What they wanted to see was the credit at the bottom of the page: 'John Burks, *Newsweek* correspondent.'"[5] *Newsweek* was also "much more left and youth-oriented than it is now," so Burks was able to not only do stories on the Monterey Jazz Festival and the self-destruction of Cream, but also an article about groupies which, as discussed in the previous chapter, Burks and other staff writers would develop into an expanded (albeit problematic from a feminist perspective) cover story on groupies that appeared in *Rolling*

Stone. Burks brought his jazz fan's perspective to many of the articles he wrote, and this, along with his habit of assigning multiple writers to a story and collectively composing articles in writerly "jam sessions," meant that he quickly became known by the rest of the *Rolling Stone* staff as a "jazz style" editor.[6]

When writing about Cream, for example, Burks suggested that "with their long rampaging improvisations, Cream, in all their virtuoso glory, gave rock a new dimension, carried the music in a direction parallel to jazz—some critics called it jazz, and the Cream themselves don't argue—and set new standards, which other, less innovative groups adopted as their own."[7] He noted that "the big influences on Jack Bruce have all been jazz players—Charlie Mingus, Jimmy Blanton, Charlie Haden."[8]

Burks also wrote a cover story for *Rolling Stone* on Sun Ra.[9] As he recalled later, the initial idea for the piece actually came from Jann Wenner's wife Jane, who was interested in hippie philosophies of the day such as numerology and cosmology—she was therefore intrigued by Sun Ra, the cosmic jazz musician who claimed to hail from outer space and for whom sci-fi mysticism was inextricable from his artistic output.[10] The thought of covering Sun Ra in *Rolling Stone* had never occurred to Burks, but once it was suggested he quickly threw his support behind the idea. Burks was a longtime fan of Sun Ra and successfully pitched the article as a cover story.[11] While the process of creating the magazine content was a cooperative effort between the staff with Wenner giving the final verdict, it is probably not insignificant that the only three cover stories of musicians who experimented with integrating avant-garde, jazz, and rock genres and performance practices—Sun Ra, Miles Davis, and Captain Beefheart—coincided with Burks's tenure at the magazine.

Burks clearly felt that the interactions between jazz and rock would be of interest to readers of *Rolling Stone*. His first published work as a record reviewer was a triple review—new albums from the Don Ellis Band, the Jimmy McGriff Organ & Blues Band, and Steve Marcus—which he felt represented "three different ways of hooking jazz up with pop music."[12] The *Rolling Stone* office subscribed to both *NME* and *Melody Maker*, but Burks was also a regular reader of *Down Beat*, and this interest occasionally manifested itself

Figure 5.1 *Sun Ra cover issue of* Rolling Stone, *April 19, 1969. Copyright 1969 © by Rolling Stone LLC. All Rights Reserved. Used by Permission.*

in the pages of *Rolling Stone*: for instance, when the annual *Down Beat* readers poll announced Gary Burton as jazz musician of the year, Burks argued it indicated an increasing overlap between the jazz and rock culture:

The 33rd annual *Down Beat* magazine readers poll offers convincing proof that the boundaries between rock and jazz are fading, or at least in the mind's eye. Jazzman of the Year—running well ahead of Miles Davis and Duke Ellington—is vibist Gary Burton, whose hair is as long as plenty of rock players, and whose rhythm section often gets into a groove like Jimi Hendrix or Cream....Also appearing on the guitar poll: Larry Coryell, Eric Clapton Mike Bloomfield, Jimi Hendrix and bluesman B.B. King. Both Ginger Baker and Mitch Mitchell turned up among the drums.[13]

John Burks also occasionally sought out well-known writers from *Down Beat* to contribute to *Rolling Stone*. These included blues reviewer Pete Welding and jazz reviewer and trombonist Michael Zwerin. Such crossover of writers working for both *Down Beat* and *Rolling Stone* is interesting because it demonstrates that the worlds of jazz and rock criticism, both at the discursive and the professional level, were not as mutually exclusive as we might assume. The most outstanding example of this kind of overlap was the cover story *Rolling Stone* did on Miles Davis at the end of 1969, just between the release of *In a Silent Way* and *Bitches Brew*.[14] The feature included a series of photographs taken of Miles working out at the boxing ring and an interview conducted by Don DeMichael, the editor of *Down Beat* before Morgenstern took over. That same week, *Down Beat* also ran a cover story on Miles Davis, also interviewed at the boxing ring by Don DeMichael.[15] The *Rolling Stone* version is more of an introduction to Miles's career, and the interview quotes focus on his views about race and rock 'n' roll. The *Down Beat* version is much shorter and is framed by DeMichael discussing Miles's passion for boxing. However, although the two stories are geared toward different audiences and contain contrasting assumptions about the reader's likely knowledge of Miles's career, they are clearly based on the same interview.

Another critic who was excited by early jazz-rock fusion was Lester Bangs. Burks was the young critic's first contact at the magazine:

Here's an 18-year-old high school dropout or no show, and he tells me he's trying to become a romular addict....He'd sent me a couple of letters that were intriguing in their own right, so I gave him a phone call to check him out. I say, "I see you want to write about Miles's latest and the MC5, and some jazz and rock 'n' roll. So where does your heart lie?" And he said, "both places."[16]

Bangs made his rock criticism debut at *Rolling Stone* and quickly developed a unique jazz-rock aesthetic that drew connections between the likes of Miles Davis, Captain Beefheart, Tony Williams, and the Velvet Underground. On Beefheart's *Trout Mask Replica*, he wrote

the whole group gets into a raucous wrangling horn dialog that reveals a strong Albert Ayler influence. The music truly meshes, flows, and excites in a way that almost none of the self-conscious, carefully crafted jazz-rock bullshit of the past year has done. And the reason for this is that while many other groups have picked upon the trappings of the new jazz, Cap and the Magic Band are into its essence.[17]

Bangs's reference to "self conscious, carefully crafted jazz-rock bullshit" is telling: it reveals that his vision of an aesthetically worthwhile dialogue between jazz and rock did not actually align with most of the music being labeled "jazz-rock" in 1969. It is difficult to guess whether his comment referred specifically to the popular big-band rock that emerged that year with best-selling albums by Blood, Sweat, and Tears and Chicago, although it is certainly clear from his later writing that he did not hold bands of that ilk in high regard.[18]

In the November 15, 1969, issue of *Rolling Stone*, Bangs had two jazz reviews published where he expanded on his earlier enthusiasm for Captain Beefheart and connected it to two new releases by Miles Davis and the Tony Williams Lifetime:

[*In a Silent Way*] is the kind of album that gives you faith in the future of music. It is not rock and roll, but it's nothing stereotyped as jazz either. All at once, it owes almost as much to the techniques developed by rock improvisers in the last four years as to Davis's jazz background. It is part of a transcendental new music which flushes categories away and, while using musical devices from all styles and cultures, is defined mainly by its deep emotion and unaffected originality.... They say that jazz has become menopausal, and there is much truth in the statement. Rock too seems to have suffered under a numbing plethora of standardized sounds. But I believe there is a new music in the air, a total art which knows no boundaries or categories, a new school run by geniuses indifferent to fashion. And I also believe that the ineluctable power and honesty of their music shall prevail. Miles Davis is one of those geniuses.[19]

[reviewing Tony Williams Lifetime album *Emergency*:] There is a new music aborning which gives the lie to all classifications by school and idiom, whose passions alone are sufficient unto its identity. It is found in the work of Miles Davis, of Captain Beefheart and Don Cherry and the Velvet Underground. More than anyone else in this company, Williams and associates stand at the frontier.[20]

Besides Burks and Bangs, another *Rolling Stone* writer who addressed jazz-rock was University of California postgraduate Langdon Winner, whom Greil Marcus had asked to write for the record review section of the magazine. Like Bangs, Winner reviewed a mix of both rock and jazz albums, ranging from Crosby, Stills, Nash, and Young to Ornette Coleman. The piece that revealed the most about Winner's attitudes toward jazz-rock experiments was his double review of Herbie Mann's *Memphis Underground* and Freddie Hubbard's *A Soul Experiment*:

Recent attempts to synthesize the mainstreams of jazz and rock have produced a peculiar collection of paste jobs, unmitigated disasters and a scant few successes. To the delight of a naïve public, rock groups like Blood, Sweat and Tears have unearthed stale twenty-year-old Stan Kenton licks and now herald them as wonderful innovations.[21] At the same time jazz players like Albert Ayler have gone scampering about hiring rock musicians for spectacularly packaged but entirely unconvincing "experimental" albums.... What Freddie [Hubbard] has done is to bring together a random collection of jazz, rock and soul players with little affinity for each other.... Whereas in *Memphis Underground* the integrity of the jazz and rock styles is carefully preserved, *A Soul Experiment* sacrifices both of them to a dream of speedy profits. "Run this up the flagpole, Ed, and see if they Boogaloo to it!" The point is, I suppose, that jazz and rock musicians can work together effectively but only if they achieve a delicate balance .... Mann found this balance and ought to be listened to. Freddie Hubbard set out to do the same but in the process lost exactly what he thought he would find—his "soul."[22]

Like Jon Landau before him, Winner condemned groups like Blood, Sweat, and Tears for their "paste-job" merger of jazz and rock. The critical buzz surrounding jazz-rock, in conjunction with increased sales from a market that was willing to buy jazz with a danceable rock beat, led to many accusations from both jazz and rock critics of jazz musicians "selling out" by incorporating rock styles. But as we have seen with critics such as Burks, Bangs, and Gleason, there was also an excitement about taking the most innovative, experimental strands of jazz and rock and merging them into a new avant-garde music.

As discussed previously in Chapter 3, both *Down Beat* and *Jazz* changed their editorial policies in 1967 to include rock coverage, with *Jazz* changing its title to *Jazz & Pop*. It is especially notable that both these magazines partly justified their inclusion of rock on the grounds that they saw aesthetic potential in a possible merging of the two genres. The term "fusion" may not have entered the critical lexicon until 1973–74,[23] but this did not prevent both jazz and rock critics in the music press from debating the possibilities of a "merging," "rapprochement," and "dissolution of boundaries" between jazz and rock from 1967 onward.[24]

In *Down Beat*, the policy of including rock coverage appeared to be more of a half-hearted gesture than a radical shift in the attitudes of its writers, as most of the veteran *Down Beat* critics—Leonard Feather, Martin Williams, Dan Morgenstern, and so on—were lukewarm, uninterested, or openly hostile to rock music. However, one of the consistent champions of rock music in the magazine was Alan Heineman, who began writing jazz and rock criticism for the magazine in 1967. Like the jazz-rock misfits at *Rolling Stone*, Heineman was interested in the prospect of a blurring of boundaries between jazz and rock:

I've been thinking a lot, recently, about rock and jazz, wondering mostly whether the terms have any meaning and, if so, whether they are names for two different sorts of music…. There is also continuing controversy, in print and in conversation, about "true" rock, "true" jazz, and about the extent to which one may profitably have to do with the other … the best we can do for a categorical definition [of jazz] is: improvised rhythm music. And much of rock also fits that definition.[25]

If rock sympathizers like Heineman stood out in *Down Beat* as the jazz sympathizers did in *Rolling Stone*, then the magazine *Jazz & Pop*, as its title suggested, tried to reconcile the two cultures. By 1969, budding guitarist and journalist Lenny Kaye felt that *Jazz & Pop* captured the spirit of the era better than any other magazine: "you look[ed] at a group like the MC5, who were cover artists, and they were covering songs by Pharaoh Sanders and John Coltrane. It was a style I liked, because I believe in free music. When you get into an improvisational situation, all the genre forms break down. *Jazz & Pop* was a good place to discover that."[26] One of the most unlikely critics at the magazine to champion jazz-rock was Frank Kofsky, who was infamous among jazz critics for his black nationalist politics and harsh critiques of white critics (Kofsky himself was white). Despite his politics, Kofsky expressed delight in hearing white rock musicians being influenced by black avant-garde jazz musicians. In an article exploring the relationship between avant-garde jazz and rock, he explained why he felt *Jazz & Pop* was an important forum to discuss these developments, because unlike *Down Beat* or *Rolling Stone*, it was no longer aligned to either jazz or rock, but tried to split the difference between these two discourses:

[I]t occurs to me that the objective need for a magazine called *Jazz & Pop* is much greater than I had foreseen. Originally, the new title was meant to signify nothing more than the fact that Jazz had expanded its coverage to include popular music too. I now see, however, that there is a more profound justification for a journal with that name. Jazz and popular music are intimately related, more so than perhaps any of us have heretofore suspected. It will be useful for both the jazz and pop communities if in the succeeding issues we can elucidate the nature of this connection in greater detail.[27]

The difference in ideologies between *Down Beat, Rolling Stone*, and *Jazz & Pop* can be shown in part by examining the results of annual "best of" lists between 1967 and 1970. These lists give some indication of the canon of artists that each magazine was respectively promoting. It is impossible to make a systematic comparison of the awards and polls, because each magazine used a different system: *Down Beat* had a jazz critics poll that did not include a rock category and a readers poll that did include rock; *Jazz & Pop* had critics and readers polls with numerous categories for both jazz and rock; and *Rolling Stone* published an irreverent annual wrap-up that included seemingly earnest awards for "Album of the Year" alongside joke awards—Led Zeppelin, for instance, received a "Platinum Lemon Squeezer" award.[28]

There are nevertheless a few noticeable differences to be found between the three magazines' annual best-of lists. In *Rolling Stone*, for instance, the canon that would come to dominate rock discourse was already in place by the late 1960s: the "best of" lists that appeared in *Rolling Stone* for 1969 and 1970 (no such list appeared in 1968) unsurprisingly ranked the Beatles, the Rolling Stones, and Bob Dylan as the top rock artists for each year, between them winning all the award categories for "best artist" and "best album."[29] But in *Down Beat* and *Jazz & Pop*, the rock canon looks quite different. Take the *Jazz & Pop* Readers Poll published in 1968, which ranked "pop musician[s] of the year" in the following order: Frank Zappa, Jimi Hendrix, Eric Clapton, Paul McCartney, John Lennon, Bob Dylan, and Mick Jagger.[30] In this poll, the traditional canonical trio of the Beatles, Stones, and Dylan is subordinated by a new trio: Zappa, Hendrix, and Clapton, all of whom were playing virtuosic, improvisatory music that clearly held more appeal for *Jazz & Pop* readers. In fact, the *Jazz & Pop* Critics Poll consistently ranked Frank Zappa or his band, the Mothers of Invention, as leaders in pop music; his albums consistently beat the Rolling Stones and Bob Dylan in the "pop album of the year" category between 1968 and 1970.[31] And in the Readers Poll, Zappa topped the "pop musician of the year" category in 1968 and 1970, placing second to Bob Dylan in 1969.[32]

Figure 5.2 *Critics poll issue of* Jazz & Pop, *February 1968.*

In *Down Beat*, 1967 was the only year when jazz critics were able to cast votes for a "best rock group" category, and although the Beatles took first place, the rest of the top five spots were notable because they all went to black musicians (Muddy Waters, The Supremes, James Brown, and B.B. King, respectively).[33] Even in rock music, then, the *Down Beat* polls tradition was carried on, where critics voted predominantly for black artists, while the magazine's readers voted for white artists. But like *Jazz & Pop*, the *Down Beat* Readers Poll suggested a fondness for rock bands that drew from jazz styles, with Cream and Jimi Hendrix in second and third place in 1968 and Blood, Sweat, and Tears topping the rock category in 1969.[34]

In summary, there was more overlap between jazz and rock discourses in the late 1960s than present-day dominant jazz and rock (and historical) discourses might lead us to believe. From the jazz-rock misfits writing for *Down Beat* and *Rolling Stone* to the alternative jazz-rock canons being constructed in the critics and readers polls of *Down Beat* and *Jazz & Pop*, there was clearly an interest in the potential dissolution of boundaries between the two genres.

Stirring up excitement for a jazz-rock festival

By the end of the 1960s, a significant number of critics in the jazz and rock press were writing with excitement about the possibility of a new music developing out of a jazz-rock merger. This group of early jazz-rock advocates included *Rolling Stone* staffers John Burks, Lester Bangs, and Langdon Winner, *Jazz & Pop* editor Pauline Rivelli and associate editor Frank Kofsky, *Down Beat* and *Village Voice* critic Michael Zwerin, and *Down Beat* critic Alan Heineman. It was Ralph Gleason, however, who led the way, predicting that this new genre of American music would not only revitalize jazz culture, but forge an alliance between avant-garde jazz musicians and a young mass rock audience. He used his *Jazz & Pop* column on numerous occasions to call out for jazz festival organizers to integrate jazz and rock in their programs:

> The jazz festival circuit has been an important factor in the exposure of this music to many people in the past decade who might ordinarily not have had the chance to hear it.... festivals ought to be places where musicians which are not ordinarily heard on the same bill will be presented. Some time, somewhere, someone is going to present a music festival which runs

the gamut of American music from Johnny Cash through the Jefferson Airplane and Albert Ayler. That's one to go to.[35]

If I could do away with all contractual barriers, I would record Miles Davis with B.B. King and Mike Bloomfield with Woody Herman. Let it all hang out, so to speak. This may yet come to pass. Bill Graham makes a conscious effort to do this from time to time (would that the Newport and Monterey Jazz Festivals did as much) and it could work in the long run.[36]

Musicians in experimental music involving improvisation—which includes both jazz and rock—are going to solve [the problem of reaching a youth audience] themselves.…. They are by nature inquiring and their ears will tell them where it's at eventually. And the rock musicians can hear the value of the jazz men and always have. The problem is getting the two together. That would be a real contribution for some jazz festival to sponsor some year.[37]

Meanwhile, John Burks wrote a harsh indictment of the 1968 Monterey Jazz Festival for *Rolling Stone*, likening the majority of the music presented to "the fixed smile on the face of a later middle-aged society page matron—weary, sagging, desperately trying to be 'with-it'.… In the main, it was old people playing the same music they've played over the decades and young people trying to master old styles, rather than give something of themselves."[38] Instead, Burks was excited by the sets from Gary Burton, Gabor Szabo, and Don Ellis, all of whom were experimenting with rock and pop forms. When interviewed, Burton seemed to agree with Burks's assessment of the festival: "Jazz isn't dying. It's changing to a point where most of *these* people"— [Burton] nodded in the direction of the Monterey audience—"probably won't be able to recognize it. It's going to draw on lots of different sources, classical and country and, of course the blues, and all kinds of music."[39] Gabor Szabo expressed similar sentiments: "we're all trying to expand the limits. Whatever 'style' emerges from this exploration is what everybody will be playing. Forget about the labels, *rock* and *jazz*."[40]

The jazz-rock outsiders at Monterey probably would have felt more at home playing at one of concert promoter Bill Graham's Fillmore venues in San Francisco or New York, where the mixing of jazz and rock was more common. Graham practiced what historian Stuart Nicholson has described as an "egalitarian booking policy that mixed jazz, folk, blues, rock, and pop artists on the same bill," often putting jazz artists with crossover appeal like John Handy, Cannonball Adderley, and Buddy Rich in supporting slots for larger rock acts, some of whom, like Electric Flag, Cream, and the Jefferson Airplane, were experimenting with long-form improvisations in their live performances.[41] Joe Zawinul played electric piano for Cannonball Adderley during his successful "Mercy, Mercy, Mercy" soul-jazz period in the late 1960s and remembered that "we were so popular that Bill Graham had us open for the Who. It might seem funny now, but people liked it! We played with Zappa, all kinds of people."[42] Charles Lloyd was another jazz artist who benefited from Graham's eclectic approach to concert programming and recalled that San Francisco audiences seemed especially open to the blending of jazz and rock:

> It was a time of idealism and there were not these lines of demarcation, kids were listening to all kinds of music. So when we played for them at the Fillmore, we were very lovingly and warmly received and it opened a door, because things were kind of depressed in the jazz scene, jazz clubs were struggling for their existence. All the San Francisco groups loved our music—Grateful Dead, the Airplane, Janis Joplin rallied around us. The Dead's favorite album at this point was *Dreamweaver* and when they heard it they wanted to improvise more. Jerry [Garcia] was always talking about us recording together. There was an exchange of ideas among musicians.[43]

However, it was one thing for jazz acts to be included at rock venues, and quite another for rock to be openly welcomed by a jazz festival. If a jazz artist supported a rock band at the Fillmore, they might be praised for bringing an underappreciated art to a large audience that might not otherwise have heard them. But the argument did not work in reverse: if a commercially successful rock band was put on a jazz festival bill, critics would complain that they were siphoning money and exposure away from jazz. Furthermore, it remained to be seen whether jazz audiences would be as open-minded hearing rock acts as the Fillmore rock audiences were listening to Graham's specially selected jazz crossover acts.

Such was the context in which Newport producer George Wein had to plan his approach to programming the 1969 Newport Jazz Festival. His stance on rock music would be condemned by critics no matter what he decided: if he brought in rock acts, he risked a backlash from jazz critics like Leonard Feather and Martin Williams, but if he ignored rock he faced criticism from Ralph Gleason and other critics supporting a jazz-rock merger. But Wein was used to this kind of dilemma, as his programming choices at Newport had incurred criticism throughout most of its history. John Gennari has analyzed the cultural politics of the Newport Jazz Festival between 1954 and 1960 and has documented the vexed relations between the festival's producer and the "influential jazz critics who had supported the festival in its first years but turned against it as the festival grew in size and began to feature popular acts that transgressed the critics' notions of jazz authenticity and purism."[44] From its inception in 1954, Wein had openly expressed his desire to "make Newport the jazz center of the world," but as Gennari explains, Wein's aggressive strategy for maximizing the festival's audience meant including the programming of pop performers that fell outside of the jazz canon:

> It soon became Wein's assumption that the jazz mission demanded a broad mainstream audience development strategy, and that this strategy in turn required the box office clout of a few big-name stars to subsidize the presentation of a wider range of lesser known artists. Jazz had just a few such stars, and increasingly Wein deemed it necessary to venture outside the jazz mainstream for big box office attractions (Chuck Berry, Ray Charles, Aretha Franklin, and the like) that helped underwrite less popular acts.[45]

As noted above, one of the more controversial acts to appear at Newport during its early years was rock 'n' roller Chuck Berry, who performed in 1958 backed by Count Basie's rhythm section. The fact that Berry was put on stage with a jazz band illustrated the second important trait in Wein's programming philosophy; Wein was driven not only by audience-growth considerations, but also by an ideological commitment to a consensus-oriented concept of a cultural "mainstream." Wein programmed eclectically, but he always tried—often didactically—to stage some sort of rapprochement between seeming disparate styles. In the 1950s, he tried to forge a consensus between the post-bop modernists and the swing-traditionalists—most tellingly, in his end-of-festival all-star jam sessions that threw musicians from all generations and schools together, or as Wein put it, "one big happy family." As Gennari argues, "Wein's 'one big happy family' was a more sentimental, middlebrow version of what jazz critics had begun to call the jazz tradition or, even more tellingly, the 'jazz mainstream,' a kind of vital jazz center that jibed with the consensual politics of the era."[46] Although Wein was not personally a fan of Chuck Berry—it was John Hammond who convinced him to put Berry on the bill—the decision to pair him with the Basie rhythm section was completely in keeping with Wein's Newport philosophy. Wein would draw criticism throughout the festival's history as a consequence of his ambitions for constant audience growth and transforming Newport into a symbol of the jazz "mainstream"; as Gennari put it, at issue here "was the question of what constitutes real jazz, whether the latest stylistic developments were authentically rooted in the already canonized tradition.... When Wein caught promoter's fever, enlarging the festival each year and aiming to pull in the burgeoning rock 'n' roll youth audience, he became a ripe target for the critics' purist righteousness."[47]

Given the history of Wein's programming policies, it perhaps should not have come as a surprise when he announced that he would be booking rock acts into the 1969 Newport Jazz Festival. Wein had programmed rock 'n' roll before and regularly included a few big-name pop acts at most of the Newport festivals in order to ensure ticket sales (Dionne Warwick, for instance, had headlined the festival in 1968). However, whereas previously Wein had not drawn explicit attention to his policy of booking non-jazz acts at a jazz festival, in 1969 there appeared to be a change in his tactics, as he intentionally made his inclusion of rock acts the central focus of his Newport publicity campaign. As Wein himself explained to *Jazz & Pop* in an interview regarding his announcement of integrating jazz and rock at Newport, "rock is not new here, you know. It's new in, shall we say, the stress put on it."[48]

In an article titled "Jazz Meets Rock," *Rolling Stone* reported that "for the first time ever, rock and roll will be a feature at the Newport Jazz Festival this year—with a special evening of its own."[49] Wein boasted that rock artists and their agents were apparently bending over backward to play a festival with the prestige of Newport: "all of the major rock artists we contacted were eager to perform at Newport. The Newport Jazz and Folk Festivals were still undisputed as the most important outdoor music events in the country, and the response…was a deluge."[50] He also claimed that "rock groups were so anxious to play here at the Jazz Festival that most of them came at their lowest rate."[51] Finally, Wein timed his unveiling of the jazz-rock booking policy for Newport 1969 to coincide with the announcement that he would be producing a series of jazz concerts at the Fillmore East in collaboration with Bill Graham.[52] As it turned out, the projected series of eight Fillmore concerts was canceled after only three performances due to "rapidly diminishing attendance" (a sign that the potential overlap between jazz and rock audiences was not as strong as critics like Gleason claimed), but at that point it hardly mattered: Wein had succeeded in stirring up coverage in both the jazz and rock press for Newport.[53]

The line-up for the 1969 festival was a diverse range of jazz, rock, and blues, with many performers falling somewhere in between those categories. It included artists firmly accepted by consensus as part of the jazz tradition, such as Art Blakey, Dave Brubeck, Gerry Mulligan, Stephane Grapelli, the World's Greatest Jazz Band, and the Newport All-Stars. However, these were outnumbered by the musicians who had earned their reputations as jazz players but by 1969 were increasingly incorporating elements of rock and pop into their music, such as George Benson, Gary Burton, Steve Marcus, Freddie Hubbard, Buddy Rich, and Miles Davis. Avant-garde jazz was under-represented on the whole, although both Roland Kirk and Sun Ra and his Solar Arkestra were booked to perform. The blues, on the other hand, was heavily represented, with sets by B.B. King, Johnny Winter, and a host of English blues-rock artists such as Jeff Beck, Ten Years After, John Mayall, and hardest rocking of all, Led Zeppelin. Finally, the line-up was rounded off with the popular acts that actively challenged the boundaries between classical, jazz, rock, pop, and soul, such as Blood, Sweat, and Tears, Jethro Tull, The Mothers of Invention, James Brown, and Sly and the Family Stone.[54]

In the notes to the 1969 Newport Jazz Festival program, Wein, with some qualification, personally endorsed the signs of a rapprochement between jazz and rock.

> The better rock kids have the enthusiasm and the drive that many young jazz musicians seem to lack. They know there is a public out there and they go get it. They improvise, jam, play with a beat, play the blues and have many of the characteristics of jazz. But is it JAZZ?.... Blood, Sweat and Tears are the most important group to emerge from the youth music as far as jazz is concerned. The amateurism of the rock movement is taking a back seat. (Some rock critics don't like this). The reason is that Berklee School and dozens of other music schools have thousands of students who know that they won't find work unless they join the rock scene. Yet they really want to play jazz. The result—Blood, Sweat and Tears, and the like.... With much emotion and soul searching, I resisted the intrusion of rock in our jazz world for over three years. Now that I've turned the corner, I really enjoy what's happening.[55]

In many ways, the diverse jazz-rock program at Newport 1969 was simply an extension of George Wein's "one big happy family" ideology; the question was whether this ideology, forged out of the jazz culture wars of the 1940s and 1950s, stood any chance in the cauldron of late 1960s cultural politics. The climate of consensus on the jazz tradition during the 1950s had aligned well with the rise of Newport, but no such agreement was to be found in 1969, especially as the avant-garde jazz movement continued to divide critics and musicians alike. Ralph Gleason and other jazz-rock advocates constituted an important voice in the music press, but even more important were the critics and magazines who were at the same time trying to shape jazz and rock discourses as separate and distinct from one another. Just as Gennari suggests that the story of Newport in the 1950s brought to light "a lively contest over jazz's meaning and public image,"[56] so would its incarnation in 1969 amplify the undercurrent of tension between jazz and rock discourses throughout the late 1960s and force it to the surface.

The unfolding and aftermath of Newport 1969

Before examining the press coverage of Newport 1969, I will begin by summarizing the unfolding of the festival from producer George Wein's perspective according to his autobiography. The festival began Thursday, July 3, with an evening bill aimed at the "the jazz aficionado." It was the most conventional jazz night of the festival, featuring Anita O'Day, Bill Evans, and Phil Woods; but also performing were players who had been influenced by pop and rock, such as George Benson and Freddie Hubbard, as well as the Sun Ra Arkestra, who did not incorporate rock into their music but whose image resonated with certain aspects of the rock counterculture, evidenced by Sun Ra's appearance on the cover of *Rolling Stone* only a few months before.[57] A total of 3,500 people attended without incident.

The Friday afternoon concert included the Canadian jazz-rock band Lighthouse and an all-star jam session, both of which were well received. Then the field began to fill up for the Friday evening concert, which was billed as "an evening of jazz-rock." On the bill were Jethro Tull, Ten Years After, Jeff Beck, Steve Marcus, Roland Kirk, and Blood, Sweat, and Tears. According to official estimates, the field was sold out and an indeterminate number of people managed to jump the fences: "in all, there were nearly 22,000 people packed onto the grounds...and another 10,000 on the adjacent hillside."[58] At one point, a 20-foot-wide section of the 10-foot-high fence was knocked down, and more crowds from the hillside poured into the field. Wein went onstage to try and establish a sense of order, but was powerless before the crowd.

On Saturday afternoon the Newport Jazz All-Stars appeared, but the real excitement came with Miles Davis, who took the opportunity to try out several early incarnations of "Miles Runs the Voodoo Down" and "Sanctuary," which would appear the following year in recorded form on *Bitches Brew*. This was followed by sets from John Mayall and Frank Zappa's Mothers of Invention, all without incident. However, the Saturday evening concert was a different story. After sets by a Finnish jazz ensemble, Dave Brubeck, Art Blakey, and the Gary Burton Quartet, Sly and the Family Stone took the stage and the crowd began to behave differently. The resulting press coverage differed in its reports of the intensity of the crowd disturbances; according to all accounts, however, shortly after Sly hit the stage rain began to fall. The perimeter fence fell down a second time and the gates were opened to prevent rioting. There was an enthusiastic audience response to Sly's performance, with some of the crowd rushing forward into the press pit. Wein, fearing a riot, went out on stage in an attempt to calm the crowd down. After Sly's performance, Wein considered canceling the final performance of the evening, but instead went ahead with the program.[59] The next group on was the World's Greatest Jazz Band, a group specializing in Dixie and traditional jazz, and therefore a bizarre musical contrast to Sly. The evening ended in chaos with Wein wondering whether to cancel the rock acts scheduled for Sunday.

The festival field calmed down again for the Sunday afternoon concert, which featured James Brown, Willie Bobo, the Buddy Rich Orchestra, B.B. King, and Johnny Winter. Fearing that Led Zeppelin's scheduled Sunday evening performance would generate even greater disruption, and without informing the band members, Wein fabricated a story about one of them being ill and announced that Led Zeppelin had cancelled. The band's manager, Peter Grant, was infuriated and warned Wein that if he didn't let Led Zeppelin play, they would set up their equipment in the street outside.[60] But by that point much of the crowd who had caused the previous night's tumult had left the city, and Led Zeppelin was allowed to perform on stage. The total attendance for the festival that weekend was 85,000 people, breaking all previous Newport records. Reflecting on it decades after the fact, Wein felt that "the rock bands that played the festival were in another league and in another world, and their scene had nothing to do with my passion as a promoter or as a musician ....I still consider it to be the nadir of my career."[61]

Newport 1969 drew largely unfavorable reviews from jazz critics covering the festival. The crowd disturbances on the Friday and Saturday nights were blamed entirely on young rock fans, as in the article by jazz critic John S. Wilson for the *New York Times*, titled "Unruly Rock Fans Upset Newport Jazz Festival."[62] In it he described the scene as follows:

> The Newport Jazz Festival was invaded last night by several hundred young people who broke down a section of the 10-foot wooden fence

surrounding Festival Field and engaged in a rock throwing battle with security guards. As they rushed toward the stage where Sly and the Family Stone, a rock group, was playing, they drove paying customers from their seats, occupied the boxes at the front of the field and filled a pit in front of the bandstand, intended for photographers.[63]

In the Canadian jazz magazine *Coda*, John Norris described the level of chaos—as well as the number of unruly rock fans—to be even greater in scale: "for three nights the Newport Jazz Festival hovered on the brink of total disaster as thousands of 'rock' fans went out of control, both inside and outside the fenced arena, causing considerable damage and generally contributing to an unsettling, uncomfortable and dangerous situation."[64] In an article titled "Rock at Newport '69: Big Crowds, Bad Vibes," *Down Beat* critic Ira Gitler described how he chose to flee during Sly's performance: "having been in the middle of Newport disturbances before (in 1960), a sixth sense made me apprehensive. Behind us, young people were beginning to vault the snow fence. Flares were being shot into the crowd from outside the park, and when Wein asked for cooperation, his voice sounded worried. So we split."[65] *Down Beat* editor Dan Morgenstern picked up where Gitler left off:

swarms of people leaped, pushed, and squeezed past us while we huddled in the rain and Sly and the Family Stone, monstrously amplified by banks of speakers, made orgiastic noises. Fences crumbled, people stood on chairs, photographers were stepped on in the pit, and a ring of police and field security protected the performers on stage. Sly milked the crowd, obviously enjoying the pandemonium.[66]

If jazz critics were offended by the audience behavior during Sly and the Family Stone's performance, they were equally distressed by the music. Their complaints were twofold: first, they felt the rock music presented at the festival was overamplified, and second, they judged the rock players to be inadequate musicians. As mentioned above, Morgenstern felt Sly and the Family Stone were "monstrously amplified" and churning out "orgiastic noises."[67] As for the other rock acts at the festival, Morgenstern applauded the Canadian group Lighthouse, the first rock act to appear on Friday, for having "a musical slant," but wished that some of the jazz guitarists at the festival like Kenny Burrell and George Benson could have been on hand "to show the [other] rockers what fine guitar playing is all about, and how amplification can be used for musical ends."[68] He also commented that "Blood, Sweat and Tears was by far the best of the rock groups (it's not a rock band, anyhow), while Ten Years After, Jethro Tull, and Jeff Beck were too over-amplified to assess properly."[69] Ira Gitler agreed, commenting "most of the time, [rock musicians] try to amplify something out of nothing, thereby creating a bigger nothing that results only in an earache."[70] Writing for *Coda*, John Norris argued that on the whole, the rock bands at the festival "demonstrated their appalling musicianship, their reliance on showbiz antics to win applause and a general inability to control the monstrous amount of electrical equipment that seems essential to a performance."[71] But it was Morgenstern who arguably gave the most damning verdict of the inclusion of rock music at Newport, when he concluded "the rock experiment was a resounding failure.... By all means, spice [the program] up with valid things like real blues and r&b, but leave rock where it belongs: in the circus or the kindergarten."[72]

The initial condemnations of rock at Newport that appeared in *Down Beat* exposed a serious tension between the tastes of the established jazz critics and newer writers, such as Alan Heineman, who covered rock for the magazine. Heineman felt that the rock performances had been unfairly criticized, especially since *Down Beat* had claimed to welcome rock as a legitimate musical culture only two years earlier. Consequently, the events of Newport 1969 were reappraised in the magazine at the end of the year in the form of two articles, with Heineman championing the merits of rock and Morgenstern defending his original critiques. On the music being overamplified, Heineman suggested that "rock music is designed to be played very loud, louder than you or most jazz critics are prepared to tolerate."[73] As for Lighthouse, he argued that "it is very clear ... that what you meant by their having 'a musical slant' on things is a 'jazz slant.'" Heineman also felt it was impossible to compare the musical conventions of a jazz guitarist like George Benson with those of a rock guitarist, writing that "if you think the electronic aspects of the guitar aren't being explored [in rock] in a thoroughly musical way—albeit violently and jarringly—then you just haven't been listening to rock."[74] Morgenstern gave himself space to respond to Heineman's comments and defend the critical stance he took on rock music. He began with a clarifying statement about his intentions in the original review:

> My reaction was quite simply that of a life-long jazz enthusiast who had witnessed the near-destruction of the oldest and most famous jazz festival in the world, brought about by a combination of carelessness and stupidity in which rock, unfortunately, was the active principle ... [It was] a clash between two kinds of fans and two kinds of music. The jazz fans had come mainly to listen, while the rock fans were mainly there to create—and be part of—a "scene." And in that difference in motivation—if I am correct in my assumption—is revealed a fundamental fact about rock: It is only incidentally music, whereas jazz, alas, is by now primarily music. Why alas? Because jazz once was also a social force as well as a great music; because, at one time, it elicited similar (if less demonstrative) spontaneous participation from its audience.[75]

Morgenstern suggested that rock is only "incidentally music" (a value judgment in itself, implying that rock's real importance is sociological rather than musical), but his comments inadvertently illustrated how rock and jazz were *both* social forces, albeit contrasting ones: the act of coming to a music festival "mainly to listen," presumably while seated in chairs provided by the organizers, is as much a socially agreed audience practice as that of preferring to stand on chairs or remove them to get as close the stage as possible. As Morgenstern implied, the social norms for audience behavior at jazz concerts were at one time not so different from those of rock in the 1960s, but these had changed dramatically over the decades, resulting in a clash of social conventions at the festival.

Newport 1969 was also criticized as a failure in the rock press, but for different reasons. In an anonymous *Rolling Stone* article on the festival, George Wein was caricatured as a "short, bald, fat, and 42-year-old" man, and criticized for lacking an understanding of rock performance conventions and failing to provide adequate sound equipment for the rock bands. After the crowd's excitement set in during Sly's performance, Wein was represented as a patronizing, uptight "high school principal" stalking the stage, "all flailing arms" and unable to relate to the young crowd.[76] The difference in audience behavioral norms for jazz and rock concerts was also noted in a separate article by Jan Hodenfield, who complained that the Newport jazz and folk festivals appeared to have been "designed by programmers who find it natural to remain stationary on a 14-inch wide wooden chair for hours at a stretch," implying that the norm for *Rolling Stone* readers would be a more physically animated response to live performance.[77]

The *Rolling Stone* article also lamented the staid professionalism of Blood, Sweat, and Tears and contrasted it with the vitality of other rock performances. Sly and the Family Stone's performance was put forth as the event that best captured the tension between jazz and rock cultures, and was described in hyperbolic detail:

> Everything went off. The rain. The crowds. Firecrackers. And, above all, establishment paranoia. The fence went again. To prevent more damage to the fence, the gates were opened and bands of wild hippies, LSD on their breath, swarmed through, pushing the bleacher audience forward, vaulting over the VIP box seats, shoving into the press section, slamming the customers into the stage, all the while Sly, monarch of his own fascist jungle, urging everyone higher! Higher! *Higher!*... [Wein] stalked the stage, crying, "Alright you kids, be cool, be cool, we don't want any riots," as firecrackers shot into the crowd, fist fights erupted between what one observer described as gas station attendants and boogalooers, and hippies leaped over the bodies—flashing the victory sign furiously—and one acid tripping lady went into her own gymnastic reverie. Sly played on, digging it, and the audience still with seats stood on them. To the encore applause for Sly, Wein replied: "that's all—Sly isn't playing anymore."[78]

Members of both the jazz and the rock press portrayed Newport 1969 as a failed attempt to integrate two disparate genres. The critical reactions suggested a clash between jazz and rock cultures—both in terms of audiences and the music itself. The electronic amplification of instruments was clearly of central concern, as *Rolling Stone* accused George Wein of being woefully unprepared for the sound equipment needs of rock bands, while several *Down Beat* critics felt heavy amplification was an aesthetic outrage. Jazz critics also accused rock musicians of relying on amplification to mask inadequate levels of musicianship, while rock critics suggested that many jazz performers, despite their improvisations, were simply rehashing the same old tired routines. Age was another source of tension: on the one hand, some jazz critics accused rock music and audiences of being immature, unruly, and fit for the kindergarten. On the other hand, *Rolling Stone* caricatured George Wein as the school principal trying to keep the kids under control. Finally, there was a tension between minorities and masses—the perennial desire for jazz to find a popular audience, undermined with trepidation at what such an audience might actually look like.

We now think of jazz and rock as quite separate traditions. Newport 1969 and its aftermath provided the first glimpse of just how bitterly fusion would divide jazz and rock cultures. The negative press coverage of the festival has been naturalized over time as both jazz and rock traditions have come to reject jazz-rock fusion from their respective musical canons. As Kevin Fellezs has pointed out, fusion has been disowned in rock discourse, and "by and large, rock critics and scholars have left analyses of fusion to jazz critics";[79] yet a similar rejection has occurred in jazz discourse, with Stuart Nicholson suggesting that it has become "distinctly fashionable to stop the clock in 1969, when electric jazz was ushered in by Miles Davis, start it again in 1982 with the arrival of that latter-day model of acoustic rectitude Wynton Marsalis, and pretend the fusion of jazz and rock never happened."[80]

However, is it accurate to represent Newport 1969 as an unequivocal failure? It may be true that there were disturbances at the festival and several negative reactions from critics, but there was also a range of interpretations of the problems raised by jazz-rock, demonstrating not only a conflict *between* jazz and rock ideologies, but *within* them as well. Whether it was Alan Heineman sympathizing with rock in the pages of *Down Beat*, or Ralph Gleason cultivating a radical aesthetic that aimed to dissolve genre boundaries, 1969 was a year that saw challenges to strict distinctions between the two genres; with Blood, Sweat, and Tears at the top of the pop charts, Sun Ra on the cover of *Rolling Stone*, and Miles Davis heralding new

Figure 5.3 *Miles Davis cover issue of* Rolling Stone, *December 13, 1969. Copyright 1969 © by Rolling Stone LLC. All Rights Reserved. Used by Permission.*

directions in music, no one knew for sure which way popular music would turn. Indeed, there are several examples of Newport 1969 being represented not as a catastrophe, but as a conquest. For a magazine like *Jazz & Pop*, whose editorial agenda depended on the overlap between the two genres, Newport

1969 became a symbol of triumph for musical integration. Pauline Rivelli, the magazine's publisher, gave the following assessment:

> Press and television coverage during the four-day fest would have you believe that the huge crowds rioted. Not so. True, tension was mounting and thousands of kids did try (successfully) to break down fences in order to get in, but there was no heavy violence.... These were the kids who couldn't buy tickets due to a complete sell-out or else didn't have the bread.... This may be the turning point: this great first effort—the Newport Jazz Festival—at mixing the two musics, rather than separating them into "pop" and/or "jazz" festivals. If all festivals were integrated as such we'd have the pop ears open up to jazz and (hopefully) jazz ears open up to pop.[81]

Miles Davis also felt Newport 1969 was a great success. According to George Wein, "Miles, who wanted to avoid the festival grounds and had arrived via sailboat the previous year for a truly perfunctory performance, now stood at my shoulder all weekend."[82] Miles himself remarked that "I enjoyed myself more than I ever have. There was life there and I specially enjoyed hearing Blood, Sweat and Tears and John Mayall, everybody. Everyone was encouraging to each other backstage. It was something to look forward to and I went every night."[83] Wein recalled that Miles "listened to every group. He scrutinized every detail of each performance. He saw those thousands of young people and their enthusiasm, and decided that he wanted to be a part of it."[84]

Conclusion

In the Burns and Ward narrative of jazz, Newport 1969 is used as a convenient prologue to Miles Davis making his "electric turn" and the recording of *Bitches Brew*, an album which has since been represented as "virtually creat[ing] the genre known as jazz-rock fusion" and "precipitating one of the great debates in jazz history."[85] However, the debates about the merging of jazz and rock were already in full flow before *Bitches Brew* was released in 1970. Newport 1969 was the watershed event that revealed both the problems *and* possibilities of what would later become fusion. Musicians had experimented with jazz-rock on record and in isolated performances before Newport, but the sheer size and symbolic weight of the festival put jazz-rock into a living, social context, one so well documented that the results of that experiment made a greater impact on critical debate in 1969 than any individual album or concert. Critics had argued about the worth of jazz-rock experiments before, but the clashes were mostly restricted to the printed page, without any real threat of violence. At Newport, however, sonic experiments had tangible social consequences; people could literally get hurt by mixing jazz and rock, and the debate about a possible merger suddenly became much more serious.

However, the positive responses from Miles Davis and *Jazz & Pop* suggest that Newport 1969 could also be represented as a symbol of optimism; the interpretation of the festival as foreshadowing the "failure" of jazz-rock only makes sense once fusion has been retrospectively marginalized in the dominant discourses of jazz and rock. Like other examples of overlap, conflict, and crossover between jazz and rock, the study of jazz-rock fusion is revealing precisely because it constitutes a problematic fit for these discourses. Having now examined several cases of how the music press has contributed to the meanings of jazz, rock, and what lies in between, I will turn to considering the role of the music press in the production of music history.

Conclusion

The Production of History

Musical history making cannot be known in any innocent sense. Arranging a vast number of sounds, words and images into musical "eras" is not a neutral activity. It involves a process of imposing patterns and order onto the many events taking place across space and through time. History is produced.

KEITH NEGUS, 1996[1]

Have you noticed that life, real honest-to-goodness life, with murders and catastrophes and fabulous inheritances, happens almost exclusively in the newspapers?

JEAN ANOUILH, 1950[2]

"If the year 1970 is remembered in connection with any outstanding event in the history of jazz, musicologists may recall it as the Year of the Whores."[3] So Leonard Feather argued in a piece titled "A Year of Selling Out" published in the 1971 *Down Beat* annual yearbook. He continued:

Never before, no matter how grievous the economic woes of jazz musicians...did so many do so little in an attempt to earn so much. It is a demonstrable fact that during the last 12 months, jazz musicians in unprecedented numbers made an attempt to get on an accelerating bandwagon by producing music in a style more representative of what they hoped might sell than of what they believed might endure. Their own profession seemingly threatened, they fled in fear at the mention of the word jazz. "Don't call me a jazzman! I always disliked categories." "I never wanted to be branded as a jazz musician." "Jazz is an Uncle Tom word."[4]

Feather was referring, of course, to the "rock-jazz rapprochement" which he claimed was characterized by jazz musicians discarding the hard-won techniques of their genre acquired through years of practice, instead using simplistic chords and pop harmonies "dictated by the need to hold onto and magnify their audiences," exchanging swing for straight rhythmic feel, sacrificing the nuances of acoustic instrumental timbre for the "noise" of electric amplification, and performing covers of pop hits rather than writing their own jazz material.[5] Interestingly, he singled out Miles Davis as an exception to the rule, an artist whose "special insight" had enabled him to create an "exciting new electronic music that cannot be classified under jazz, rock, or any hyphenate form." Yet in terms of abandoning swing rhythm for straight rock feel, digging into funk-inspired forms rather than standard jazz chord changes, using electronic and amplified instruments, and outright rejecting the label "jazz," Miles led the charge. Indeed, it was in his *Rolling Stone* cover story interview that Miles declared "I don't like the word rock and roll and all that shit. Jazz is an Uncle Tom word. It's a white folks word. I never heard that shit until I read it in a magazine."[6]

It is no coincidence that Miles singles out magazines as a source of genre labels. From the Jazz Age of the 1920s to the dawn of the rock era in the late 1960s, the music press had become a driving force in categorizing music, popularizing new genre labels, debating—and in many cases, defining—the boundaries between them. There was only a small handful of critics Miles respected, and while Feather was one of them, it was Ralph Gleason who got the call to write the liner notes for *Bitches Brew*.[7] Recorded six weeks after the 1969 Newport Jazz Festival and released in 1970, the album was a landmark statement that pointed to a potentially rich dialogue between jazz and rock. Many of the musicians who played on the album—including Chick Corea, John McLaughlin, Joe Zawinul, and Billy Cobham—would become leaders in their own right creating music that would later be classified as "fusion." Ralph Gleason described the music with a kind of different label in the album's liner notes:

This music is new. This music is new music and it hits me like an electric shock and the word "electric" is interesting because the music is to some degree electric music. . . . Electric music is the music of this culture and in the breaking away (not the breaking down) from previously assumed forms a new kind of music is emerging.[8]

None of the leading magazines in the American music press wholly embraced the fusion experiments of the 1970s or indeed any ideology of popular music culture where jazz, rock, and music in between were all valued equally. Most of the staff at *Rolling Stone* who had shown interest in jazz in the magazine's first years—such as John Burks, Ralph Gleason, and Langdon Winner—either quit or were fired from the magazine by Wenner between 1970 and 1971. This was partly a matter of chance: in what Chet Flippo described as the "Great Purge of 1970," Burks and those staff who were loyal to him left in 1970 after a blowout with Wenner over the political direction of the magazine. According to Burks, Wenner decided that *Rolling Stone* "was going to stick with the rock and roll trip, and not get into all this troublesome political shit. The advertisers (I learned from our ad side) had complained that with the repression that's coming they weren't sure whether they could get behind a paper that didn't do just about a hundred per cent rock and roll."[9] Wenner saw things differently: "Everybody got swell-headed, I mean everybody. They thought they were something other than what they really were and that we were something other than what we really were. It was a money crisis, so we dumped some bad people."[10] Whatever the cause, *Rolling Stone* did continue to publish political journalism including extensive and irreverent coverage of the 1972 U.S. presidential campaign written by Hunter S. Thompson. It was coincidental that several of those staffers who left in the early 1970s were also the key jazz sympathizers on staff, and indeed some left for personal reasons and without acrimony—Gleason abandoned full-time writing to work for Fantasy Records, while Winner pursued postgraduate studies in political theory. But the net result was that what limited jazz coverage had existed during the late 1960s all but ceased at the magazine.

Meanwhile, *Down Beat* editor Dan Morgenstern was primarily focused on using the magazine as a forum to support jazz in whatever way possible.

Writing in 1970, he expressed his deep concern for what he called the "economic strangulation" of jazz over the previous decade:

> Night clubs withered and darkened; audiences dwindled; broadcast studios cut down their musical staffs; films were increasingly scored abroad; festivals flopped; record companies practically ceased to produce ungimmicked jazz ... More and more, jazz was becoming an accepted art form; i.e., it was no longer the music of the day but rapidly moving toward the unenviable status of a cultural asset—something in need of artificial life supports.... The best hopes for the true nourishment and survival of jazz as a creative force lie in a rebuilding of its vanishing audience.... Nothing in this present world can be accomplished without organization, and the jazz world is totally unorganized (except into small, essentially divisive cells). It is high time to band together and support the music we love. If we do not, the time will come—and maybe soon—when the depressing sixties will look in retrospect like a golden age, as we sift through our records, tapes and memories.[11]

According to the *Down Beat*'s official history on its website, during the early 1970s the magazine learned to deal with rock "without submitting to it": "*Jazz-Blues-Rock* became part of the cover logo, even as Morgenstern fought to moderate the magazine's commitment to the pop sensibility." A plethora of other youth-market music magazines had appeared by the early 1970s. Audited paid circulation figures from 1973 show *Rolling Stone* well in the lead selling 330,000 copies, *Circus* 168,000, *Zoo World* 40,000, *Creem* 100,000, *Rock* 15,000, *Crawdaddy!* 30,000, *Hit Parader* 90,000, *Country Music* 30,000, *Guitar Player* 20,000, and *Down Beat* 90,496.[12] Both the relationship of jazz to the wider popular music culture and the music press as an industry had changed beyond recognition since the early days of *Down Beat* in the swing era:

> By the 1970s *Down Beat* had survived its old rival *Metronome* and numerous other jazz magazines that had come and gone. Now, however, there loomed *Rolling Stone*, which targeted a distinctly different readership but many of the same advertisers.... [Owner Jack] Maher and Morgenstern recognized

Rolling Stone as a force to be reckoned with. They talked about it. But in the end, the only way to directly fight back was to start another magazine. *Down Beat* could not become *Rolling Stone* without undermining its own heritage and its readership. And the prospects of succeeding at a new magazine were dim. First, Chicago was not the place to do it. But to go to L.A. or New York would take a huge investment. More important than money would be the right people. Jann Wenner was young and hungry when *Rolling Stone* appeared in November 1967. *Down Beat* was neither.[13]

Jazz & Pop was perhaps the only magazine which, as its name suggested, seriously promoted an ideology that aimed to bridge the gap between jazz and the rest of popular music, featuring columns by critics like Gleason who explicitly framed jazz and rock as part of a shared and longstanding American popular music culture. Tellingly, however, *Jazz & Pop* ultimately failed to find a readership and folded in 1970.

Ways of writing music history

Few people question the assumption that rock 'n' roll is not a form of jazz. But as Keith Negus suggests in the quote at the outset of this chapter, musical history making is not a neutral activity. Writing history is an act of production, of choosing what to leave in the story and what to leave out, of viewing events through a lens that filters out inconvenient details to project a coherent narrative. The starting point of rock 'n' roll (and popular music studies for that matter) is often represented as a departure from the musical cultures that came before—a narrative of revolution rather than evolution. This approach to history privileges discontinuity over continuity. But writing any music history is inevitably an act of interpretation—an imagining, even, albeit with evidence—of how events unfolded. There is no single history of American popular music but many histories, and all of them, are to some extent imagined.

Scott DeVeaux once wrote that "history is not the passive imprint of the past but an active search for meaning, a creative reading of the past to suit the needs of the present."[14] As a fan of both jazz and rock, I have often wondered why the two genres maintained such a distance from one another in both journalistic and academic discourses, despite having so much in common and potentially much to benefit from a more open dialogue. The need here is for contemporary popular music studies to open its doors more fully to jazz studies and vice versa and, therefore, my historical research has been guided by a desire to consider jazz and rock music before the genre distinctions we now take for granted were so rigid. Rock did not simply arrive fully formed, nor did jazz. I am interested in the historical moments where those processes of genre formation happened.

This book is a history of the formative years of American jazz and rock journalism on the one hand, and a history of the relationship between jazz, rock 'n' roll, and rock in the years leading up to fusion on the other. It by no means aims to be a comprehensive history of either but is instead an attempt to draw from accounts in the music press to dig up an alternative perspective that challenges assumptions often taken for granted: that interwar jazz culture bore little relation to 1950s rock 'n' roll culture; that the jazz press largely ignored the birth of R&B and rock 'n' roll; that rock 'n' roll was a revolution; that no one was writing about rock 'n' roll prior to the advent of dedicated rock periodicals like *Crawdaddy!* and *Rolling Stone*; that critics universally dismissed interactions between jazz and rock, and did not consider the two genres to be part of a shared American popular music culture.

Jazz and rock are different genres, but this difference is historically constructed: rock could have been part of jazz, but did not become so for particular reasons, and it is possible to reconsider key periods in music history when the boundary between the two was not nearly so clear. In this respect my own investigation aligns with the recent work of David Brackett on the practice of music categorization and the emergence of music genres. The differences between jazz and rock may seem self-evident in the twenty-first century, but Brackett argues that for music scholars "the question becomes how the self-evidence of these truths comes into being."[15] Like Brackett, I have taken a genealogical approach to music categorization which "does not assume that categories are pre-given and universal, but rather encourages an analysis of the processes through which they are formed," and have worked on the premise that genres must be understood in relation to one another (and that such relationships inevitably change over time).[16] However, if Brackett has focused on "how a certain concept of a category becomes accepted at a particular time and place, i.e., how it becomes legible," my interest has been in the instability of this legibility, particularly when genres are contested or come into conflict.[17]

The timeline for this book ends at the beginning of the 1970s, just when one might expect a history of interactions between jazz and rock to begin. Instead, I have focused on the fortification of boundaries more than their blurring, on walls between popular music going up rather than coming down. In 1955, Duke Ellington could claim, albeit provocatively, that "rock 'n' roll was the most raucous form of jazz," whereas by 1970 any potential jazz-rock fusion seemed destined to be rejected by the dominant discourses of jazz and rock. In his history of fusion, Kevin Fellezs notes that "the very existence of genre mixing is tethered to notions of fixed identities and cultures—there is no mixing where there are no lines...There are differences in the different music genres and traditions, and it is between those real distinctions that fusion music was realized."[18] Fellezs argues that fusion never coalesced into a genre, but instead occupied a "broken middle" which prized musical hybridity. But on either side of the broken middle lay boundaries policed in part by institutions like the music press.

The music press then and now

As we have seen throughout this book, the differences between jazz and rock are sources of disagreement and dispute, and are defined differently throughout history according to shifting categories of age, race, gender, performance convention, audience behavior, language, and so on. The popular music press has played a crucial role in simultaneously reflecting and shaping these discourses. In other words, the American music press has historically been involved in the production of music history. Over time, *Down Beat* has become an authoritative magazine for scholars and journalists researching jazz history, just as *Rolling Stone* has for rock history.

I realize I will not have convinced everyone with the arguments in this book. When I interviewed rock critic Robert Christgau during the course of my research, for instance, he did not shy away in telling me that despite "having a considerable interest in jazz" himself, from his perspective jazz criticism had very little influence on rock criticism:

> I think *Little Sandy Review* and *Sing Out!* were far more influential on rock criticism than any jazz criticism, but clearly there was a present discourse, and clearly there were people, notably Ralph Gleason, who clearly had a profound effect on *Rolling Stone*, but you see, not in terms of jazz! Did jazz criticism have an effect on rock criticism or did rock 'n' roll have an effect on that jazz critic? I think it's more like that. It really changed him a lot.[19]

I believe that there is a middle ground between suggesting that jazz criticism and rock criticism are the same thing on the one hand and that jazz criticism bore no relation to rock criticism on the other; more importantly, any version of the history of either genre that adheres too strictly to an "evolutionary" or "revolutionary" narrative will inevitably have its limitations.

In his recent overview of popular music criticism, Simon Frith acknowledges such a middle ground, arguing that the "critical model" of 1960s rock critics "was clearly jazz writing, which had established that a music critic was not bound by the technical language or aesthetic sensibility of the classical world."[20] However, he goes on to argue that rock criticism differentiated itself from earlier jazz writing in two ways. First, most rock writers identified themselves as fans, "writing as and for music consumers rather than music makers."[21] Second, rock writers were "less concerned than jazz writers with musical skill and technique, more concerned with musicians' ability to articulate the communal values of their fans," an approach that owed more to folk than jazz discourse.[22] Even here there are arguably precedents: as we have seen, some jazz writers wrote for a readership of musicians (*Down Beat* targeted professional musicians in its first two decades of existence and learning musicians thereafter), but many were also writing as fans (and for fans). Many jazz writers were concerned with musical skill and technique, but as with folk revivalists writing for *Little Sandy Review* and *Sing Out!* in the 1950s and 1960s, the "moldy fig" New Orleans jazz purists of the 1940s pitted themselves in direct opposition to such discourses of musicianship and technical proficiency, preferring to fetishize the first generation of jazz musicians (the older and more obscure, the better) and championing their authenticity by virtue of being "close to the source" (even if they were sometimes demonstrably less technically proficient than later generations of jazz musicians).

It is worth noting that it suits the first generation of rock critics to claim that rock criticism was an entirely new way of writing about music because it bolsters an ideology that positions them firmly as pioneers. My view is that rock writers and rock writing were not without precedent. This argument applies not just to rock criticism as a general discourse but to many of its individual leading voices. Jon Landau, a rock critic who wrote with precision and authority, commanded the respect of musicians, and eventually went to pursue a career in record production (beginning with the MC5) and then management (with Bruce Springsteen, whom Landau continues to manage to this day), walked the lines between critic and industry insider not unlike John Hammond in previous decades (coincidentally, Springsteen was one of Hammond's final signings during his tenure at Columbia Records). Greil Marcus, who convincingly made the case for rock music's vital social and cultural significance in American culture, was following a similar path (albeit with different results) as jazz critics like Amiri Baraka and Nat Hentoff had before him. And Jann Wenner, a self-professed fan of rock 'n' roll rather than a musician, found his initial mentor in jazz critic (and fan) Ralph Gleason. Music histories may emphasize the similarities between jazz and rock (as well as criticism and scholarship of those genres) or the points where they diverge. Both approaches contain truths that enhance our understanding of popular music.

Most of the jazz and rock periodicals discussed peripherally in this book have long since ceased publication, but the central case studies of *Down Beat* and *Rolling Stone* have survived into the twenty-first century. Throughout the 1980s and 1990s, *Down Beat* remained a jazz-focused publication and maintained features that its former writers pioneered including the Blindfold Test column, the annual readers and critics' poll, and the *Down Beat* Jazz

Hall of Fame. It also occasionally continued to flirt with coverage of music outside the jazz canon in a bid to reach new readers. Writing for the *Chicago Tribune Magazine*, Howard Reich noted that in the 1990s, "[*Down Beat*] has annoyed and infuriated some fans by celebrating on its cover Lyle Lovett, Lou Reed, Kenny G, and Stevie Wonder. When covers such as these alternate with pieces on major jazz artists such as Wynton Marsalis, Dizzy Gillespie, and Miles Davis, *Down Beat* still gives the impression that it doesn't know exactly what it wants."[23] This was of course a strategy that *Down Beat* employed since its earliest decades of publication. In the twenty-first century, the magazine's approach appears to have changed, with the vast majority of the artists gracing the magazine's cover participating first and foremost in jazz culture. Its focus on learning musicians is also still apparent: the magazine's website hosts a "Jazz 101" feature which provides summaries of over a dozen sub-genres of jazz (rock 'n' roll is not among them).

Rolling Stone continues to be the most widely circulated magazine with a focus on popular music, with an audited circulation close to 1.5 million in the United States in 2015 and international editions in countries around the world (it should be noted that David Hepworth has challenged the accuracy of its U.S. circulation figures).[24] The magazine's headquarters moved from San Francisco to New York in 1977, and over the 1980s and 1990s the magazine shifted its focus toward increasing coverage of television and film stars as well as popular music. As a dominant forum for music journalism, *Rolling Stone* has ironically become a target of derision by many contemporary pop critics in much the same way that its earliest critics dismissed existing forms of popular music writing in the 1960s. Jim Derogatis has argued, for instance, that far from its anti-establishment roots, the mature *Rolling Stone* became "the institution most dedicated to charting the sounds we need to venerate," with an approach to the popular music canon that remains "old-fashioned," "conservative," and "boomer-centric."[25] Likewise, Jody Rosen memorably described the ideology of the magazine as "unrepentant rockist fogeyism."[26] In 1983, Jann Wenner was part of a consortium of music industry professionals who founded the Rock and Roll Hall of Fame, which held its first annual Induction Ceremony in 1986. Wenner has since become chairman of the Rock and Roll Hall of Fame Foundation and was inducted himself with a Lifetime Achievement Award in 2004.

The landscape of the music press has of course changed dramatically since the historical scope of this book, with the biggest impact caused by the shift toward online journalism since the advent of the internet, with websites such as *Pitchfork*, *Pop Matters*, *The Line of Best Fit*, *Drowned in Sound*, *Pop Justice*, and dozens of others all competing for the attention of readers. The details of this shift have been documented elsewhere, including an overview of the field by Simon Warner where he summarizes the situation:

> There is a clear paradox: while popular music writing remains in demand in markets around the world, the inclination of readers to pay for such material has reduced dramatically in the last decade and a half... Writing and reporting on rock, pop and its variants have never been so available, never so abundant. But the traditional model, in which a cover price and advertising income sustained print magazines and allowed publishing houses to train and pay journalists, has been significantly undermined by those websites which permit free access to their pages and, in most cases, pay their writers little or nothing at all.[27]

This is not to say the music press no longer matters, not least because the same trends that have changed the economics of music journalism have also affected music production and distribution. It is as easy for amateur musicians to put their music online as it is for amateur critics to publish their writing, but just because more people can publicly express themselves online does not mean it has become easier to be heard. In this age of abundant music and music writing, gatekeepers that can provide a trusted filter to music worth hearing (or writers worth reading) are still important.[28] There is a perception that a smaller percentage of both recording artists and music critics are paid a living wage for their labor (how one would actually measure this is unclear). However, even in the heyday of the rock era, the majority of artists trying to make a living from writing, performing, and recording original material—and critics trying to make a living from writing about that music—were both still pursuing precarious professions. Yet in the struggle to legitimize jazz and rock as culturally significant rather than mere commercial entertainment, music critics played an important part in opening up another professional avenue for taking popular music seriously—the academy.

The power of genre cultures

In an online discussion debating whether academics were over-represented in popular music studies, Eric Weisbard noted the importance of "partial academics" in the history of the field: "independent scholars who sometimes taught and not always at the university level. I think that lineage, blurry boundaries between critic, activist, performer, scholar, and so on, is not a random one: it constituted the International Association for the Study of Popular Music and continues to shape much of the work I learn the most from."[29] Music critics and journalists are a key constituency in both jazz and rock scholarship and institutions beyond the academy. Studying the music press reveals not only that the process of genrification is a very messy business, but also how over time certain genres become increasingly stable through the organizations that structure dominant culture. Universities and state funding bodies arrive at a consensus on what jazz and rock mean in part through discussions that begin in the pages of the music press. Musical gatekeepers who began as music journalists have gone on to become writers of history books, consultants on television documentaries, members of arts funding institutions, university lecturers, and curators of music halls of fame. The legitimization of genre cultures as they move into cultural institutions is always written *backward*, with gatekeepers choosing selectively from what was actually the disorderly field of music making, consuming, and debating. It is also generally *written* backward: the opinions of musicians and audiences may provide the basis for historical accounts, but critics, journalists, and other writers are the ones who typically fix these views into print; they therefore have a privileged role in mediating and shaping the language and formal rules of an art world.

What I hope to have demonstrated is merely that music genre discourses did not emerge organically but rather were surprisingly unstable, and remain in a process of negotiation: researching the history of the music press and its legacy in popular music scholarship allows us to bring those rough edges to the surface and reconsider current genre boundaries and rules. I suggest that this is of particular importance when studying the relationship between jazz and rock, because the discourses of both of these genres tend to operate with an all-encompassing logic. In David Ake et al's overview of the current state of jazz studies, for instance, they note that "jazz boundaries have been drawn and redrawn," and that many scholars in New Jazz Studies "hold that jazz possesses no essential characteristics," allowing for almost any music to be approached through a jazz lens.[30] Similarly, Scott DeVeaux has argued that "there is no single workable definition of jazz, no single list of essential characteristics":

> Attempts to base a definition even on such seemingly unassailable musical fundamentals as improvisation and "swing" inevitably founder. Exceptions overwhelm and trivialize the rule.... The writing of jazz history is accordingly obsessed with continuity and consensus, even—perhaps *especially*—when the historical record suggests disruption and dissent.[31]

Interestingly, Keir Keightley makes an argument not dissimilar from the jazz scholars above in his influential essay, "Reconsidering Rock":

> [Rock has] stood for much more than a single style of musical performance. Very diverse sounds and stars, including country blues, early Bob Dylan, Motown, Otis Redding, Kraftwerk, P-Funk, salsa, Run-DMC, Garth Brooks and Squirrel Nut Zippers, have all been called "rock" at one time or another, even though they are also equally describable as non-rock. If this eclectic set of performers and sounds can be grouped under the heading "rock," it is not because of some shared, timeless, musical essence; rather, specific historical contexts, audiences, critical discourses, and industrial practices have worked to shape particular perceptions of this or that music or musician as belonging to "rock."[32]

Neither jazz nor rock occupies the center of popular music culture in the twenty-first century, but through such open definitions, jazz and rock discourses continue to wield influence over debates about American popular music. This is especially clear when analyzing jazz and rock in relation to one another. As David Brackett has noted, "simply because a musical text may not (to paraphrase Derrida) 'belong' to a genre with any stability does not mean that it does not 'participate' in one."[33] One could apply this notion to genres as a whole. Has rock *participated* in jazz, or does it *belong* to jazz (or vice versa)? Or to take a related and more contemporary example, what does it mean for the Rock & Roll Hall of Fame to induct hip-hop artists such as Grandmaster Flash, Run D.M.C., and N.W.A., locating them within the rock tradition? Such questions are beyond the scope of this book, but they illustrate how the difference between belonging and participating can cause tension by virtue of the fact that "belonging" implies a kind of ownership. This is why moments of overlap, intersection, fusion, or "crossing over" can often be viewed as acts of betrayal or defecting to the enemy: they may expose struggles for institutional power, whether the institution granting power is the music industry, the academy, or government funding bodies. It is a natural instinct for some critics to dislike fusions and crossovers due to suspicions of selling out, commercialization, or corruption.[34] Rock critics accuse rock bands of incorporating jazz as a calculated way of finding a niche market or to take a fast track to the cultural prestige or "art" status associated with jazz; meanwhile, jazz critics accuse jazz musicians of incorporating rock idioms merely to sell more records, betraying the original principles of the music. In fact, it has been argued that the very definition of bad music in many cases is that of a performer from one genre trying to work in another genre which they do not understand (classical singers trying to sing rock songs, for instance).[35] But this only makes comparative studies of the interaction, overlap, and crossover of genres all the more important—to highlight the fissures in these discourses in order to better understand them.

Jazz and rock worlds have continued to intersect and collide since the time frame of my research. A significant part of the postpunk movement incorporated jazz and the avant-garde, while the Downtown New York jazz scene of Anthony Coleman, John Zorn, Don Byron, and others openly embraced punk.[36] Long after jazz discourse had distanced itself from dance music, musicians continued to make jazz for dancing using the rhythms of rock, funk, and soul, and jazz became an important ideological touchstone for popular DJs such as Gilles Peterson, who has made a career out of rediscovering forgotten and abandoned jazz hybrid records from the 1960s to 1970s and exposing them to new audiences of dance fans. Miles Davis, a longstanding posthumous member of the Jazz Hall of Fame, was inducted into the Rock and Roll Hall of Fame in 2006. More recently, the collaborations between Los Angeles hip-hop artist Kendrick Lamar and electronic music producer Flying Lotus with jazz-rooted, multi-genre musicians such as Stephen Bruner (aka Thundercat) and Kamasi Washington indicate that artists continue to reap benefits from crossing the boundaries between jazz and other forms of popular music.

The definitions of jazz, rock, and popular music continue to be negotiated, as they have been throughout their existences. The forces of institutionalization may have had a strong stabilizing impact on music genres, but through exploring the instability of their histories we can hopefully create a more diverse, less monolithic understanding of what these musical cultures can and should mean to us in the present.

Notes

Introduction

1   George Gerswhin, "The Composer in the Machine Age," reprinted in *The George Gershwin Reader*, ed. Robert Wyatt and John Andrew Johnson (Oxford: Oxford University Press, 2007), 121.

2   Duke Ellington, *The Future of Jazz* (Newport Jazz Festival Program, 1955).

3   Tony Whyton (ed.), *Jazz* (Farnham: Ashgate, 2011).

4   Mark Tucker (ed.), *The Duke Ellington Reader* (New York: Oxford University Press, 1993), 324–325.

5   David Ake, Charles Hiroshi Garrett, and Daniel Goldmark (eds.), *Jazz/Not Jazz: The Music and Its Boundaries* (Berkeley: University of California Press, 2012), 1.

6   Simon Frith, 2007. "Is Jazz Popular Music?" *Jazz Research Journal* 1(1), 9–10.

7   David Ake, *Jazz Cultures* (Berkeley: University of California Press, 2002a), 263.

8   Ibid.

9   Matt Betton, 1968. "N.A.J.E. Seattle Meeting," *National Association of Jazz Educators Newsletter* 1(1), 1.

10 Ibid., 2.

11 Sidney Fox, 1970. "To All Chairmen," *National Association of Jazz Educators Newsletter* 3(1), 9.

12 Scott DeVeaux, "Historicist Jazz. History of Jazz Lecture Notes," 2005b. Available online: http://people.virginia.edu/~skd9r/MUSI212_new/ (accessed September 10, 2005).

13 Wynton Marsalis, Acceptance speech for Grammy award for "Best Jazz Instrumental Performance, Soloist," 1983.

14 Ake, *Jazz Cultures*, 45.

15 Ibid., 46–47.

16 Sherrie Tucker, 2005. "Deconstructing the Jazz Tradition: The 'Subjectless Subject' of New Jazz Studies," *The Source* 2, 34.

17 Andy Bennett and Steve Waksman, *The Sage Handbook of Popular Music* (London: Sage, 2015), 1.

18 Keith Negus and D. Hesmondhalgh, *Popular Music Studies* (London: Arnold, 2002), 1–9.

19 Dave Laing, *The Sound of Our Time* (London: Sheed and Ward, 1969); Charlie Gillett, *The Sound of the City*, 2nd ed. (1971; New York: Pantheon Books, 1983); Greil Marcus, *Mystery Train* (New York: Dutton, 1975).

20 Negus and Hesmondhalgh, *Popular Music Studies*, 9.

21 Ibid., 3.

22 Lawrence Levine, 1989. "Jazz and American Culture," *Journal of American Folklore* 102, 18.

23 "Jazz snob" definition available online: http://www.urbandictionary.com/define .php?term=Jazz%20Snob (accessed July 27, 2016).

24 Douglas Wolk, "Thinking About Rockism," *Seattle Weekly*, 9 October 2006. Available online: http://archive.seattleweekly.com/2005-05-04/music/thinking-about-rockism/ (accessed July 26, 2016).

25 Miles Parks Grier, 2013. "Said the Hooker to the Thief: Some Way Out of Rockism," *Journal of Popular Music Studies* 25(1), 31.

26 Jody Rosen, "The Perils of Poptimism," *Slate*, 9 May 2006. Available online: http:// www.slate.com/articles/arts/music_box/2006/05/the_perils_of_poptimism.html (accessed July 26, 2016).

27 Nat Shapiro and N. Hentoff, *Hear Me Talkin' to Ya: The Story of Jazz as Told by the Men Who Made It*, 1955, repr. (New York: Dover Publications, 1966); Marshall Stearns, *The Story of* Jazz (New York: Oxford University Press, 1956); Leroi Jones, *Blues People* (New York: William Morrow and Co., 1963); Francis Newton, *The Jazz Scene* (New York: Monthly Review Press, 1960).

28 Gunther Schuller, *Early Jazz: Its Roots and Musical Development* (New York: Oxford University Press, 1968); Hughes Panassié, *Hot Jazz* (London: Cassell and Co., 1936); Winthrop Sargeant, *Jazz: Hot and Hybrid* (New York: Arrow Editions, 1938); André Hodeir, *Jazz: Its Evolution and Essence*, trans. David Noakes (New York: Grove Press, 1956).

29 Theodor Adorno and M. Horkheimer, *The Dialectic of Enlightenment*, 1936, repr. (London: Verso, 1979); Theodor Adorno, *On Popular Music*, 1941, repr. in *On Record*, ed. Simon Frith and A. Goodwin (London: Routledge, 1990); There has been much debate about whether Adorno was listening to "real" jazz at the time of his writings.

See, for instance, Evelyn Wilcock, 1996. "Adorno, Jazz and Racism: Uber Jazz and the 1934-7 British Jazz Debate," *Telos* 107, Spring. However, the existence of this debate merely reinforces my point that jazz has been constructed in opposition to the rest of popular music.

30   Howard S. Becker, 1951. "The Professional Dance Musician and His Audience," *American Journal of Sociology* 57, 136–144.

31   Neil Leonard, *Jazz and the White Americans* (University of Chicago Press, 1962); Robert A. Stebbins, 1996. "Class, Status, and Power Among Jazz and Commercial Musicians," *The Sociological Quarterly* 7, 197–213.

32   Richard Peterson, "A Process Model of the Folk, Pop and Fine Art Phases of Jazz." In *American Music: From Storyville to Woodstock*, ed. C. Nanry (New Brunswick: Transaction Books, 1972), 135–151; Simon Frith, *The Sociology of Rock* (London: Constable, 1978).

33   Negus and Hesmondhalgh, *Popular Music Studies*, 1–6.

34   Philip Tagg, "Why IASPM? Which Tasks?" In *Popular Music Perspectives 2* ,ed. David Horn (Exeter: IASPM, 1985), 502.

35   Simon Frith, Interview with the author. Glasgow, March 8, 2006.

36   Charles Hamm, 2004. "Popular Music and Historiography," *Popular Music History* 1(1), 10–13.

37   I would like to single out the pioneering work of *Philip Ennis's The Seventh Stream: The Emergence of Rocknroll in American Popular Music* (Hanover: Wesleyan University Press, 1992). For more recent examples, see: Keir Keightley, "Reconsidering Rock." In *The Cambridge Companion to Pop and Rock*, ed. Simon Frith, Will Straw, and John Street (Cambridge: Cambridge University Press, 2001), 109–142; Bruce Johnson, "Jazz as Cultural Practice." In *The Cambridge Companion to Jazz*, ed. Mervyn Cooke and David Horn (Cambridge: Cambridge University Press, 2002), 96–113; Ake, *Jazz Cultures*; Scott DeVeaux, 2005a. "Cores and Boundaries," *The Source* 2, 15–30; Peter Doyle, *Echo and Reverb: Fabricating Space in Popular Music Recording 1900-1960* (Wesleyan University Press, 2005); Elijah Wald, *How the Beatles Destroyed Rock and Roll* (London: Oxford University Press, 2009); Karl Hagstrom-Miller, *Segregating Sound* (Durham: Duke University Press, 2010); Steven Pond, *Head Hunters: The Making of Jazz's First Platinum Album* (London: University of Michigan, 2005); Kevin Fellezs, *Birds of Fire: Jazz, Rock, Funk, and the Creation of Fusion* (London: Duke University Press, 2011).

38   As Dave Laing has pointed out, the aphorism "journalism is the first draft of history" is a popular misquotation, and was actually part of

> a statement made in an address to foreign correspondents of *Newsweek* in 1963 by Philip Graham, proprietor of the *Washington Post* in the 1960s. The exact words used by Graham were "our inescapably impossible task of providing every week a first rough draft of history that will never really be completed about a world we can never really understand." (Laing 2006: 237)

39 The *Down Beat* logo has changed numerous times over its history, appearing as *DOWN BEAT, down beat, DownBeat,* and *Down Beat.* I will refer to the title as *Down Beat* throughout this book.

40 Marshall Stearns, Leonard Feather, Barry Ulanov, Nat Hentoff, Martin Williams, LeRoi Jones (Amiri Baraka), and Gary Giddins are only the most famous to write for *Down Beat* before publishing bestselling histories of jazz. Meanwhile, Greil Marcus, Robert Palmer, Charlie Gillett, and Peter Guralnick all wrote for *Rolling Stone* as well as producing influential histories of rock, while *Rolling Stone* itself has produced its own highly successful self-branded rock history books.

41 John McDonough, "60 Years of Down Beat." In *Down Beat: 60 Years of Jazz,* ed. Frank Ayler (Winona: Hal Leonard Corporation, 1995), 6–17.

42 Robert Sam Anson, *Gone Crazy and Back Again: The Rise and Fall of the Rolling Stone Generation* (New York: Doubleday, 1981); Robert Draper, *The Rolling Stone Story* (Worcester: Mainstream, 1990).

43 Devon Powers, *Writing the Record: The Village Voice and the Birth of Rock Criticism* (Boston: University of Massachusetts Press, 2013).

44 John Gennari, *Blowin' Hot and Cool* (Chicago: University of Chicago Press, 2006); Lindberg et al., *Rock Criticism from the Beginning;* Bernard Gendron, *Between Montmartre and the Mudd Club* (Chicago: University of Chicago Press, 2002); Fabian Holt, *Genre in Popular Music* (Chicago: University of Chicago Press, 2007); Steve Jones (ed.), *Pop Music and the Press* (Philadelphia: Temple University Press, 2002).

45 John Gennari, *Blowin' Hot and Cool,* 11.

46 Ibid., 3.

47 Ibid., 14.

48 Ibid., 14.

49 Lindberg et al., *Rock Criticism from the Beginning,* 3–4.

50 Ibid., 7.

51 Franco Fabbri, "A Theory of Musical Genres: Two Applications." In *Popular Music Perspectives,* ed. David Horn and Philip Tagg (Göteberg and London: IASPM, 1982), 52–81.

52 Holt, *Genre in Popular Music,* 7.

53 Ibid., 19.

54 Ake, Garrett, and Goldmark (eds.), *Jazz/Not Jazz,* 3.

55 Holt, *Genre in Popular Music,* 3.

56 Fellezs, *Birds of Fire,* 15.

57 David Brackett, *Categorizing Sound: Genre and Twentieth-Century Popular Music* (Berkeley: University of California Press, 2016), 5–6.

58   David Brackett, "Popular Music Genres." In *The Sage Handbook of Popular Music*, ed.
     Bennett and Waksman, 203–204.

59   Fellezs, *Birds of Fire*, 3.

60   Ibid., 226.

Chapter 1

1   Ralph Gleason, *Jam Session: An Anthology of Jazz* (New York: G.P. Putnam's Sons,
     1958), 278.

2   Simon Frith, 1981. "The Magic That Can Set You Free: The Ideology of Folk and the
     Myth of the Rock Community," *Popular Music* 1, 167.

3   Ibid., 129–130.

4   Gene Santoro, *Highway 61 Revisited: The Tangled Roots of American Jazz, Blues, Rock,
     & Country Music* (New York: Oxford University Press, 2004), 1–7; Phillip H. Ennis,
     The Seventh Stream: The Emergence of Rocknroll in American Popular Music (Hanover:
     Wesleyan University Press, 1992), 17–41.

5   Chris McDonald, 2006. "Rock, Roll and Remember? Addressing the Legacy of Jazz in
     Popular Music Studies," *Popular Music History* 1(2), 125.

6   According to Jon Savage, the terms "teenage," "teenager," and "youth culture"
     were popularized during the 1940s (see Savage's *Teenage*, New York: Viking, 2007,
     452–453). The word "subculture" did not become a routine term to describe musical
     cultures until the 1970s.

7   Paul Lopes, *The Rise of a Jazz Art World* (Cambridge: Cambridge University
     Press, 2002).

8   Ibid., 12.

9   Ibid., 15.

10   *Metronome*, "The Degeneration of Our Popular Song," January 1914, 8.

11   Lopes, *The Rise of a Jazz Art World*, 6.

12   Ibid., 12.

13   Neil Lenoard, "The Impact of Mechanization." In *American Music: From Storyville to
     Woodstock*, ed. Charles Nanry (New Brunswick: Transaction Books, 1972), 44.

14   Theodore Gracyk, *Rhythm and Noise: An Aesthetics of Rock* (London: Duke University
     Press, 1996), 37.

15   Gracyk, *Rhythm and Noise*.

16 David Brackett, *Categorizing Sound: Genre and Twentieth-Century Popular Music* (Berkeley: University of California Press, 2016), 154.

17 Scott DeVeaux, *The Birth of Bebop: A Social and Musical History* (Berkeley: University of California Press, 1997).

18 Ibid., 45; for reference to the "pre-recording era," see Brackett, *Categorizing Sound*, 44.

19 Ibid., 50.

20 McDonald, "Rock, Roll and Remember?," 134.

21 John Gennari, *Blowin' Hot and Cool* (Chicago: University of Chicago Press, 2006), 77. There is plenty of research documenting the growth of similar hot record-collecting clubs in France (Jeffrey Jackson, *Making Jazz French: Music and Modern Life in Interwar Paris,* London: Duke University Press, 2003) and England (Simon Frith, 1988. "Playing with Real Feeling: Making Sense of Jazz in Britain," *New Formations* 4, 7–24), which in many instances predated the spread of record-collecting clubs in America.

22 McDonald, "Rock, Roll and Remember?," 135.

23 Paula S. Fass, *The Damned and the Beautiful: American Youth in the 1920's* (Oxford: Oxford University Press, 1979), 308.

24 Ibid., 301.

25 Karl Koenig, *Jazz in Print (1859–1929)* (Hillsdale: Pendragon Press, 2002), 153.

26 Ron Welburn has noted that it is difficult to precisely distinguish between criticism of ragtime and jazz in the early twentieth century, as "once the term 'jazz' became a means to describe this phenomenon, writers used it and 'ragtime' interchangeably until they fell into the habit of using the term 'jazz' almost exclusively, without being clear about what they meant" (Ron Welburn, 1987. "James Reese Europe and the Infancy of Jazz Criticism." *Black Music Research Journal* 7, 35). In terms of much of the newspaper discourse of African-American music, "'jazz replaced 'ragtime' in newspapers, magazines, and popular thought because it was a new style and 'ragtime' as a term was shopworn" (Ibid., 35).

27 Morroe Berger, "Jazz: Resistance to the Diffusion of a Culture." In *American Music,* ed. Charles Nanry (New Brunswick: Transaction Books, 1972), 11–12.

28 Ibid., 12.

29 Ronald Welburn, *American Jazz Criticism, 1914–1940.* PhD dissertation (New York University, New York, 1983); Lopes, *The Rise of a Jazz Art World.*

30 DeVeaux, *The Birth of Bebop*, 18.

31 C.L. Graves, 1926. "Two Views of Jazz," *Sunday Province,* April 4, 1.

32 Lopes, *The Rise of a Jazz Art World*, 79.

33 Ron Welburn, 1986. "Duke Ellington's Music: The Catalyst for a True Jazz Criticism." *International Review of the Aesthetics and Sociology of Music* 17, 114.

34 Ibid.

35 Gene Lees, *Singers and the Song* (New York: Oxford University Press, 1987), 88.

36 Lilliam Breslau, "Letter to the Editor," *New York Times*, February 26, 1939, 51.

37 Lewis A. Erenberg, *Swingin' the Dream: Big Band Jazz and the Rebirth of American Culture* (London: University of Chicago Press, 1998), 39.

38 Ibid., 44.

39 "About Down Beat: A History as Rich as Jazz Itself." Available online: http://www .DownBeat.com/default.asp?sect=about (accessed July 2, 2016).

40 David Stowe, *Swing Changes: Big Band Jazz in New Deal America* (Cambridge: Harvard University Press, 1944), 74–75.

41 Ibid.

42 See, for instance, Paul Eduard Miller, *Miller's Yearbook of Popular Music* (Chicago: PEM Publications, 1943).

43 Paul Eduard Miller, "Disc-Cussin'," *Down Beat*, September 1937, 22–23.

44 Ibid.

45 Ibid.

46 Ibid.

47 Ibid.

48 Stowe, *Swing Changes*, 60.

49 Ibid., 124.

50 Christopher J. Wells, *Chick Webb and His Dancing Audience During the Great Depression*. PhD dissertation (Chapel Hill: University of North Carolina, 2014), 181.

51 Ibid., 181, 184.

52 Gennari, *Blowin' Hot and Cool*, 11.

53 Leonard Feather, "Feather's Nest," *Down Beat*, January 11, 1956, 43.

54 Erenberg, *Swingin' the Dream*, 170.

55 DeVeaux, *The Birth of Bebop*.

56 Ibid., 125.

57 Stowe, *Swing Changes*, 124–125.

58 Brackett, *Categorizing Sound*, 169.

59   Bernard Gendron, "'Moldy Figs' and Modernists: Jazz at War 1942–1946." In
     Jazz Among the Discourses, ed. Krin Gabbard (Durham: Duke University Press,
     1995), 32 . Gendron located thirteen revivalist journals operating in the United
     States alone, but there were ten others in Europe as well. The American journals
     included *H.R.S. Society Rag, Jazz Information, Record Changer* (which featured writer
     Ernest Borneman), and *The Jazz Record* (Bernard Gendron, 1995. "'Moldy Figs' and
     Modernists: Jazz at War 1942–1946." In *Jazz Among the Discourses*, ed. Krin Gabbard
     (Durham: Duke University Press, 1995), 51).

60   Ibid., 32.

61   Erenberg, *Swingin' the Dream*, 141.

62   Ibid., 35.

63   Gendron, "*Moldy Figs,*" 37.

64   DeVeaux, *The Birth of Bebop*, 274.

65   Gendron, "*Moldy Figs,*" 150–151.

66   Ibid., 230.

67   Bernard Gendron, *Between Montmartre and the Mudd Club* (Chicago: University of
     Chicago Press, 2002), 148.

68   Ibid., 155–156.

69   David Ake, *Jazz Cultures* (Berkeley: University of California Press, 2002a).

70   Ibid., 43.

71   Ibid.

72   Ibid., 49.

73   Ibid., 53.

74   Ibid., 55.

75   Ibid.

76   Ibid., 56.

77   Scott DeVeaux, 2005a. "Cores and Boundaries." *The Source* 2, 15–30.

78   Ibid., 19.

79   Brackett, *Categorizing Sound*, 18.

80   Ibid., 176.

81   Ibid.

82   Ibid., 181.

83   Leonard Feather, *Inside Be-bop* (New York: JJ Robbins and Sons, 1949); Barry Ulanov,
     A History of Jazz in America (New York: Viking Press, 1952).

84 Gennari, *Blowin' Hot and Cool*, 162.

85 Ibid., 162.

86 Steven B. Elworth, "Jazz in Crisis, 1948–1958: Ideology and Representation." In *Jazz Among the Discourses*, ed. Krin Gabbard (Durham: Duke University Press, 1995), 60.

87 Gendron, *Between Montmartre and the Mudd Club*, 156.

88 Scott DeVeaux, 1991. "Constructing the Jazz Tradition: Jazz Historiography," *Black American Literature Forum* 25(3), 544.

Chapter 2

1 Scott DeVeaux, 2005. "Cores and Boundaries," *The Source* 2, 15–30.

2 Edith Schonberg, "You Can't Fool Public, Says Haley," *Down Beat*, May 30, 1956, 10.

3 John McDonough, "60 Years of Down Beat." In *Down Beat: 60 Years of Jazz*, ed. Frank Ayler (Winona: Hal Leonard Corporation, 1995), 13.

4 David Brackett, *Categorizing Sound: Genre and Twentieth-Century Popular Music* (Berkeley: University of California Press, 2016), 30.

5 John McDonough, "60 Years of Down Beat." In *Down Beat: 60 Years of Jazz*, ed. Frank Ayler (Winona: Hal Leonard Corporation, 1995), 13.

6 Fabian Holt, *Genre in Popular Music* (Chicago: University of Chicago Press, 2007), 82.

7 Richard Peterson, *Creating Country Music: Fabricating Authenticity* (Chicago: University of Chicago Press, 1997), 188.

8 Ibid., 1987.

9 Bernard Gendron, *Between Montmartre and the Mudd Club* (Chicago: University of Chicago Press, 2002), 154.

10 Peterson, *Creating Country Music*, 7.

11 Michael Bertrand, *Race, Rock, and Elvis* (Urbana: University of Illinois Press, 2000), 144.

12 Peterson, *Creating Country Music*, 189.

13 *Down Beat,* Multivox amplifier advertisement. June 16, 1950, 7.

14 Bill Bailey, "Country & Western," *Down Beat*, January 13, 1954, 36.

15 Ibid.

16 Leo Zabelin, "Line Between Popular, C&W Growing Thinner," *Down Beat,* November 18, 1953, 6.

17 James Denny, "Why the Upsurge in Country Music?," *Down Beat*, June 30, 66.

18 Ibid.

19 Joli Jensen, *The Nashville Sound: Authenticity, Commercialization, and Country Music* (Nashville: Vanderbilt University Press, 1998), 196.

20 Norman Weiser, "Memo from the Publisher," *Down Beat*, June 30, 1954, 1.

21 Phillip H. Ennis, *The Seventh Stream: The Emergence of Rocknroll in American Popular Music* (Hanover: Wesleyan University Press, 1992).

22 Ibis., 217.

23 Nelson King, "Country & Western: Who's to Blame for Dip in Country Music Field?," *Down Beat*, October 20, 1954, 18.

24 Ibid.

25 Nelson King, "Country Music for Pop's Sake; Not Country Music for Country Music's Sake," *Down Beat*, November 3, 1954, 16.

26 Ibid.

27 David Brackett, *The Pop, Rock, and Soul Reader* (New York: Oxford University Press, 2005), 84.

28 Ibid., 86.

29 *Down Beat*, "C&W DJ Parley Supports Action to Combat Blue Lyrics," December 29, 1954, 6.

30 *Down Beat*, "Are Pop DJs Being Unfair to C/W Disc Artists?," January 26, 1955, 18.

31 Randy Blake, "Disc Jockey Urges Return to Spinning Only Country Music," *Down Beat,* January 26, 1955, 1.

32 *Down Beat,* January 12, 1955, 23.

33 *Down Beat*, November 19, 1952, 10.

34 Ruth Cage, "Rhythm and Blues Notes," *Down Beat*, September 22, 1954, 16.

35 Peter Guralnick, *Last Train to Memphis: The Rise of Elvis Presley* (London: Little Brown, 1994), 186–187.

36 Ruth Cage, "Rhythm and Blues Notes," *Down Beat*, February 9, 1955, 4.

37 Ruth Cage, "Rhythm and Blues Notes," *Down Beat,* December 1, 1954, 17.

38 *Variety*, February 23, 1955, quoted in Brackett, *The Pop, Rock, and Soul Reader*, 77.

39 Ibid., 77–80.

40 Ibid., 79.

41 Michael T. Bertrand, "Conquering the Bias of Taste: The Postwar Guardians of Culture and the Critique of 1950s' Rock 'n' Roll." In *Race, Rock, and Elvis* (Chicago: University of Illinois Press, 2000), 141–142.

42 Ruth Cage, "Horrors! Recognition Finally Comes to R&B," *Down Beat*, April 6, 1955, 1.

43 Ibid., 17; Cage is referring to "All of You," written by Cole Porter.

44 Ibid., 1, 17.

45 Ralph Gleason, "Perspectives," *Down Beat*, March 9, 1955, 18.

46 Les Elgart, "R&B Boom Won't Stick," *Down Beat*, March 23, 1955, 1.

47 Ruth Cage, "Horrors! Recognition Finally Comes to R&B," *Down Beat*, April 6, 1955, 17.

48 Al Portch, "Manager of Bill Haley Defends the Real Thing," *Down Beat*, September 19, 1956, 43.

49 Ruth Cage, "Rhythm and Blues Notes," *Down Beat*, March 23, 1955, 20.

50 Ibid.

51 Cage, September 22, 1954, 16.

52 Cage, "Rhythm and Blues Notes," *Down Beat*, December 1, 1954, 17.

53 Cage, February 9, 1955, 4.

54 Ruth Cage, "Rhythm and Blues Notes," *Down Beat*, May 4, 1955, 27.

55 Ibid. (my italics).

56 Ibid., 6.

57 Ibid.

58 Ruth Cage, "Rhythm and Blues Notes," *Down Beat*, May 18, 1955, 5.

59 Ruth Cage, "Arranger Quincy Jones Says Quality of R&B Sides Better," *Down Beat*, September 21, 1955, 42.

60 Ibid.

61 Ruth Cage, "Rhythm and Blues Notes," *Down Beat*, December 14, 1955, 13.

62 Eric Porter, "Incorporation and Distinction in Jazz History and Jazz Historiography." In *Jazz/Not Jazz: The Music and Its Boundaries*, ed. Ake et al. (Berkeley: University of California Press, 2012), 24.

63 Ibid., 25.

64 Paul Lopez, *The Rise of a Jazz Art World* (Cambridge: Cambridge University Press, 2002), 225–230.

65 Keir Keightley, 2004. "Long Play: Adult-Oriented Popular Music and the Temporal Logics of the Post-war Sound Recording Industry in the USA," *Media, Culture and Society* 26(3), 385.

66 *Down Beat*, "Music Educators Will Talk Jazz," March 21, 7.

67 Ibid.

68 It should be noted that years later, the rise of popular music studies in Europe was preceded by a similar move from secondary schoolteachers lobbying for rock music to be taught in schools, and that, as with the case of jazz, the pressure for change came from a younger generation of teachers wanting the music curriculum to reflect their own tastes, rather than pressure from pupils for rock to be taught in school (see Martin Cloonan, "What Is Popular Music Studies? Some Observations," *British Journal of Music Education* 22(1), 79).

69 McDonough, "60 Years of Down Beat," 14.

70 Ralph Gleason, "Perspectives," *Down Beat*, July 11, 1956, 34.

71 Nat Hentoff, "Musicians Argue Values of Rock and Roll," *Down Beat*, May 30, 1956, 12.

72 Ibid.

73 Les Brown, "Can Fifty Million Americans Be Wrong?," *Down Beat*, September 19, 1956, 41.

74 Ibid.

75 Barry Ulanov, "Column," *Down Beat*, January 23, 1957, 40.

76 Ibid.; for an examination of similar mass culture critiques by Ulanov's contemporaries, see Joli Jensen, "Considering Commercialism." In *The Nashville Sound: Authenticity, Commercialization and Country Music* (Nashville: Vanderbilt University Press, 1998).

77 Barry Ulanov, "Column," *Down Beat*, May 2, 1957, 36.

78 Ulanov, January 23, 1957, 40.

79 Schonberg, "You Can't Fool Public, Says Haley," 10.

80 Raymond Williams, *Culture and Society* (New York: Columbia University, 1958), 289.

81 Cage, May 4, 1955, 26–27.

Chapter 3

1 Robert Draper, *The Rolling Stone Story* (Worcester: Mainstream, 1990), 367.

2 Ralph Gleason, "Like a Rolling Stone," *Jazz & Pop*, September 14, 1967, 14.

3 Dan Morgenstern, "A Message to Our Readers," *Down Beat*, June 29, 1967, 13.

4   Ibid.

5   *Down Beat,* Subscription advertisement. April 6, 1967, 51.

6   Draper, *The Rolling Stone Story,* 70.

7   Brackett, *Categorizing Sound,* 268.

8   Lerone Bennett Jr., "The Soul of Soul," *Ebony,* December 1961, 114–116.

9   Ibid., 112.

10 John S. Wilson, "Expanding Market for Better Jazz," *New York Times,* March 12, 1961, Section X, 15.

11 John Tynan, "FunkGrooveSoul," *Down Beat,* November 24, 1960, 18–19.

12 Bennett, "The Soul of Soul," 114.

13 Kevin Fellezs, *Birds of Fire: Jazz, Rock, Funk, and the Creation of Fusion* (London: Duke University Press, 2011), 38–39.

14 Pete Welding and John A. Tynan, "Double View of a Double Quartet," *Down Beat,* January 18, 1962, 28.

15 Ibid.

16 Fellezs, *Birds of Fire,* 39.

17 LeRoi Jones, *Blues People* (New York: William Morrow and Co., 1963), 219.

18 Bernard Gendron, *Between Montmartre and the Mudd Club* (Chicago: University of Chicago Press, 2002), 186.

19 Ibid., 172–174.

20 Ibid., 186.

21 Ibid., 187.

22 For an extended discussion of the influence of jazz on rock musicians during this period, see Stuart Nicholson, *Jazz-Rock: A History* (New York: Schirmer, 1998).

23 Nicholson, *Jazz-Rock: A History,* 29.

24 Dan Morgenstern, Interview with the author. Newark, February 3–4, 2005.

25 The term "stage band" is not widely used outside of North America and it refers to a school or college ensemble with big band instrumentation designed to play Jazz & Pop charts, as opposed to a concert or symphonic band. "Stage band" was seemingly invented to be a euphemism for "jazz band," as there was still opposition by some to the teaching of jazz in schools in the 1950s.

26 *Down Beat,* Subscription advertisement. September 7, 1967, 45.

27 *Down Beat,* Vox amplifier advertisement. July 1, 1965, 49.

28 Morgenstern, Interview with the author.

29 Ibid.

30 Ibid.; Morgenstern's announcement also coincided with the departure of Don DeMichael, who had edited *Down Beat* since 1961. At first glance one might assume that the change in editorial policy and DeMichael's leaving was linked, but Morgenstern contended that this was not the case; he had worked under DeMichael as an associate editor for several years, and the two were good friends. DeMichael had been planning his departure for some time. According to Morgenstern, "Don had been editor for seven years, which was a very long time to be in that catbird seat, and he was ready to go. We talked a lot about all this [leaving and changes in editorial policy], so that wasn't what triggered it" (Morgenstern, Interview with the author).

31 Pauline Rivelli, "Editorial," *Jazz & Pop*, August 5, 1967, 17.

32 Ibid.

33 John McDonough, "60 Years of Down Beat." In *Down Beat: 60 Years of Jazz*, ed. Frank Ayler (Winona: Hal Leonard Corporation, 1995), 15.

34 Rivelli, August 5, 1967, 17.

35 *Down Beat*, "Chords and Dischords: Letters," August 24, 1967, 8; Morgenstern, Interview with the author.

36 *Down Beat,* "Chords and Dischords: Letters," August 10, 1967, 7.

37 *Down Beat*, August 24, 1967, 8.

38 Morgenstern, Interview with the author.

39 For an account of music coverage in Playboy, Monique Bourdage, "Beyond the Centerfold: Technology, Culture, and Masculinity in Playboy's Multimedia Empire, 1953–1972." PhD dissertation (Ann Arbor: University of Michigan, 2016).

40 John Gabree, "The World of Rock," *Down Beat*, July 13, 1967, 19–20.

41 John Gabree, "The Beatles in Perspective," *Down Beat*, November 16, 1967, 22.

42 *Down Beat*, "Chords and Dischords: Letters," December 28, 1967, 8.

43 Edward A. Spring, "The Grateful Dead," *Down Beat*, September 21, 1967, 31.

44 Mark Wolf, "Their Satanic Majesties Request," *Down Beat*, May 30, 1968, 30.

45 Morgenstern, Interview with the author.

46 Horace Silver, Psychedelic Sally (sheet music supplement), *Down Beat*, April 18, 1968.

47 Harvey Pekar, "From Rock to???," *Down Beat*, May 2, 1968, 20.

48 Bob Perlongo, "The Widening Mainstream: A Look at the Sound of Now," *Down Beat* '68 annual, 1968, 31.

49 Draper, *The Rolling Stone Story*; Fred Goodman, *The Mansion on the Hill: Dylan, Young, Geffen, Springsteen, and the Head-On Collision of Rock and Commerce* (New York: Vintage, 1998).

50 Leonard Feather, "Pop=Rock=Jazz: A False Musical Equation Dissected," *Down Beat* '68 annual, 1968, 16.

51 Ibid.

52 Ibid.

53 Ibid., 17.

54 Ibid., 16–17.

55 Ibid., 17.

56 For an excellent consideration of Jimi Hendrix's jazz legacy, read Charles Shaar Murray, "Hear My 'Trane A-comin.'" In *Crosstown Traffic* (Canongate books, 2001).

57 Ibid., 19.

58 Martin Williams, "Bystander," *Down Beat*, June 27, 1968, 15.

59 Gleason, September 14, 1967, 14.

60 Ralph Gleason, "Like a Rolling Stone," *Jazz & Pop*, November 1967, 12.

61 Russ Wilson, "The Future of Jazz: On the Rocks?" *Down Beat*, June 15, 1967, 17.

62 Ralph Gleason, "Buddy Rich: A Note of Hope," *Jazz & Pop*, January 1969, 39.

63 Ralph Gleason, "Like a Rolling Stone," *Jazz & Pop*, April 1969, 14.

64 Ibid.

65 Dan Morgenstern, "The Year in Review: 1967," *Down Beat Music '68* annual, 12.

66 For more on the economic hardships of jazz in the late 1960s, see Paul Lopes, *The Rise of a Jazz Art World* (Cambridge: Cambridge University Press, 2002), 266–268.

67 Morgenstern, "The Year in Review: 1967," 12–13.

Chapter 4

1 Robert Christgau, "Chords and Discords," *Down Beat*, September 19, 1968, 10.

2 Jann Wenner, *The Rolling Stone Record Review* (New York: Pocket Books, 1971), viii.

3 See Sam Robert Anson, *Gone Crazy and Back Again: The Rise and Fall of the Rolling Stone Generation* (New York: Doubleday, 1981); Robert Draper, *The Rolling Stone Story* (Worchester: Mainstream, 1990); Chet Flippo, 1974a. "The History of

Rolling Stone: Part I," *Popular Music and Society* 3(3), 159–188; Ulf Lindberg et al., *Rock Criticism from the Beginning: Amusers, Bruisers, and Cool-Headed Cruisers* (New York: Peter Lang, 2005).

4   Simon Frith, *Sound Effects: Youth, Leisure and the Politics of Rock 'n' Roll* (London: Constable, 1983), 168.

5   Ibid., 168–169.

6   A recent and notable exception that provides a more nuanced account is Simon Warner, "In Print and On Screen: The Changing Character of Popular Music Journalism." In *The Sage Handbook of Popular Music*, ed. Andy Bennett and Steve Waksman (London: Sage, 2015), 439–455.

7   Paul Gorman, *In Their Own Write: Adventures in the Music Press* (London: Sanctuary Press, 2001); Robert Christgau, Interview with the author. Seattle, April 27, 2006; Jon Landau, Phone interview with the author. Connecticut, August 3, 2006; Greil Marcus, Interview with the author. Seattle, April 29, 2006.

8   Marcus, Interview with the author.

9   Jerry Wexler and D. Ritz, *Rhythm and the Blues: A Life in American Music* (New York: St. Martin's Press, 1993), 62.

10   Lindberg et al., *Rock Criticism from the Beginning*, 71.

11   Robert Wolfe, "The First Issue," *Sing Out*, May 1959, 2.

12   There was also a small but significant country music press, which included publications such as *Country Song Roundup* and *C&W Jamboree*, but none of the rock critics I interviewed or researched mentioned reading these when they were young.

13   Gorman, *In Their Own Write*, 24.

14   Landau, Phone interview with the author.

15   Gorman, *In Their Own Write*, 25.

16   Gorman, *In Their Own Write*, 24–29.

17   Ibid., 174–175.

18   Ibid.

19   John Burks, "The Underground Press," *Rolling Stone*, October 4, 1969, 11–30.

20   Warner, "In Print and On Screen," 439–455.

21   Lindberg et al., *Rock Criticism from the Beginning*, 132; the significant exceptions to this rule were Richard Goldstein's *Village Voice* column from 1966 to 1969 and Robert Christgau's *Esquire* column from 1967 to 1968 (Christgau took over Goldstein's position at the *Voice* in 1969).

22   Paul Williams, "Get Off My Cloud!" *Crawdaddy!*, February 7, 1966, 1.

23 Paul Williams, "Editorial," *Crawdaddy!*, February 14, 1966, 1; Williams announced that the comparative reviews would be featured in the next issue of *Crawdaddy!*, but they were never published.

24 Dave Harris, "Editorial: A Reply to *The Oracle's* 'Indo-Rock'," *Mojo-Navigator*, September 7, 1966, 7; Harris noted the article in question appeared in a recent issue of the underground paper *The Oracle*, but did not specify the name of the "jazz buff" critic.

25 There were a few notable exceptions to the largely male-dominated profession of rock criticism in the 1960s such as Ellen Willis.

26 Lindberg et al., *Rock Criticism from the Beginning*, 133.

27 Jann Wenner televised interview with Andrew Denton, *Enough Rope*, October 6, 2008. Transcript available online: http://www.abc.net.au/tv/enoughrope/transcripts/s2382889.htm (accessed May 23, 2016).

28 Draper, *The Rolling Stone Story*, 44.

29 Wenner interview with Denton, 2008.

30 Draper, *The Rolling Stone Story*, 44–50.

31 Williams and Shaw quoted in Gorman, *In Their Own Write*, 54.

32 Draper, *The Rolling Stone Story*, 64.

33 Wenner quoted in Dalton, David, "We Visit Mr. Zeitgeist; or How I Learned to Stop Worrying and Love Jann Wenner," *Gadfly*, July 1999. Available online: http://www.gadflyonline.com/home/archive/July99/archive-zeitgeist.html (accessed May 23, 2016).

34 Jann Wenner, "A Letter from the Editor," *Rolling Stone*, November 9, 1967, 2.

35 Wenner, Jann in televised interview with Charlie Rose, May 26, 1992. Transcript available online: https://charlierose.com/videos/449 (accessed May 23, 2016).

36 Lydon quoted in Stephanie M. Lee, "The Origins of *Rolling Stone*," *The Daily Californian*, August 20, 2007. Available online: http://archive.dailycal.org/article.php?id=25647 (accessed May 23, 2016).

37 John Burks, Phone interview with the author. San Francisco, August 20, 2005.

38 Draper, *The Rolling Stone Story*, 49, 58.

39 Lindberg et al., *Rock Criticism from the Beginning*, 91.

40 Burks, Phone interview with the author.

41 Draper, *The Rolling Stone Story*, 67.

42 Morgenstern,   Interview with the author.

43 Wenner quoted in Jon Fine, "An In-Depth Interview with Jann Wenner," *Business Week*, November 2, 2007. Available online: http://www.bloomberg.com/news/articles/2007-11-01/an-in-depth-interview-with-jann-wenner (accessed May 23, 2016).

44 Jann Wenner in televised interview with Charlie Rose, February 5, 2007. Transcript available online: https://charlierose.com/videos/12131 (accessed May 23, 2016).

45 Draper, *The Rolling Stone Story*, 61.

46 Fong-Torres quoted in ibid., 98.

47 Ralph Gleason, "Perspectives: When Down to Seeds and Stems," *Rolling Stone*, December 14, 1967, 10.

48 Ralph Gleason, "Perspectives: A Power to Change the World," *Rolling Stone*, June 22, 1968, 10.

49 Burks, Phone interview with the author.

50 Fred Goodman, *The Mansion on the Hill: Dylan, Young, Geffen, Springsteen, and the Head-On Collision of Rock and Commerce* (New York: Vintage, 1998), 19–20.

51 Draper, *The Rolling Stone Story*, 90.

52 Gorman, *In Their Own Write*, 52.

53 Landau, Phone interview with the author.

54 Ibid.

55 The locally produced *Boston Broadside* should not be mistaken with the better known and more widely circulated *Broadside* folk magazine, which covered the national folk scene.

56 Ibid.

57 Jon Landau, "Mitch Ryder and the Detroit Wheels—Breakout!" *Crawdaddy!*, September 6, 1966, 6.

58 Landau quoted in Flippo, "The History of Rolling Stone: Part I," 162. It should be noted that *Crawdaddy!* was not without fine music writers, notably Paul Williams, Sandy Pearlman, Richard Meltzer, and Peter Guralnick. But Landau's writing was distinct from all of them—more concerned with what made rock successful as music rather than what made it culturally important.

59 Lindberg et al., *Rock Criticism from the Beginning*, 143.

60 Ibid.

61 Jon Landau, "Stones," *Rolling Stone*, February 10, 1968, 18.

62 Jon Landau, March 1968, quoted in Landau, *It's Too Late to Stop Now* (San Francisco: Straight Arrow, 1972), 155.

63 Ibid., 150–154.

64 Cream fan Graeme Pattingale (2002) has devoted a website to the comparison of these two reviews with a bootleg recording of the concert. I thank Mr. Pattingale for alerting me to the existence of the second review; my interpretations of these two reviews are my own. It should also be noted that Heineman and Landau did not know one another while studying at Brandeis (Heineman 2006; Landau 2006).

65 Alan Heineman, "'Trippin': Impressions of Cream and Jefferson Airplane," *Down Beat*, July 25, 1968, 16; Jon Landau, "Cream," *Rolling Stone*, May 11, 1968, 14.

66 Heineman, July 25, 1968, 16.

67 Ibid., 15.

68 Jon Landau, "Cream on Its Way," *The Justice*, March 26, 1968, 4.

69 Christgau, "Chords and Discords," 10.

70 Jon Landau, "Blood, Sweat and Tears," *Rolling Stone*, March 1, 1969, 28.

71 Marcus, Interview with the author.

72 Greil Marcus, "The Woodstock Festival," *Rolling Stone*, September 20, 1969, 8–9.

73 Draper, *The Rolling Stone Story*, 86.

74 Marcus quoted in Draper, *The Rolling Stone Story*, 87.

75 Marcus, Interview with the author.

76 Lindberg et al., *Rock Criticism from the Beginning*, 159.

77 Ibid., 160.

78 Draper, *The Rolling Stone Story*, 131–132.

79 Norma Coates, "Teenyboppers, Groupies, and Other Grotesques: Girls and Women and Rock Culture in the 1960s and early 1970s," *Journal of Popular Music Studies* 15(1), 2003, 77.

80 Ibid, 80.

81 Ibid, 82.

82 Patricia Kennealy-Morrison, "Rock Around the Cock," reprinted in *Rock She Wrote*, ed. Evelyn McDonnell and Ann Powers (London: Plexus, 1995), 357–363.

83 Marcus, September 20, 1969, 8.

84 Wenner interview with Denton, 2008.

85 Jon Landau, "What's Wrong with Rock 'Art,'" *Rolling Stone*, July 20, 1968, 18.

86 Robert Christgau, *Any Old Way You Choose It* (Baltimore: Penguin, 1973), 3, 6.

Chapter 5

1   Dan Morgenstern 1970, quoted in Dan Morgenstern, *Living with Jazz*, ed. Sheldon Meyer (New York: Pantheon Books, 2004), 673

2   Geoffrey C. Ward, *Jazz: A History of America's Music* (New York: Knopf, 200), 444.

3   Dan Morgenstern, "The Year That Was," *Down Beat Music '69*, 1969, 12.

4   Jann Wenner, *The Rolling Stone Record Review* (New York: Pocket Books, 1971), viii.

5   John Burks, Phone interview with the author. San Francisco' August 20, 2005.

6   Robert Draper, *The Rolling Stone Story* (Worcester: Mainstream, 1990), 97.

7   John Burks, "The Goose That Laid the Golden Rock," *Rolling Stone,* November 23, 1968, 22.

8   This stood in contrast to Jon Landau's perspective: as we have seen, earlier that year Landau based many of his criticisms of Cream on the assumption that their music was decidedly not jazz.

9   John Burks, "Sun Ra," *Rolling Stone*, April 19, 1969, 16–17.

10 Burks, Phone interview with the author.

11 Ibid.

12 John Burks, "Records," *Rolling Stone*, March 14, 1969, 28.

13 *Rolling* Stone, "Gary Burton Named Jazzman of the Year," February 1, 1969, 12.

14 Don DeMichael, "Miles Davis," *Rolling Stone*, December 13, 1969, 23–26.

15 Don DeMichael, "Miles Davis, Boxer: An Offbeat Interview," *Down Beat*, December 11, 1969, 12.

16 Burks, Phone interview with the author.

17 Lester Bangs, "Review of *Captain Beefheart: Trout Mask Replica*," *Rolling Stone*, July 26, 1969, 37.

18 On a 1972 Chicago release, he wrote that the band "have no trace of originality .... They saw a void and they filled it. With putty and plaster of Paris, but they *did* fill it" (Lester Bangs, *Psychotic Reactions and Carburetor Dung* (New York: Knopf, 1988), 97). To me, this description agrees well with his earlier allusion to "self-conscious, carefully crafted jazz-rock bullshit."

19 Lester Bangs, "Review of *Miles Davis: In a Silent Way*," *Rolling Stone*, November 15, 1969, 33.

20 Ibid.

21 Here Winner identifies precisely the kind of rock audience that constituted *Down Beat's* target readership (see Chapter 3). This suggests that rather than existing as a kind of critical anomaly without a mass audience, *Down Beat* and its ideology actually reflected certain tastes of a significant, visible "public" that Winner frames in opposition to himself (and presumably other *Rolling Stone* readers). Interestingly, certain aspects of this taste group—the audience that was exhilarated by virtuosic, large ensemble rock performances with a jazz flavor—continue to survive decades later in high-school music programs. High-school stage bands continue to compete in festivals with other school bands from Canada and the United States performing arrangements of jazz-rock songs from the late 1960s, such as "Spinning Wheel" by Blood, Sweat, and Tears and "Peaches En Regalia" by Frank Zappa.

22 Langdon Winner, "Reviews—Memphis Underground by Herbie Mann and a Soul Experiment by Freddie Hubbard," *Rolling Stone*, July 12, 1969, 36.

23 Stuart Nicholson, "Fusions and Crossovers." In *The Cambridge Companion to Jazz*, ed. Mervyn Cooke and David Horn (Cambridge: Cambridge University Press, 2002), 217.

24 Nicholson suggests that the earliest appearance of the word "fusion" in jazz was in 1963 "by record producer Orrin Keepnews as the title of an album guitarist Wes Montgomery, who in mixing light, accessible improvisation with strings created an easy-listening album with an appeal extending beyond jazz audiences to 'crossover' into the popular market." (Stuart Nicholson et al., "The Song of the Body Electric: Jazz-Rock." In *The Future of Jazz*, ed. Yuval Taylor (Chicago: A Cappella, 2002), 218). Two more notable appearances of the word are in a 1967 *Down Beat* interview with long-time critic Stanley Dance, who discusses the possibility of a "pop-jazz fusion," as well as a *Rolling Stone* advertisement in 1970 for a band called "Fusion": "Fusion is more than a name. It's the sound of an exciting new group, Fusion, who bring together the sound of jazz, rock, and blues …. Tune in and catch up with the jazz-rock-blues sound of Fusion" (Dance quoted in Jim Delehant, "Is Jazz Going Longhair?," *Down Beat Yearbook Music '67*, 1967, 56; *Rolling Stone*, advertisement, February 7, 1970, 43).

25 Alan Heineman, "Rocks in My Head," *Down Beat*, January 8, 1970, 8.

26 Paul Gorman, *In Their Own Write: Adventures in the Music Press* (London: Sanctuary Press, 2001), 51.

27 Frank Kofsky, "The Scene," *Jazz & Pop*, January 1968, 37.

28 *Rolling Stone*, "Awards for Idiocy, Evil …," February 7, 1970, 28.

29 Ibid.; *Rolling Stone*, "It Happened in 1968," February 1, 1969, 15.

30 *Jazz & Pop*, "Readers Poll," May 1968, 22.

31 *Jazz & Pop*, "Critics Poll," February 1968, 14; *Jazz & Pop* "Critics Poll," February 1969, 17; *Jazz & Pop* "Critics Poll," February 1970, 17.

32 *Jazz & Pop* "Readers Poll," May 1968, 22; *Jazz & Pop* "Readers Poll," May 1969, 22; *Jazz & Pop* "Readers Poll," May 1970, 27.

33 *Down Beat*, "Jazz Critics Poll," August 24, 1967, 15.

34 *Down Beat* Readers Poll, December 26, 1968, 21; *Down Beat* Readers Poll, December 25, 1969, 16.

35 Ralph Gleason, "Like a Rolling Stone," *Jazz & Pop*, December 1968, 14.

36 Gleason, January 1969, 39.

37 Gleason, "Like a Rolling Stone," *Jazz & Pop*, February 1969, 12.

38 John Burks, "The Monterey Jazz Festival," *Rolling Stone*, November 9, 1968, 14.

39 Ibid.

40 Ibid.

41 Stuart Nicholson, *Jazz-Rock: A History* (New York: Schirmer, 1998), 87.

42 Ibid., 162.

43 Ibid., 79.

44 John Gennari, "Hipsters, Bluebloods, Rebels, and Hooligans, The Cultural Politics of the Newport Jazz Festival, 1954–1960." In *Uptown Conversation: The New Jazz Studies*, ed. Robert G. O'Meally, Brent Hayes Edwards, and Farah Jasmine Griffin (New York: Columbia University Press, 2004), 129.

45 Ibid., 144.

46 Ibid., 131.

47 Ibid., 138.

48 George Wein, "An interview with George Wein," *Jazz & Pop*, April 1969, 47.

49 *Rolling Stone*, "Jazz Meets Rock," March 1, 1969, 6.

50 George Wein with Nate Chinen, *Myself Among Others: A Life in Music* (Cambridge: Da Capo, 2004), 281.

51 Burt Goldblatt, *Newport Jazz Festival: The Illustrated History* (New York: Dial Press, 1977), 172.

52 *Rolling Stone*, March 1, 1969, 6.

53 *Rolling Stone*, "Jazz Takes Gas at Fillmore," April 19, 1969, 10.

54 I have mentioned most of the important acts that played at the 1969 Newport Festival, but it is not a comprehensive list. In my research I have found conflicting accounts of the exact program, since the advertised line-up did not match the line-up that actually performed. None of the press accounts I have found offer a comprehensive program list.

55 George Wein, "Newport Festival Program Notes," 1969.

56 Gennari, "Hipsters, Bluebloods, Rebels, and Hooligans," 128.

57 *Rolling Stone*, Sun Ra cover, April 19, 1969.

58 Wein, *Myself Among Others*, 283.

59 Ibid., 284.

60 Ibid., 285.

61 Ibid., 286.

62 John S. Wilson, "Unruly Newport Fans Upset Newport Jazz Festival," *New York Times*, July 7, 1969, 28; it is interesting to note that according to George Wein, John S. Wilson was indebted to Newport for his position as the jazz critic for the *New York Times*. As Wein recalled the coverage for the first Newport Jazz Festival in 1954: "Without any full-time jazz reviewers on staff, the *New York Times* had asked the esteemed opera critic Harold Schonberg, who happened to be in Newport at that time, to cover the festival" (Wein, *Myself Among Others*, 148). An ensuing letter-writing campaign to the *Times* protesting Schonberg's inability to cover jazz properly "was so successful that the editors of the *Times* not only apologized; they hired John S. Wilson as the first full-time jazz critic on any major U.S. metropolitan newspaper. This set a crucial precedent for jazz coverage everywhere, and it was a direct result of Newport" (ibid., 148).

63 Ibid., 28.

64 John Norris, "Newport '69," *Coda*, August 1969, 13.

65 Ira Gitler and Dan Morgenstern, "Rock at Newport '69: Big Crowds, Bad Vibes," *Down Beat*, August 21, 1969, 26; it is beyond the scope of this chapter to examine the Newport riots of 1960, but for an excellent analysis see Gennari's *Hipsters, Bluebloods, Rebels, and Hooligans*.

66 Gilter and Morgenstern, August 21, 1969, 31.

67 Ibid.

68 Ibid.

69 Ibid.

70 Ibid., 25.

71 Norris, August 1969, 15.

72 Gitler and Morgenstern, August 21, 1969, 45.

73 Alan Heineman and Dan Morgenstern, "Rock, Jazz, and Newport: An Exchange," *Down Beat*, December 25, 1969, 22.

74 Ibid.

75 Ibid.

76 *Rolling Stone*, "Rock Too Much for Newport," August 9, 1969, 10.

77 Jan Hodenfield, "The Newport Folk Festival," *Rolling Stone*, August 23, 1969, 20.

78 *Rolling Stone*, August 9, 1969, 10.

79 Kevin Fellezs, "Between Rock and a Jazz Place: Intercultural Interchange in Fusion Musicking," PhD thesis (University of California, 2004), 5.

80 Nicholson, "Fusions and Crossovers," 43.

81 Pauline Rivelli, "Newport Jazz Festival 1969," *Jazz & Pop*, September 1969, 31–32.

82 Wein, *Myself Among Others*, 463.

83 *Rolling Stone* August 9, 1969, 10.

84 Wein, *Myself Among Others*, 463–464.

85 Ward, *Jazz: A History of America's Music*, 445–449; Tom Jurek, Allmusic review of *Bitches Brew*. Available online: http://www.allmusic.com/album/bitches-brew -mw0000188019 (accessed July 25, 2016); Eric Porter, "It's About That Time: The Response to Miles Davis's Electric Turn." In *Miles Davis and American Culture*, ed. Gerald Early (St. Louis: Missouri Historical Society Press, 2001), 130–147.

Conclusion

1   Keith Negus, *Popular Music in Theory* (Cambridge: Polity, 1996), 138.

2   Jean Anouilh (*The Rehearsal*, 1950) quoted in Forbes, October 5, 2010. Available online: http://www.forbes.com/global/2010/0510/quotes-sayings-proverbs-thoughts .html (accessed July 13, 2016).

3   Leonard Feather, "A Year of Selling Out," *Down Beat Music '71*, 1971, 10.

4   Ibid.

5   Ibid., 11.

6   Don DeMichael, "Miles Davis," *Rolling Stone*, December 13, 1969, 23–26.

7   Miles Davis with Quincy Troupe, *The Autobiography* (New York: Simon and Schuster, 1989), 253.

8   Ralph Gleason, "Liner notes for Miles Davis," *Bitches Brew*. Columbia Records, 1970.

9   Chet Flippo, 1974a, "The History of Rolling Stone: Part I," *Popular Music and Society* 3(3), 181.

10 Ibid., 184.

11 Dan Morgenstern, "Farewell to the Sixties," *Down Beat Music '70*, 1970, 9–10.

12 Chet Flippo, 1974b. "The History of Rolling Stone: Part II," *Popular Music and Society* 3(4), 259.

13 "About Down Beat: A History as Rich as Jazz Itself." Available online: http://www .DownBeat.com/default.asp?sect=about (accessed July 2, 2016).

14 Scott DeVeaux, *The Birth of Bebop: A Social and Musical History* (Berkeley: University of California Press, 1997), 443.

15 David Brackett, *Categorizing Sound: Genre and Twentieth-Century Popular Music* (Berkeley: University of California Press, 2016), 330.

16 Ibid., 31.

17 Ibid., 331.

18 Kevin Fellezs, *Birds of Fire: Jazz, Rock, Funk, and the Creation of Fusion* (London: Duke University Press, 2011), 226–227.

19 Robert Christgau, Interview with the author. Seattle, April 27, 2006.

20 Simon Frith, "Writing About Popular Music." In *The Cambridge History of Music Criticism*, ed. Christopher Dingle (Cambridge: Cambridge University Press, 2017), forthcoming.

21 Ibid., forthcoming.

22 Ibid.

23 "About Down Beat: A History as Rich as Jazz Itself." Available online: http://www. DownBeat.com/default.asp?sect=about (accessed July 2, 2016).

24 Alliance for Audited Media consumer magazine circulation figures, available online: http://abcas3.auditedmedia.com/ecirc/magtitlesearch.asp (accessed July 2, 2016); David Hepworth, "The gob-smacking 'sales' figures of *Rolling Stone*," September 5, 2013. Available online: http://whatsheonaboutnow.blogspot.co.uk/2013/09/the-gob -smacking-sales-figures-of.html (accessed July 18, 2016).

25 Jim Derogatis, *Kill Your Idols: A New Generation of Rock Writers Reconsiders the Classics* (Fort Lee: Barricade Books, 2004). Foreword available online: http://www .jimdero.com/KillYourIdols/Idolsforeword.htm (accessed July 2, 2016).

26 Jody Rosen, "The Perils of Poptimism," *Slate*, May 2006. Available online: http://www .slate.com/articles/arts/music_box/2006/05/the_perils_of_poptimism.html (accessed July 2, 2016).

27 Simon Warner, "In Print and On Screen: The Changing Character of Popular Music Journalism." In *The Sage Handbook of Popular Music*, ed. Andy Bennett and Steve Waksman (London: Sage, 2015), 452–453.

28 Tom Davies, European Marketing Director for the Secretly Group (a consortium of independent record labels), put it to the author this way in 2015:

> The importance of the music press differs depending on what genre of music you're trying to sell. But in the world we loosely refer to as 'indie,' a great review

in a well-known publication is always of huge importance. A great review in *Pitchfork*, the *Guardian*, *Mojo*: this can be the difference between a band sinking or surviving, and as a label we work very hard to get our bands reviewed and featured in those publications for that reason. For certain genres of music, though not all of course, the music press can be more important than radio or video play because some of these records are never likely to receive a lot of airtime—so you rely on press to deliver the message. The printed music press may have much smaller circulation figures than it used to, but the people who buy and read those magazines and papers are largely the hardcore music fans—the same ones who still pay for music, be that buying records or going to shows. In this era, it is likely that the ones who stop reading the music press are the ones who stop paying for music period.

E-mail correspondence with the author, November 7, 2015.

29 Eric Weisbard, IASPM mailing list discussion, May 5, 2015.

30 David Ake, Charles Hiroshi Garrett, and Daniel Goldmark (eds.), *Jazz/Not Jazz: The Music and Its Boundaries* (Berkeley: University of California Press, 2012), 3–5.

31 Deveaux, *The Birth of Bebop*, 6.

32 Keir Keightley, "Reconsidering Rock." In *The Cambridge Companion to Rock and Pop*, ed. Simon Frith, John Street, and Will Straw (Cambridge: Cambridge University Press, 2002), 109.

33 Brackett, *Categorizing Sound*, 55.

34 For recent examples of critics making cheap shots at fusion and hybrid genres, see, for instance, the Ian Gittins review of Acoustic Ladyland in the *Guardian* which opens with the line, "It is a given that any band looking to marry jazz and rock produces a soggy fusion that combines the worst of both genres" (2006).

35 Simon Frith, "What Is Bad Music?" In *Bad Music*, ed. Christopher J. Washburne and Maiken Derno (New York: Routledge, 2004), 15–36.

36 Simon Reynolds, *Rip It Up and Start Again: Postpunk 1978–1984* (London: Faber and Faber, 2005), 73–91; Lester Bangs, *Psychotic Reactions and Carburetor Dung* (New York: Knopf, 1988), 315.

Bibliography

Adorno, Theodor. *On Popular Music*, 1941. Reprinted in *On Record*, edited by Simon Frith and Andrew Goodwin (London: Routledge, 1990) 256–267.

Adorno, Theodor and Max Horkheimer. *The Dialectic of Enlightenment*, 1936. Reprint. (London: Verso, 1979).

Ake, David. *Jazz Cultures* (Berkeley: University of California Press, 2002a).

Ake, David. "Learning Jazz, Teaching Jazz," in *The Cambridge Companion to Jazz*, edited by Mervyn Cooke and David Horne (Cambridge: Cambridge University Press, 2002b), 255–269.

Ake, David, Charles Hiroshi Garrett, and Daniel Goldmark (eds.). *Jazz/Not Jazz: The Music and Its Boundaries* (Berkeley: University of California Press, 2012).

Alliance for Audited Media consumer magazine circulation figures. Available online: http://abcas3.auditedmedia.com/ecirc/magtitlesearch.asp (accessed July 2, 2016).

Anouilh, Jean. Quoted in *Forbes*, October 5, 2010. Available online: http://www .forbes.com/global/2010/0510/quotes-sayings-proverbs-thoughts.html (accessed July 13, 2016).

Anson, Robert Sam. *Gone Crazy and Back Again: The Rise and Fall of the Rolling Stone Generation* (New York: Doubleday, 1981).

Ayler, Frank. *Down Beat: 60 Years of Jazz* (Winona: Hal Leonard Corporation, 1995).

Bailey, Bill. "Country & Western." *Down Beat*, January 13, 1954, 36.

Baker, David N. *New Perspectives on Jazz* (London: Smithsonian Institution, 1990)

Balliett, Whitney. "Musical Events: Newport News." *New Yorker*, July 19, 1969, 73–75.

Bangs, Lester. *Psychotic Reactions and Carburetor Dung* (New York: Knopf, 1988).

Bangs, Lester. "Review of *Captain Beefheart: Trout Mask Replica*." *Rolling Stone*, July 26, 1969, 37.

Bangs, Lester. "Review of *Miles Davis: In a Silent Way*." *Rolling Stone*, November 15, 1969, 33.

Bangs, Lester. "Reviews—Tony Williams Lifetime: Emergency!" *Rolling Stone*, November 15, 1969, 33.

Becker, Howard S. *Art Worlds* (Berkeley: University of California Press, 1984).

Becker, Howard S. "Art Worlds and Social Types." *American Behavioral Scientist*, 19(6), 1976, 703–719.

Becker, Howard S. "The Culture and Career of the Dance Musician," 1953. Reprinted in *American Music*, edited by Charles Nanry (New Brunswick: Transaction, 1972), 65–98.

Becker, Howard S. *Outsiders* (New York: Free Press of Glencoe, 1963).

Becker, Howard S. "The Professional Dance Musician and His Audience." *American Journal of Sociology*, 57, 1951, 136–144.

Bennett, Andy and Steve Waksman (eds.). *The Sage Handbook of Popular Music* (London: Sage, 2015).

Bennett, Lerone Jr. "The Soul of Soul." *Ebony*, December 1961, 114–116.

Berger, Morroe. "Jazz: Resistance to the Diffusion of a Culture," in *American Music*, edited by Charles Nanry (New Brunswick: Transaction Books, 1972), 11–43.

Bertrand, Michael T. *Race, Rock, and Elvis* (Urbana: University of Illinois Press, 2000).

Betton, Matt. "N.A.J.E. Seattle Meeting." *National Association of Jazz Educators Newsletter*, 1(1), 1968, 1–2.

Blake, Randy. "Disc Jockey Urges Return to Spinning Only Country Music." *Down Beat*, January 26, 1955, 1.

Borneman, Ernest. *A Critic Looks at Jazz* (London: Chilton, 1946).

Bourdage, Monique. "Beyond the Centerfold: Technology, Culture, and Masculinity in Playboy's Multimedia Empire, 1953–1972." PhD dissertation (Ann Arbor: University of Michigan, 2016).

Bourdieu, Pierre. *The Field of Cultural Production: Essays on Art and Literature* (New York: Columbia University Press, 1993).

Bourdieu, Pierre. *On Television and Journalism* (London: Pluto, 1998).

Brackett, David. *Categorizing Sound: Genre and Twentieth-Century Popular Music* (Berkeley: University of California Press, 2016).

Brackett, David. *The Pop, Rock, and Soul Reader* (New York: Oxford University Press, 2005).

Brennan, Matt. "The Rough Guide to Critics: Musicians Discuss the Role of the Music Press." *Popular Music*, 25(2), 2006, 221–234.

Breslau, Lillian. "Letter to the Editor." *New York Times*, February 26, 1939, 51.

Brown, Les. "Can Fifty Million Americans Be Wrong?" *Down Beat*, September 19, 1956, 41.

Brown, Les. "In The Whirl." *Down Beat*, September 19, 1956, 45.

Burks, John. "The Goose That Laid the Golden Rock." *Rolling Stone*, November 23, 1968, 1, 20, 22, 30.

Burks, John. "The Monterey Jazz Festival." *Rolling Stone*, November 9, 1968, 14.

Burks, John. Phone interview with the author. San Francisco, August 20, 2005.

Burks, John. "Records." *Rolling Stone*, March 4, 1969, 28.

Burks, John. "Sun Ra." *Rolling Stone*, April 19, 1969, 16–17.

Burks, John. "The Underground Press." *Rolling Stone*, October 4, 1969, 11–30.

Burns, Ken. *Jazz* VHS (London: Florentine Films and British Broadcasting Corporation, 2000).

Cage, Ruth. "Arranger Quincy Jones Says Quality of R&B Sides Better." *Down Beat*, September 21, 1955, 42.

Cage, Ruth. "Horrors! Recognition Finally Comes to R&B." *Down Beat*, April 6, 1955, 1, 17.

Cage, Ruth. "Rhythm and Blues Notes." *Down Beat*, August 25, 1954, 17.

Cage, Ruth. "Rhythm and Blues Notes." *Down Beat*, September 22, 1954, 16.

Cage, Ruth. "Rhythm and Blues Notes." *Down Beat*, December 1, 1954, 17.

Cage, Ruth. "Rhythm and Blues Notes." *Down Beat*, February 9, 1955, 4.

Cage, Ruth. "Rhythm and Blues Notes." *Down Beat*, March 23, 1955, 20.

Cage, Ruth. "Rhythm and Blues Notes." *Down Beat*, April 20, 1955, 41.

Cage, Ruth. "Rhythm and Blues Notes." *Down Beat*, May 4, 1955, 26.

Cage, Ruth. "Rhythm and Blues Notes." *Down Beat*, May 18, 1955, 5.

Cage, Ruth. "Rhythm and Blues Notes." *Down Beat*, December 14, 1955, 13.

Cameron, William Bruce. "Sociological Notes on the Jam Session." *Social Forces*, 33, 1954, 177–182.

Christgau, Robert. *Any Old Way You Choose It* (Baltimore: Penguin, 1973).

Christgau, Robert. "Chords and Discords." *Down Beat*, September 19, 1968, 10.

Christgau, Robert. Interview with the author. Seattle, April 27, 2006.

Christgau, Robert. "The Pop-Boho Connection: History as Discourse, or Is It the Other Way Around?" *Bookforum*, June 2002. Available online: http://www.robertchristgau.com/xg/bkrev/gendron-02.php (accessed September 25, 2016)

Cloonan, Martin. "What Is Popular Music Studies? Some Observations." *British Journal of Music Education*, 22(1), 2005, 77–93.

Coates, "Teenyboppers, Groupies, and Other Grotesques: Girls and Women and Rock Culture in the 1960s and Early 1970s." *Journal of Popular Music Studies*, 15(1), 2003, 77.

Collier, James Lincoln. *The Reception of Jazz in America: A New View* (Brooklyn: I.S.A.M. Monographs, 1988).

Cooke, Mervyn and David Horn. *The Cambridge Companion to Jazz* (Cambridge: Cambridge University Press, 2002).

Dalton, David, "We Visit Mr. Zeitgeist; or How I Learned to Stop Worrying and Love Jann Wenner." *Gadfly*, July 1999. Available online: http://www.gadflyonline.com/home/archive/July99/archive-zeitgeist.html (accessed May 23, 2016).

Davies, Tom. E-mail correspondence with the author, November 7, 2015.

Davis, Nathan T. *Writings in Jazz* (Dubuque: Kendall/Hunt, 1996).

Davis, Miles with Quincy Troupe, *The Autobiography* (New York: Simon and Schuster, 1989).

Delehant, Jim. "Is Jazz Going Longhair?" *Down Beat Yearbook Music '67*, 1967, 54–57.

DeMichael, Don. "Miles Davis." *Rolling Stone*, December 13, 1969, 23–26.

DeMichael, Don. "Miles Davis, Boxer: An Offbeat Interview." *Rolling Stone*, December 11, 1969, 12.

Denny, James. "Why the Upsurge in Country Music?" *Down Beat*, June 30, 1954, 66.

Derogatis, Jim. *Kill Your Idols: A New Generation of Rock Writers Reconsiders the Classics* (Fort Lee: Barricade Books, 2004). Available online: http://www.jimdero.com/KillYourIdols/Idolsforeword.htm (accessed July 2, 2016).

DeVeaux, Scott. *The Birth of Bebop: A Social and Musical History* (Berkeley: University of California Press, 1997).

DeVeaux, Scott. "Constructing the Jazz Tradition: Jazz Historiography." *Black American Literature Forum*, 25(3), 1991, 525–560.

DeVeaux, Scott. "Cores and Boundaries." *The Source*, 2, 2005a, 15–30.

DeVeaux, Scott. "Historicist Jazz. History of Jazz Lecture Notes." 2005b. Available online: http://people.virginia.edu/~skd9r/MUSI212_new/ (accessed September 10, 2005)

Down Beat. "About Down Beat: A History as Rich as Jazz Itself." Available online: http://www.DownBeat.com/default.asp?sect=about (accessed July 2, 2016).

Down Beat. "Advertisement." April 20, 1955, 66.

Down Beat. "Are Pop DJs Being Unfair to C/W Disc Artists?" January 26, 1955, 18.

Down Beat. "Bands Dug by the Beat: Louis Jordan." September 1, 1944, 4.

Down Beat. "C&W DJ Parley Supports Action to Combat Blue Lyrics." December 29, 1954, 6.

Down Beat. "C&W Notes." August 10, 1955, 29.

Down Beat. "Cover." October 19, 1967.

Down Beat. "Cover." April 4, 1968.

Down Beat. "Chords and Dischords: Letters." August 10, 1967, 7.

Down Beat. "Chords and Dischords: Letters." August 24, 1967, 8.

Down Beat. "Chords and Dischords: Letters." December 28, 1967, 8.

Down Beat. " 'Diggin' the Discs with Don." September 10, 1947, 13–15.

Down Beat. "Down Beat Readers Poll." December 26, 1968, 21, 25.

Down Beat. "Editorial Masthead." March 9, 1955, 2.

Down Beat. "Jazz Critics Poll." August 24, 1967, 15.

Down Beat. "Maher Publications." April 20, 1955, 3.

Down Beat. "Multivox Amplifier Advertisement." June 16, 1950, 7.

Down Beat. "Music Educators Will Talk Jazz." March 21, 1956, 7.

Down Beat. " 'Quit Rockin': It's Time to Get Rollin." September 19, 1956, 39.

Down Beat. "R&B Boom Won't Stick: Elgart." March 23, 1955, 1.

Down Beat. "Readers Poll." December 25, 1969, 16.

Down Beat. "Record Reviews." November 19, 1952, 52.

Down Beat. "Record Reviews." January 24, 1954, 10.

Down Beat. "Record Reviews: C&W." January 27, 1954, 10.

Down Beat. "Rock 'n' Roll Has Got to Go." September 19, 1956, 39.

Down Beat. "Subscription Advertisement." January 12, 1955, 23.

Down Beat. "Subscription Advertisement." April 20, 1955, 66.

Down Beat. "Subscription Advertisement." November 28, 1956, 55.

Down Beat. "Subscription Advertisement." April 6, 1967, 51.

Down Beat. "Subscription Advertisement." September 7, 1967, 45.

Down Beat. "Vox amplifier Advertisement." July 1, 1965, 49.

Doyle, Peter. *Echo and Reverb: Fabricating Space in Popular Music Recording 1900–1960* (Middletown, CT: Wesleyan University Press, 2005).

Draper, Robert. *The Rolling Stone Story* (Worcester: Mainstream, 1990).

Ellington, Duke. "The Future of Jazz." *Newport Jazz Festival program notes*, 1955.

Elworth, Steven B. "Jazz in Crisis, 1948–1958: Ideology and Representation," in *Jazz Among the Discourses*, edited by Krin Gabbard (Durham: Duke University Press, 1995), 57–75.

Ennis, Philip H. *The Seventh Stream: The Emergence of Rocknroll in American Popular Music* (Hanover: Wesleyan University Press, 1992).

Erenberg, Lewis A. *Swingin' the Dream: Big Band Jazz and the Rebirth of American Culture* (London: University of Chicago Press, 1998).

Evans, Nicholas. *Writing Jazz: Race, Nationalism and Modern Culture in the 1920s* (New York: Garland, 2000).

Fass, Paula S. *The Damned and the Beautiful: American Youth in the 1920's* (Oxford: Oxford University Press, 1979).

Feather, Leonard. "The 30's." *Down Beat*, September 1989, 16.

Feather, Leonard. "America Crazy but England's Crazier Still!" *Down Beat*, September 1989, 24.

Feather, Leonard. "Blindfold Test—Carmen Blanches on Hearing R&B." *Down Beat*, May 18, 1955, 25.

Feather, Leonard. *The Book of Jazz* (New York: Horizon, 1957).

Feather, Leonard. "Feather's Nest." *Down Beat*, July 14, 1954, 21.

Feather, Leonard. "Feather's Nest." *Down Beat*, May 4, 1955, 6.

Feather, Leonard. "Feather's Nest." *Down Beat*, January 11, 1956, 43.

Feather, Leonard. *Inside Be-bop* (New York: JJ Robbins and Sons, 1949).

Feather, Leonard. "Pop=Rock=Jazz: A False Musical Equation Dissected." *Down Beat Music '68* annual, 1968, 16–19.

Feather, Leonard. "A Year of Selling Out." *Down Beat Music '71*, 1971, 10.

Fellezs, Kevin. "Between Rock and a Jazz Place: Intercultural Interchange in Fusion Musicking." PhD dissertation (University of California, Santa Cruz, 2004).

Fellezs, Kevin. *Birds of Fire: Jazz, Rock, Funk, and the Creation of Fusion* (London: Duke University Press, 2011).

Fine, Jon, "An In-Depth Interview with Jann Wenner." *Business Week*, November 2, 2007. Available online: http://www.bloomberg.com/news/articles/2007-11-01/an-in-depth -interview-with-jann-wenner (accessed May 23, 2016).

Flippo, Chet. "The History of Rolling Stone: Part I." *Popular Music and Society*, 3(3), 1974a, 159–188.

Flippo, Chet. "The History of Rolling Stone: Part II." *Popular Music and Society*, 3(4), 1974b, 258–280.

Fowler, Bridget. *Pierre Bourdieu and Cultural Theory* (London: Sage, 1997).

Fox, Sidney. "To All Chairmen." *National Association of Jazz Educators Newsletter*, 3(1), 1970, 9–10.

Frith, Simon. Interview with the author. Glasgow, March 8, 2006.

Frith, Simon. "Is Jazz Popular Music?" *Jazz Research Journal*, 1(1), 2007, 7–23.

Frith, Simon. "'The Magic That Can Set You Free': The Ideology of Folk and the Myth of the Rock Community." *Popular Music*, 1, 1981, 159–168.

Frith, Simon. *Performing Rites: On the Value of Popular Music* (Cambridge, MA: Harvard University Press, 1996).

Frith, Simon. "Playing with Real Feeling: Making Sense of Jazz in Britain." *New Formations*, 4, 1988, 7–24.

Frith, Simon. *The Sociology of Rock* (London: Constable, 1978).

Frith, Simon. *Sound Effects: Youth, Leisure and the Politics of Rock 'n' Roll* (London: Constable, 1983).

Frith, Simon. "What Is Bad Music?" in *Bad Music*, edited by Christopher J. Washburne and Maiken Derno (New York: Routledge, 2004), 15–36.

Frith, Simon. "Writing About Popular Music," in *The Cambridge History of Music Criticism*, edited by Christopher Dingle (Cambridge: Cambridge University Press, forthcoming 2017).

Frith, Simon, Will Straw, and John Street. *The Cambridge Companion to Rock and Pop* (Cambridge University Press, 2001).

Gabree, John. "The Beatles in Perspective." *Down Beat*, November 16, 1967, 22.

Gabree, John. "The World of Rock." *Down Beat*, July 13, 1967, 19–20.

Gendron, Bernard. *Between Montmartre and the Mudd Club* (Chicago: University of Chicago Press, 2002).

Gendron, Bernard. "'Moldy Figs' and Modernists: Jazz at War 1942–1946," in *Jazz Among the Discourses*, edited by Krin Gabbard (Durham: Duke University Press, 1995), 31–56.

Gennari, John. *Blowin' Hot and Cool* (Chicago: University of Chicago Press, 2006).

Gennari, John. "Hipsters, Bluebloods, Rebels, and Hooligans: The Cultural Politics of the Newport Jazz Festival, 1954–1960," in *Uptown Conversation: The New Jazz Studies*, edited by Robert G. O'Meally, Brent Hayes Edwards, and Farah Jasmine Griffin (New York: Columbia University Press, 2004), 126–149.

Gennari, John. "Jazz Criticism: Its Development and Ideologies." *Black American Literature Forum*, 25(3), 1991, 449–523.

Gershwin, George. "The Composer in the Machine Age," reprinted in *The George Gershwin Reader*, edited by Robert Wyatt and John Andrew Johnson (Oxford: Oxford University Press, 2007) 119–122.

Gillett, Charlie. *The Sound of the City*, 2nd ed. (New York: Pantheon Books, 1983).

Gitler, Ira and Dan Morgenstern. "Rock at Newport '69: Big Crowds, Bad Vibes." *Down Beat*, August 21, 1969, 25–26, 31, 45.

Gittins, Ian. "Acoustic Ladyland." *The Guardian*, February 9, 2007. Available online: http://music.guardian.co.uk/jazz/livereviews/story/0,,2009106,00.html (accessed July 26, 2016).

Gleason, Ralph. "Buddy Rich: A Note of Hope." *Jazz & Pop*, January 1969, 39.

Gleason, Ralph. *Jam Session: An Anthology of Jazz* (New York: G.P. Putnam's Sons, 1958).

Gleason, Ralph. "Like a Rolling Stone." *Jazz & Pop*, September 1967, 14.

Gleason, Ralph. "Like a Rolling Stone." *Jazz & Pop*, November 12, 1967.

Gleason, Ralph. "Like a Rolling Stone." *Jazz & Pop*, December 1968, 14.

Gleason, Ralph. "Like a Rolling Stone." *Jazz & Pop*, February 1969, 12.

Gleason, Ralph. "Like a Rolling Stone." *Jazz & Pop*, April 1969, 14.

Gleason, Ralph. Liner notes for Miles Davis, *Bitches Brew*. Columbia Records, 1970.

Gleason, Ralph. "Perspectives: A Power to Change the World." *Rolling Stone*, June 22, 1968, 10.

Gleason, Ralph. "Perspectives: When Down to Seeds and Stems." *Rolling Stone*, December 14, 1967, 10.

Gleason, Ralph. "Perspectives." *Down Beat*, March 9, 1955, 18.

Gleason, Ralph. "Perspectives." *Down Beat*, July 11, 1956, 34.

Gleason, Ralph. "Perspectives." *Down Beat*, September 5, 1957, 18.

Goldblatt, Burt. *Newport Jazz Festival: The Illustrated History* (New York: Dial Press, 1977).

Goodman, Fred. *The Mansion on the Hill: Dylan, Young, Geffen, Springsteen, and the Head-On Collision of Rock and Commerce* (New York: Vintage, 1998).

Gorman, Paul. *In Their Own Write: Adventures in the Music Press* (London: Sanctuary Press, 2001).

Gracyk, Theodore. *Rhythm and Noise: An Aesthetics of Rock* (London: Duke University Press, 1996).

Graves, C.L. "Two Views of Jazz." *Sunday Province*, April 4, 1926, 1.

Gridley, Mark. *Jazz Styles: History and Analysis*, 7th ed. (Upper Saddle River, NJ: Prentice Hall, 2000).

Grier, Miles Parks. "Said the Hooker to the Thief: Some Way Out of Rockism." *Journal of Popular Music Studies*, 25(1), 2013, 31–55.

Guralnick, Peter. *Last Train to Memphis: The Rise of Elvis Presley* (London: Little Brown, 1994).

Hagstrom-Miller, Karl. *Segregating Sound* (Durham: Duke University Press, 2010).

Hamm, Charles. "Popular Music and Historiography." *Popular Music History*, 1(1), 2004, 9–14.

Harris, Dave. "Editorial: A Reply to *The Oracle's* 'Indo-Rock.'" *Mojo-Navigator*, September 7, 1966, 7.

Heineman, Alan. Phone interview with the author. January 10, 2006.

Heineman, Alan. "Rocks in My Head." *Down Beat*, January 8, 1970, 8.

Heineman, Alan. "'Trippin': Impressions of Cream and Jefferson Airplane." *Down Beat*, July 25, 1968, 15–16.

Heineman, Alan and Dan Morgenstern. "Rock, Jazz, and Newport: An Exchange." *Down Beat*, December 25, 1969, 22–23.

Hentoff, Nat. 1956. "Musicians Argue Values of Rock and Roll." *Down Beat*, May 30, 1956, 12.

Hepworth, David. "The Gob-smacking "Sales" Figures of *Rolling Stone*." September 5, 2013. Available online: http://whatsheonaboutnow.blogspot.co.uk/2013/09/the-gob-smacking-sales-figures-of.html (accessed July 18, 2016).

Hesmondhalgh, David. "Bourdieu, the Media and Cultural Production." *Media, Culture and Society*, 28(2), 2006, 211–231.

Hodeir, André. *Jazz: Its Evolution and Essence*, trans. David Noakes (New York: Grove Press, 1956).

Hodenfield, Jan. 1969. "The Newport Folk Festival." *Rolling Stone*, August 23, 1969, 20.

Holly, Hal. "What About R&B 'Leerics'?" *Down Beat*, May 4, 1955, 31.

Holt, Fabian. *Genre in Popular Music* (London: University of Chicago Press, 2007).

Jackson, Jeffrey. *Making Jazz French: Music and Modern Life in Interwar Paris* (London: Duke University Press, 2003).

Jazz & Pop. "Critics Poll." February 1968, 14.

Jazz & Pop. "Critics Poll." February 1969, 17.

Jazz & Pop. "Readers Poll." May 1969, 22.

Jazz & Pop. "Critics Poll." February 1970, 17.

Jazz & Pop. "Readers Poll." May 1970, 27.

Jensen, Joli. *The Nashville Sound: Authenticity, Commercialization, and Country Music* (Nashville: Vanderbilt University Press, 1998).

Johnson, Bruce. "Jazz as Cultural Practice," in *The Cambridge Companion to Jazz*, edited by Mervyn Cooke and David Horn (Cambridge: Cambridge University Press, 2002), 96–113.

Johnson, Randal. "Editor's Introduction: Pierre Bourdieu on Art, Literature and Culture," in *The Field of Cultural Production*, edited by Pierre Bourdieu (Cambridge: Polity Press, 1993), 1–28.

Jones, Leroi (Amiri Baraka). *Black Music* (New York: William Morrow, 1967).

Jones, Leroi (Amiri Baraka). *Blues People* (New York: William Morrow, 1963).

Jones, Nick. "Unnerving Jazz with Rock." *Rolling Stone*, February 10, 1968, 18.

Jones, Steve. *Pop Music and the Press* (Philadelphia: Temple University Press, 2002).

Jones, Steve and Kevin Featherly. "Re-Viewing Rock Writing: Narratives of Popular Music Criticism," in *Pop Music and the Press*, edited by Steve Jones (Philadelphia: Temple University Press, 2002), 19–40.

Jurek, Tom. Allmusic review of *Bitches Brew*. Available online: http://www.allmusic.com/album/bitches-brew-mw0000188019 (accessed July 25, 2016).

Keightley, Keir. "Long Play: Adult-Oriented Popular Music and the Temporal Logics of the Post-war Sound Recording Industry in the USA." *Media, Culture and Society*, 26(3), 2004, 375–391.

Keightley, Keir. "Reconsidering Rock," in *The Cambridge Companion to Pop and Rock*, edited by Simon Frith, Will Straw, and John Street (Cambridge: Cambridge University Press, 2001), 109–142.

Kennealy-Morrison, Patricia. "Rock Around the Cock," reprinted in *Rock She Wrote*, edited by Evelyn McDonnell and Ann Powers (London: Plexus, 1995), 357–363.

King, Nelson. "Country & Western: Who's to Blame for Dip in Country Music Field?" *Down Beat*, October 20, 1954, 18.

King, Nelson. "True C&W Music Called Key to Return of Hits." *Down Beat*, November 3, 1954, 16.

Koenig, Karl. *Jazz in Print (1859–1929)* (Hillsdale: Pendragon Press, 2002).

Kofsky, Frank. "The Scene." *Jazz & Pop*, January 1968, 36–39.

Laermans, Rudi. "The Relative Rightness of Pierre Bourdieu: Some Sociological Comments on the Legitimacy of Postmodern Art, Literature and Culture." *Cultural Studies*, 6(2), 1992, 248–259.

Laing, Dave. "Introduction to the Special Issue." *Popular Music History*, 1(3), 2006, 237–240.

Laing, Dave. *The Sound of Our Time* (London: Sheed and Ward, 1969).

Landau, Jon. "Blood, Sweat and Tears." *Rolling Stone*, March 1, 1969, 28.

Landau, Jon. "Cream." *Rolling Stone*, May 11, 1968, 14.

Landau, Jon. "Cream on Its Way." *The Justice*, March 26, 1968, 4.

Landau, Jon. *It's Too Late to Stop Now* (San Francisco: Straight Arrow, 1972).

Landau, Jon. "Mitch Ryder and the Detroit Wheels—Breakout! *Crawdaddy!*" September 1966, 6.

Landau, Jon. Phone interview with the Author. Connecticut, August 3, 2006.

Landau, Jon. "Stones." *Rolling Stone*, February 10, 1968, 18.

Landau, Jon. "What's Wrong with Rock 'Art.'" Rolling Stone, July 20, 1968, 18–20.

Lee, Stephanie M., "The Origins of *Rolling Stone*." *The Daily Californian*, August 20, 2007. Available online: http://archive.dailycal.org/article.php?id=25647 (accessed May 23, 2016).

Lees, Gene. *Singers and the Song* (New York: Oxford University Press, 1987).

Leonard, Neil. "The Impact of Mechanization," in *American Music: From Storyville to Woodstock*, edited by Charles Nanry (New Brunswick: Transaction Books, 1972), 44–64.

Leonard, Neil. *Jazz and the White Americans* (University of Chicago Press, 1962).

Levine, Lawrence. *Highbrow/Lowbrow: The Emergence of Cultural Hierarchy in America* (Cambridge: Harvard University Press, 1988).

Levine, Lawrence. "Jazz and American Culture." *Journal of American Folklore*, 102, 1989, 6–22.

Lindberg, Ulf, Gestur Guomundsson, Morten Michelsen, and Hans Weisethaunet. *Amusers, Bruisers and Cool-Headed Cruisers: The Fields of Anglo-Saxon and Nordic Rock Criticism* (Arhus: University of Arhus, 2000).

Lindberg, Ulf, Gestur Guomundsson, Morten Michelsen, and Hans Weisethaunet. *Rock Criticism from the Beginning: Amusers, Bruisers, and Cool-Headed Cruisers* (New York: Peter Lang, 2005).

Longhurst, Brian. *Popular Music and Society* (Cambridge: Polity, 1995).

Lopes, Paul. *The Rise of a Jazz Art World* (Cambridge: Cambridge University Press, 2002).

Lydon, Michael. "Wild Bill Haley Still Rocking Away." *Rolling Stone*, November 9, 1967, 21.

Marcus, Greil. "Bob Dylan—*Self Portrait*." *Rolling Stone*, July 23, 1970, 15.

Marcus, Greil. Interview with the author. Seattle, April 29, 2006.

Marcus, Greil. *Mystery Train* (New York: Dutton, 1975).

Marcus, Greil. *Rock and Roll Will Stand* (Boston: Beacon Press, 1969).

Marcus, Greil. "The Woodstock Festival." *Rolling Stone*, September 20, 1969, 16–18.

Marsalis, Wynton. Acceptance speech for Grammy award for "Best Jazz Instrumental Performance, Soloist," February 28, 1984. Available online: https://www.youtube.com/watch?v=YHytOMuSnUA (accessed July 26, 2016).

Martin, Peter J. *Music and the Sociological Gaze: Art Worlds and Cultural Production* (Manchester: Manchester University Press, 2006).

McDonald, Chris. "Rock, Roll and Remember? Addressing the Legacy of Jazz in Popular Music Studies." *Popular Music History*, 1(2), 2006, 125–145.

McDonough, John. "60 Years of Down Beat," in *Down Beat: 60 Years of Jazz*, edited by Frank Ayler (Winona: Hal Leonard Corporation, 1995), 6–17.

Metronome. "The Degeneration of Our Popular Song." January 1914, 8.

Middleton, Richard. *Pop Music and the Blues* (London: Victor Gollancz, 1972).

Miller, Paul Eduard. "Disc-Cussin." *Down Beat*, September 1937, 22–23.

Miller, Paul Eduard. *Miller's Yearbook of Popular Music* (Chicago: PEM Publications, 1943).

Moore, Allan. *The Cambridge Companion to Blues and Gospel Music* (Cambridge: Cambridge University Press, 2002).

Morgenstern, Dan. "Farewell to the Sixties." *Down Beat Music '70*, 1970, 9–10.

Morgenstern, Dan. Interview with the author. Newark, February 3–4, 2005.

Morgenstern, Dan. *Living with Jazz*. Edited by Sheldon Meyer (New York: Pantheon Books, 2004).

Morgenstern, Dan. "A Message to Our Readers." *Down Beat*, June 29, 1967, 13.

Morgenstern, Dan. "The Year in Review: 1967." *Down Beat Music '68* annual, 1968, 10–14.

Morgenstern, Dan. "The Year That Was." *Down Beat Music '69*, 1969, 11–14.

Murray, Charles Shaar. *Crosstown Traffic: Jimi Hendrix and Post-war Pop* (London: Faber and Faber, 2001).

Nanry, Charles. *American Music: From Storyville to Woodstock* (New Brunswick: Transaction, 1972).

National Endowment for the Arts. Jazz Masters Fellowships. Available online: http://www .nea.gov/national/jazz/index.html (accessed May 14, 2007).

Negus, Keith. *Popular Music in Theory* (Cambridge: Polity, 1996).

Negus, Keith and David Hesmondhalgh. *Popular Music Studies* (London: Arnold, 2002).

Newton, Francis. *The Jazz Scene* (New York: Monthly Review Press, 1960).

Nicholson, Stuart. "Fusions and Crossovers," in *The Cambridge Companion to Jazz*, edited by Mervyn Cooke and David Horn (Cambridge: Cambridge University Press, 2002), 217–254.

Nicholson, Stuart. *Jazz-Rock: A History* (New York: Schirmer, 1998).

Nicholson, Stuart et al. "The Song of the Body Electric: Jazz-Rock," in *The Future of Jazz*, edited by Yuval Taylor (Chicago: A Cappella, 2002), 43–63.

Norris, John. "Newport '69." *Coda*, August 1969, 13–15.

Nowell, William Robert. *The Evolution of Rock Journalism at the New York Times and the Los Angeles Times, 1956–1978: A Frame Analysis*. PhD dissertation (Indiana University, Bloomington, 1987).

Pattingale, Graeme. A Tale of Two Concerts, 2002. Available online: http://twtd .bluemountains.net.au/cream/a_tale_of_two_concerts.htm (accessed May 14, 2007)

Pekar, Harvey. "From Rock to???" *Down Beat*, May 2, 1968, 20–21, 39–40.

Perlongo, Bob. "The Widening Mainstream: A Look at the Sound of Now." *Down Beat '68* annual, 1968, 28–31.

Peterson, Richard A. *Creating Country Music: Fabricating Authenticity* (Chicago: University of Chicago Press, 1997).

Peterson, Richard A. "A Process Model of the Folk, Pop and Fine Art Phases of Jazz," in *American Music: From Storyville to Woodstock*, edited by C. Nanry (New Brunswick: Transaction Books, 1972), 135–151.

Peterson, Richard A. "Why 1955? Explaining the Advent of Rock Music." *Popular Music*, 9(1), 1990, 97–116.

Pond, Steven. *Head Hunters: The Making of Jazz's First Platinum Album* (London: University of Michigan, 2005).

Portch, Al. "Manager of Bill Haley Defends the Real Thing." *Down Beat*, September 19, 1956, 43.

Porter, Eric. "'It's About That Time': The Response to Miles Davis's Electric Turn," in *Miles Davis and American Culture*, edited by Gerald Early (St. Louis: Missouri Historical Society Press, 2001), 130–147.

Powers, Devon. *Writing the Record: The Village Voice and the Birth of Rock Criticism* (Boston: University of Massachusetts Press, 2013).

Purvis, Trevor and Alan Hunt. "Discourse, Ideology, Discourse, Ideology, Discourse, Ideology." *British Journal of Sociology*, 44(3), 1993, 473–499.

Regev, Motti. "Producing Artistic Value: The Case of Rock Music." *Sociological Quarterly*, 35(1), 1994.

Reynolds, Simon. *Rip It Up and Start Again: Postpunk 1978–1984* (London: Faber and Faber, 2005).

Rivelli, Pauline. "Editorial." *Jazz & Pop*, August 1967, 5, 17.

Rivelli, Pauline. "Newport Jazz Festival 1969." *Jazz & Pop*, September 1969, 31–33.

Rolling Stone. "Awards for Idiocy, Evil . . . ." February 7, 1970, 28.

Rolling Stone. Fusion advertisement. February 7, 1970, 43.

Rolling Stone. "Gary Burton Named Jazzman of the Year." February 1, 1969, 12.

Rolling Stone. "It Happened in 1968." February 1, 1969, 15.

Rolling Stone. "Jazz Meets Rock." March 1, 1969, 6.

Rolling Stone. "Jazz Takes Gas at Fillmore." April 19, 1969, 10.

Rolling Stone. "Rock Too Much for Newport." August 9, 1969, 10, 38.

Rolling Stone. Sun Ra cover. April 19, 1969.

Rosen, Jody. "The Perils of Poptimism." *Slate*, May 9, 2006. Available online: http://www .slate.com/articles/arts/music_box/2006/05/the_perils_of_poptimism.html (accessed July 26, 2016).

Santoro, Gene. *Highway 61 Revisited: The Tangled Roots of American Jazz, Blues, Rock, & Country Music* (New York: Oxford University Press, 2004).

Sargeant, Winthrop. *Jazz: Hot and Hybrid* (New York: Arrow Editions, 1938).

Schmutz, Vaughan. "Retrospective Cultural Consecration in Popular Music: *Rolling Stone's* Greatest Albums of All Time." *American Behavioral Scientist*, 48(11), 2005, 1510–1523.

Schonberg, Edith. "You Can't Fool Public, Says Haley." *Down Beat*, May 30, 1956, 10.

Schuller, Gunther. *Early Jazz: Its Roots and Musical Development* (New York: Oxford University Press, 1968).

Shapiro, Nat and Nat Hentoff. *Hear Me Talkin' to Ya: The Story of Jazz as Told by the Men Who Made It*, 1955. Reprint (New York: Dover Publications, 1966).

Shuker, Roy. *Understanding Popular Music*, 1st ed. (London: Routledge, 1994).

Shuker, Roy. *Understanding Popular Music*, 2nd ed. (London: Routledge, 2001).

Silver, Horace. "Psychedelic Sally" sheet music supplement. *Down Beat*, April 18, 1968.

Spring, Edward A. "The Grateful Dead." *Down Beat*, September 21, 1967, 31.

Stearns, Marshall W. *The Story of Jazz* (New York: Oxford University Press, 1956).

Stebbins, Robert A. "Class, Status, and Power Among Jazz and Commercial Musicians." *The Sociological Quarterly*, 7, 1996, 197–213.

Stowe, David. *Swing Changes: Big Band Jazz in New Deal America* (Cambridge: Harvard University Press, 1994).

Tagg, Philip. "Why IASPM? Which Tasks?" in *Popular Music Perspectives 2*, edited by David Horn (Exeter: IASPM, 1985), 501–507.

Tosh, John. *The Pursuit of History* (London: Longman, 1984).

Tucker, Mark (ed.). *The Duke Ellington Reader* (New York: Oxford University Press, 1993).

Tucker, Sherrie. "Deconstructing the Jazz Tradition: The 'Subjectless Subject' of New Jazz Studies." *The Source*, 2, 2005, 31–36.

Tynan, John. "FunkGrooveSoul." *Down Beat*, November 24, 1960, 18–19.

Ulanov, Barry. Column. *Down Beat*, January 11, 1956, 14.

Ulanov, Barry. Column. *Down Beat*, August 22, 1956, 32–33.

Ulanov, Barry. Column. *Down Beat*, January 23, 1957, 40.

Ulanov, Barry. Column. *Down Beat*, May 2, 1957, 36.

Ulanov, Barry. *A History of Jazz in America* (New York: Viking Press, 1952).

Urban Dictionary. "Jazz Snob Definition." Available online: http://www.urbandictionary .com/define.php?term=Jazz%20Snob (accessed July 27, 2016).

Vann, Kimberley. *Black Music in Ebony: An Annotated Guide to the Articles on Music in Ebony Magazine, 1945–1985* (Chicago: Center for Black Music Research Monographs, 1990).

Wald, Elijah. *How the Beatles Destroyed Rock and Roll* (London: Oxford University Press, 2009).

Ward, Geoffrey C. *Jazz: A History of America's Music* (New York: Knopf, 2000).

Warner, Simon. "In Print and On Screen: The Changing Character of Popular Music Journalism," in *The Sage Handbook of Popular Music,* edited by Andy Bennett and Steve Waksman (London: Sage, 2015), 439–455.

Webb, Jen, Tony Schirato, and Geoff Danaher. *Understanding Bourdieu* (London: Sage, 2002).

Wein, George. "An Interview with George Wein." *Jazz & Pop,* April 1969, 44–47.

Wein, George. Newport Jazz Festival program notes, 1969.

Wein, George with Nate Chinen. *Myself Among Others: A Life in Music* (Cambridge: Da Capo, 2004).

Weisbard, Eric. IASPM mailing list discussion, May 5, 2015.

Weiser, Norman. "Memo from the Publisher." *Down Beat,* June 30, 1954, 1.

Weiser, Norman. "A Message from the Publisher." *Down Beat Music '56,* 1956, 6.

Welburn, Ron. "Duke Ellington's Music: The Catalyst for a True Jazz Criticism." *International Review of the Aesthetics and Sociology of Music,* 17, 1986, 111–122.

Welburn, Ron. "James Reese Europe and the Infancy of Jazz Criticism." *Black Music Research Journal,* 7, 1987, 35–44.

Welburn, Ronald. *American Jazz Criticism, 1914–1940.* PhD dissertation: New York University, New York, 1983).

Welding, Pete and John A. Tynan "Double View of a Double Quartet," *Down Beat,* January 18, 1962, 28.

Wells, Christopher J. *Chick Webb and His Dancing Audience During the Great Depression.* PhD dissertation (Chapel Hill: University of North Carolina, 2014).

Wenner, Jann. "A Letter from the Editor." *Rolling Stone,* November 9, 1967, 2.

Wenner, Jann. *The Rolling Stone Record Review* (New York: Pocket Books, 1971).

Wenner, Jann. Televised interview with Andrew Denton, *Enough Rope,* October 6, 2008. Transcript available online: http://www.abc.net.au/tv/enoughrope/transcripts/ s2382889.htm (accessed May 23, 2016).

Wenner, Jann. Televised interview with Charlie Rose, May 26, 1992. Transcript available online: https://charlierose.com/videos/449 (accessed May 23, 2016).

Wenner, Jann. Televised interview with Charlie Rose, February 5, 2007. Transcript available online: https://charlierose.com/videos/12131 (accessed May 23, 2016).

Wexler, Jerry and David Ritz. *Rhythm and the Blues: A Life in American Music* (New York: St. Martin's Press, 1993).

Whyton, Tony (ed.). *Jazz* (Farnham: Ashgate, 2011).

Wilcock, Evelyn. "Adorno, Jazz and Racism: Uber Jazz and the 1934–7 British Jazz Debate." *Telos,* 107, Spring, 1996, 63–80.

Wilson, John S. "Expanding Market for Better Jazz," *New York Times*, March 12, 1961, Section X, 15.

Williams, Martin. "Bystander." *Down Beat,* June 27, 1968, 15.

Williams, Paul. "Editorial." *Crawdaddy!*, February 14, 1966, 1.

Williams, Paul. "Get Off of My Cloud!" *Crawdaddy!*, February 7, 1966, 1.

Williams, Raymond. *Culture and Society* (New York: Columbia University, 1958).

Williams, Raymond. *The Long Revolution* (London: Chatto and Windus, 1961).

Wilson, John S. 1969. "Unruly Newport Fans Upset Newport Jazz Festival." *New York Times*, July 7, 1969, 28.

Wilson, Russ. "The Future of Jazz: On the Rocks?" *Down Beat*, June 15, 1967, 17.

Winner, Langdon. "Reviews—Memphis Underground by Herbie Mann and a Soul Experiment by Freddie Hubbard." *Rolling Stone*, July 12, 1969, 36.

Wolf, Mark. "Their Satanic Majesties Request." *Down Beat*, May 30, 1968, 30.

Wolfe, Robert. "The First Issue." *Sing Out*, May 1950, 2.

Wolk, Douglas. "Thinking About Rockism." *Seattle Weekly*, October 9, 2006. Available online: http://archive.seattleweekly.com/2005-05-04/music/thinking-about-rockism/ (accessed July 26, 2016).

Zabelin, Leo. "Line Between Popular, C&W Growing Thinner: Rex Allen." *Down Beat*, November 18, 1953, 6.

Index

Note: The letter 'n' following locators refers to notes